Creative

Counterpoint

Excerpt from p. 144, *Clavier-Büchlein vor Wilhelm Friedemann Bach*, by Johann Sebastian Bach, ed. by Ralph Kirkpatrick. New Haven, Conn.: Yale University Press, 1959. Reprinted by permission.

Creative Counterpoint

Maurice Lieberman

Professor of Music
Brooklyn College

Allyn and Bacon, Inc.
Boston
1966

To my wife,
Bertha

Preface

THROUGHOUT THE HISTORY OF POLYPHONY, theorists maintained divergent views about melody appropriate to the style, the treatment of discord, the relevance of harmonic influence and the structure of various types of polyphonic music. Theory generally lagged behind practice, so it is not surprising that shortly after Bach's time, such theorists as Albrechtsberger, Cherubini and Marpurg considered Bach's music too radical a model for student imitation. J. J. Fux, a minor composer and contemporary of Bach, sought to check the current harmonic counterpoint, to reverse the trend toward instrumental melodic style and to counteract the freedom or "licences" in the music of the time by upholding sixteenth century polyphony as a standard of perfection. In his *Gradus ad Parnassum* he reverts to vocal diatonic melody in the modes, insists on strict handling of discords and employs a series of artificial rhythm schemes with canti firmi which presumably would eventuate in Palestrina-style counterpoint.

Paradoxically, Fux's outlook and the species technique which was intended to countervail the influence of music such as Bach's, was adopted by eighteenth and nineteenth century pedagogues in teaching tonal harmonic counterpoint. Treatises multiplied, with mechanical repetition of arbitrary rules and prohibitions which often had no relevance to the practices of Bach, Handel, Purcell and other eminent contrapuntists. No other musical discipline has been so resistant to the need for a realistic approach or been shackled for so long to outmoded rules and a technique so ill suited to its objective. While Bach was acquainted with the species approach, he evidently found the methods of earlier and a few contemporary German masters to be more practical. According to Kirnberger, his disciple and ardent admirer, Bach urged his students to absorb his style by playing his music before mastering thorough-bass. Nonharmonic tones were employed in chorale harmonizations. Contrapuntal instruction began with the four lines of figurated harmony and then moved on to the composition of inventions, canons and fugues.

Harmony as a prerequisite for the study of counterpoint, has long been taken for granted. Current thinking regards these disciplines as complementary, if not two phases of the same thing. The present trend toward integrating various disciplines embraces the concurrent study of tonal harmony and eighteenth century counterpoint. This orientation and the continual quest for a satisfactory approach based directly on Bach's music, prompts our effort in meeting the needs of the general music student with a practical study of counterpoint. Students who have taken a course in harmony without achieving sufficient command of its use in conjunction with nonharmonic tones will profit from reviewing the material in the parallel studies.

The procedure in two-part counterpoint takes the following pattern: As each class of chords is taken up in four-part progressions, the texture is reduced to two-part harmony which serves as the framework for two contrapuntal lines. This takes the place of the harmonically indeterminate intervals of species counterpoint. The student is trained to plan passages with a clear harmonic and key direction, a modus operandi which is especially necessary in three-part counterpoint. One line remains at first a series of chord tones; the other is elaborated with unaccented passing, auxiliary and chord tone skips. Chord tones for a limited time are retained on the beat. In subsequent exercises, both lines are developed. All of the essentials of tonal harmony are adequately covered. As a rule, the material presented is applied directly in harmony and counterpoint. Some material is presented in part and amplified later, *e.g.*, suspensions and later delayed resolutions. The student is neither required to digest a mass of information before he has occasion to use it nor to memorize a profusion of rules. Each voice moves alone in uniform and varied rhythm, which is then transferred from voice to voice in reciprocal rhythmic activity and in imitations.

The melodic line becomes more plastic with the substitution of accented nonharmonic tones and suspensions on the beat and the subordination of the underlying harmony to melodic necessity. The concept of melody appropriate to the style is gradually developed. We do not devote an opening chapter to single line melody the content of which is difficult to remember or apply immediately, since the single line is conditioned by its harmonic-modulatory scaffolding and by the rhythm, contour, direction and climax of a concurrent line or lines. The method employed here results in controlled writing and provides an understanding of the function of nonharmonic tones in analysis. Specific means of melodic unity, variety and structure which are discussed from time to time, are summarized and amplified in Ch. 7. The work is creative, in the sense that no canti firmi are given nor is the completion of partially written exercises required. The work is entirely the student's, from the earliest contrapuntal exercises to the complete fugue.

Canon at the octave, fifth and fourth precedes the composition of two-part inventions as preparation for canonic episodes and the canonic invention. Double counterpoint, at this time, is restricted to the octave. The simple two-part invention with imitation at the octave and with double theme precedes the fugal invention with answer at the fifth. Tonal answers and double counterpoint at the twelfth are discussed prior to the composition of three-part inventions and fugues.

Three-part counterpoint is first written in nonthematic passages based on each class of chords and then with modulations. These passages embody sequences, canonic imitation and other devices which approximate the episodes in a fugue. Three-part inventions and fugues are studied simultaneously since, except for auxiliary basses and some minor differences, the former are similar to three-part fugues. Exercises in writing subjects, answers, countersubjects, codettas, various types of episode, triple counterpoint, pedal points, stretto, augmentation and diminution precede the composition of three-part fugues.

A noteworthy feature of *Creative Counterpoint* is the step-by-step demonstration of how to build various kinds of episode, how to extract episodic material from a subject, how to proceed in canon writing, how to plan an invention and fugue, etc. The material, covering as much as can be realistically accomplished in a year, is carefully organized and amply illustrated with excerpts from Bach. Designed to deepen the understanding, performance and critical analysis of the future performer, conductor, musicologist and teacher, *Creative Counterpoint* also lays a solid foundation for advanced work in canon and fugue. The practical value of its methodology has been amply demonstrated in the course of its author's long experience.

Maurice Lieberman

Table of Contents

Creative
Counterpoint

Introduction

COUNTERPOINT IS THE ART OF weaving two or more strands of melody together to produce a musical texture, polyphony. The terms *counterpoint* and *polyphony* are synonymous in common usage and are applied without distinction to music in which different melodic lines are heard simultaneously. In a technical sense, any melodic line or "voice" added to a theme or fixed melody is called "the counterpoint."

Polyphony from Organum to Bach

Polyphony developed from *organum*—the practice of singing ecclesiastical melody known as *Gregorian plain chant*, accompanied by the same melody sung uniformly four or five tones lower. The term *counterpoint* was derived from the Latin, *punctus contra punctus*, note against note. Each note of the accompanying line, the *vox organalis*, was set against a note of the plain chant, the *vox principalis* or principal voice.

In two-voice texture both voices started on the same tone; one voice moved scalewise up four tones, both voices then moved in parallel lines four tones apart and then converged to a close on the same tone. Duplicating the principal voice an octave lower and the accompanying voice an octave higher produced a four-voice texture moving in parallel lines eight, five and four tones apart. From the origin of organum in the

1

late ninth century and in polyphony for centuries thereafter, the counterpoint revolved around a liturgical plain chant as the *cantus firmus* or fixed melody.

A freer type of organum developed at a later stage, characterized by embellished melody flowing over the long tones of the plain chant. Melodic lines diverged or ran in oblique motion with a purposeful introduction of intervals other than the octave, fifth and fourth. Rhythmic freedom in the vox organalis and departure from exclusive parallel motion made each line melodically independent of the other. In the early thirteenth century the *motet* emerged. This was a three-voiced composition usually based on a sacred Latin text, with the plain chant assigned to the lowest voice. Machaut, Dunstable and Dufay, composers of a later period (1325–1475), produced notable examples of the motet, among other works. The *rota*, another polyphonic type, appeared around 1240. In this form the melody of the first voice is picked up successively by other voices, overlapping itself as in the common round. This device of *imitation*, applied to shorter melodic units, became a characteristic feature of the motet and other polyphonic forms. In the sixteenth century motet, different phrases of liturgical text were set to different melodic units, each of which was treated in imitative style. Superimposed on traditional Gregorian chant, imitation played an important role in the setting of the *Mass*. After Dunstable (d. 1453), outstanding composers of the Franco-Flemish school who contributed to the evolution of sacred polyphonic music from the last half of the fifteenth to the early sixteenth century were Okeghem, Obrecht and Josquin des Prés.

The gradual secularization of European life after the eleventh century was reflected in both texts and music of *chansons* and *ballads*. Melodies from these sources served at times as canti firmi for late thirteenth century secular and religious motets. Other secular music in polyphonic style followed— *virelais, rondeaux, frottolas* and *madrigals*. Voice movement in parallel thirds and sixths gained favor. Passages in chordal style were interlarded in polyphonic contexts in some music of this period.

By the beginning of the sixteenth century the texture had increased to five, six and more voices with occasional evidence of a trend away from the modal system. The *modes,* scales derived from the ancient Greeks and from the nature of Medieval melody, were gradually yielding to the tonal *major-minor system.* Various contrapuntal devices had long been explored; *i.e.*, *augmentation* and *diminution*, the doubling and halving of the rhythmic values of melodic units; *inversion*, a reversal in direction of a melodic line; and *cancrizans*, melodic movement from the last note to the beginning of a melodic unit. Polyphonic music for multiple choirs enhanced the grandeur of religious services. Surfeited with intricate devices and dense voice texture, sixteenth century composers wrote music distinguished for its clarity and expressiveness. Pre-eminent in the first half of this century was the Netherlander, Willaert, a composer at St. Marks in Venice.

Instrumental music was of secondary importance prior to the seventeenth century. In the transitional stage, pieces written for voices were often intended for instrumental performance as well. Madrigals were frequently vocal solos with polyphonic instrumental accompaniment. The vocal motet, with its imitative construction, served as a model for the instrumental *ricercar*. Simple variations over a melodic fragment in bass led to the *passacaglia*, polyphonic variations over a bass melody. The fifteenth century *chanson*, a folk tune-like setting of secular verse in chordal or thin polyphonic texture, was the precursor of the animated sixteenth century *canzona*.

The religious schism of the sixteenth century, resulting in the establishment of Protestantism, brought in its wake a return to simplicity in sacred music best exemplified by *chorales*, simple hymn tunes sung with chordal accompaniment or imbedded in clear polyphonic texture. These melodies became the basis for instrumental *chorale preludes, variations* and *fantasias*. The Counter Reformation in turn favored a simpler and intrinsically religious type of music. The Council of Trent, without explicit directions, proposed the elimination of secular canti while encouraging simpler polyphony, purity of melodic line and clarity in textual setting. Now common in practice was the inclusion of harmonic passages, the "familiar style" which broke ground for seventeenth century *homophony*, melody accompanied by chords. This, together with the gradual displacement of the modes, set the stage for the music of the next era. Outstanding composers of sixteenth century vocal polyphony, the "golden age," were Palestrina, di Lasso, Vittoria, Goudimel and Wilbye.

Solo melody accompanied by chords was one characteristic feature of the Baroque period (ca. 1600–1750) which influenced the style of music in subsequent centuries. The bass line for songs and for the accompaniment in early seventeenth century opera—called the *continuo* or *thorough-bass*—carried a series of numerical symbols denoting precise harmonic progressions. In Baroque polyphonic music, upper contrapuntal lines of madrigals and various types of chamber music were harmonically controlled by the continuo played on a keyboard instrument. Various polyphonic compositions, written without continuo, were also governed by harmonic factors, a feature distinguishing them from sixteenth century works.

Equal temperament, a method of keyboard tuning better suited to key changes than the pure tone tuning of the modes, gained wider acceptance. Compositions that were wholly or partially contrapuntal multiplied, overtures, suites, fantasias, toccatas, capriccios, concerti grossi, sonatas and concerti. The *fugue* which is thematically unified, richer in episodic development and based on clear key relationships, superseded the simpler ricercar. All polyphonic and considerable harmonic means had been explored by the early eighteenth century, providing the resources for the outstanding composers of this time, Vivaldi, Handel and J. S. Bach.

Bach left a monumental heritage of works unsurpassed in grandeur of conception, creative imagination, wealth of ideas, masterly craftsmanship and eloquent expressiveness. He attained an eminence in eighteenth century harmonic polyphony equal to that achieved by Palestrina in modal counterpoint. His compositions display a superlative command of form, thematic originality, technical perfection in passages of exceptional ingenuity and a remarkable equilibrium between harmonic and polyphonic polarities. Absorbing the techniques and styles of his predecessors, Bach forged a unique style of his own. His music remains an inspiration to composers, a model for students and a source of deep satisfaction to performers and their audiences. Although homophony gradually gained ascendency, the polyphony of Bach left its impress on the music of later composers. Polyphonic passages abound in the works of Haydn, Mozart and Beethoven. Polyphonic and homophonic texture is fused in the music of Brahms, Wagner, Richard Strauss and other nineteenth century composers. Contemporary music is relatively more polyphonic than homophonic. Modern composers, abandoning tonality, nevertheless utilize the contrapuntal forms and devices of their predecessors.

Counterpoint is one of the basic disciplines preparatory to professional work in various musical fields. The literature of eighteenth century music is extensive, vital and interesting. Performers, choral and orchestral conductors cannot convey

4

meaningful interpretations of these works without a feeling for the style and a knowledge of contrapuntal techniques. They must be conscious of subtle relationships and significant detail while recognizing the presence of various devices. Musicologists and instrumental teachers should have a solid foundation in counterpoint to analyze these works with understanding. Prominent composer-teachers require their students to have a background in counterpoint.

This text is based on the keyboard music of Bach. Imitating his music will bring you into closer communion with its essence, its artistry and technique. Make it a matter of daily routine to play a page of Bach with conscious attention to the character of his melody, to diverse yet complementary rhythms, to melodic contours and climaxes. You should have at your disposal the *Two-* and *Three-Part Inventions*, the *Well-Tempered Clavier* and the chorale harmonizations.

The illustrations, unless noted otherwise, are excerpts from the works of Bach. Titles are abbreviated as follows: *Well-Tempered Clavier*, W.T.C.; Book I or II, as I, II; Prelude, P.; Fugue, F., followed by the specific number, #. *Two-* and *Three-Part Inventions* and their number, I, #2; II, #9, etc.; Partita, Part.; Little Preludes and Fugues, L.P.F. Chorales are identified by the first words of the text. Sources of other examples are given when used. References in the text to illustrations are to figure numbers in chapters; *e.g.*, Fig. 2-8b means Fig. 8b in Ch. 2.

Johann Sebastian Bach

1

Intervals; Triad Progressions; The Passing Tone; Two-part Harmony

HARMONY AND COUNTERPOINT ARE FREQUENTLY juxtaposed—the first as chordal study, tone blocks heard vertically; the second as the study of linear music, tones heard horizontally in concurrent melodic lines. These disciplines are neither antithetical nor mutually exclusive, since a chord series in four-part harmony is at the same time a set of four melodic lines. Unlike the polyphony of the Palestrinian age, harmonic progression and modulation are important factors in eighteenth century polyphonic composition. While each line in such texture fulfills its musical purpose, it contributes tones from point to point which delineate the harmonic direction of a composition. Mentally aware of his harmonic objectives, the practiced composer evolves each line as freely as possible. Our studies in counterpoint therefore proceed with a parallel study or review of harmony.

Intervals

The harmonic underpinning of two-part counterpoint is represented by the two tones of successive intervals. Two tones sounded together, regardless of the distance separating them or the effect produced, form an *interval*. Examined vertically, the melodic lines of a two-part invention form intervals at each instant from start to finish. This, of course, is a wholly artificial view of a polyphonic composition, but it illuminates the importance of a thorough grasp of intervals. Leading two or more concurrent lines of melody also requires, among other factors, discrimination in the choice of concords and discords that imply the harmony influencing the interplay of melodic lines.

An interval receives its name from the tonal distance between its notes. The name indicates the gross size, qualified by terms describing its precise size. The *gross size* is the number of letters spanned, including bottom and top notes. There are three letters in the interval C–E: C–D–E. The interval is a *third*. The interval D to upper C spans seven letters: D–E–F–G–A–B–C. This is a *seventh*. Such qualifying terms as *major third* and *minor seventh* denote the precise size of this third and seventh. Distinctions like major and minor, as used in this sense, do not refer to major and minor scales. The terms simply modify the gross size and mean slightly larger or smaller; a minor third is a half step smaller than a major third. There are minor intervals in major keys, and vice versa.

An accurate but cumbersome way of reckoning the size of an interval is to count the number of half steps it includes. A simpler method is: (1) disregard the key of the composition; (2) think of the lower tone as if it were a momentary step 1 or "do"; (3) note whether the upper tone is in the major scale of that "do": if it is, the interval will be *major* or *perfect–major*, if the gross size is a second, a third, a sixth or a seventh (Fig. 1-1a); *perfect*, if it is a prime, a fourth, a fifth or an octave (Fig. 1-1b). (The *prime* is an interval in which both voices have the same pitch.) We therefore speak of a major third, a perfect fourth, etc.

For example, the notes D–F♯ may appear as an interval in a piece in the key of C. Think of D as "do." F♯ is in the D–

major scale. This is a major third(M3). D–G is a perfect fourth(P4).

Compound intervals are those comprising a simple interval like a major second or a perfect fifth plus one or more octaves. Thus a major second plus an octave is a major ninth; a major third plus an octave is a major tenth, and a perfect fourth plus an octave is a perfect eleventh. Since rules governing the use of simple intervals generally apply to compound intervals, one can often refer to compound intervals in simpler terms, *e.g.*, calling a tenth a third. Intervals in which the upper note is not in the major scale of the lower note are described below.

Figure 1-1

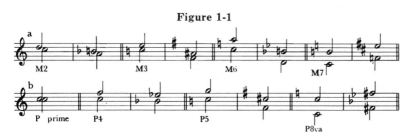

Exercise 1a. Examine each point in the *Two-part Invention #1* where two tones are played at the same time, finding and naming all major and perfect intervals.

We cited the major third D–F♯ as an instance in which an interval includes tones outside the key in which it appears. Both tones of a given interval may be tones of the prevailing key. For instance, starting with each note of the C-scale, we find major thirds in addition to C–E. These are F–A and G–B. Similarly, there are major seconds in that scale other than C–D, and major sixths and sevenths other than C–A and C–B.

Exercise 1b. Starting with each note of the C-major scale, write out each major second, third, sixth, seventh, ninth and tenth. Do this with the perfect fourths, fifths and octaves. Write the major and perfect intervals in the major scales of F, G, D, B♭, A and E♭.

Intervals narrower than major by a half step are *minor* (Fig. 1-2a). C–E is a major third; C–E♭ and C♯–E are minor thirds (m3). Use the same yardstick discussed earlier for minor intervals, conditioned by the half-step difference. Is the upper tone in the scale of the lower (*e.g.*, D–F♯)? If not, is it a half step lower (D–F♮)? This is, then, a minor third.

Figure 1-2a

Exercise 2a. Re-examine the same invention for all minor seconds, thirds, sixths, sevenths and composite minor intervals.

Exercise 2b. Starting with each note of the C-major scale, write the minor intervals including composite intervals. Write them starting from each note of the chromatic scale.

Intervals smaller than perfect by a half step (Fig. 1-2b) are *diminished; e.g.,* C–G is a perfect fifth (P5); C–G♭ is a diminished fifth (d5). Although these tones and C–F♯ are the same in sound and on the keyboard, C–G♭ contains five letters; however, C–F♯ is a fourth. Two intervals written differently but sounding alike are *enharmonic intervals* (Fig. 1-2c). The difference in spelling is due to differences in chords of which each interval is a component. The diminished fifth and the enlarged fourth (augmented fourth) encompass three whole steps. These intervals are therefore called *tritones.*

Intervals smaller than major by a whole step are also diminished. The most commonly used diminished intervals are the fifth and seventh (measures 2 and 3, Fig. 1-2b). In the major scale the d5 is from step 7 up to step 4; in minor, these steps and step 2 to step 6-flat. The d7 used in major and minor keys are the notes step 7 up to step 6-flat. This interval is enharmonic with the major sixth.

Figure 1-2b

Exercise 3a. Write out the d5, d7, d12 in C, then write diminished intervals starting from each note of the chromatic scale.

Intervals larger than perfect and major by a half step are *augmented.* The most common augmented intervals are the fourth, step 4 up to step 7, the second, steps 6–7 of the harmonic minor scale (Fig. 4-14a), the fifth, steps 5 to 2-sharp and the sixth in chords—called augmented sixth chords. Augmented sixths in C are: steps 6-flat up to 4-sharp, 2-flat up to 7 and 4 up to 2-sharp.

Exercise 3b.   The augmented fourth (a4) is enharmonic with the d5. What is the enharmonic equivalent of the a2 and a5? Write the a4th, the a5th and the a6ths in C, then write augmented intervals starting from each note of the chromatic scale.

Exercise 3c.   Find all the diminished and augmented intervals in #6 of the two-part inventions. Find the d7ths in #13 of these inventions, starting from measure 14.

Intervals larger than perfect and major by a whole step, double augmented, smaller than major by a whole step, diminished, and smaller than perfect by a whole step, or double diminished, are rarely encountered.

Interval Inversion

A simple interval is inverted when the upper note is written an octave lower or the bottom note an octave above its original location. A shift of two octaves is required for inversion of compound intervals. Inverted seconds become sevenths, and sevenths become seconds, as seen in Fig. 1-3. Subtract the gross size of an interval from the number 9 for the gross size of its inversion. Minor intervals become major, and vice versa; perfect remain perfect, diminished intervals become augmented, and vice versa. A knowledge of interval inversion is required when melodic lines are interchanged, *i.e.*, when upper line melody is used below as lower line or the reverse.

Figure 1-3

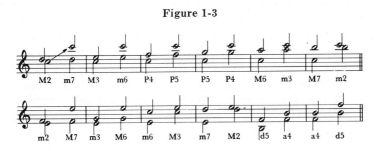

Exercise 4. Invert and name each major, perfect, minor, diminished and augmented interval in the keys of D and B♭. Do the same with compound intervals in A and E♭.

Consonance and Dissonance

Concepts of concord and discord have undergone modification from the Middle Ages to the present. Forbidden discords of one era received acceptance at a later time. Discords in sixteenth century counterpoint were carefully prepared and resolved. Bach and his contemporaries used discords with comparative frequency and freedom. The following distinctions may be deduced from their music. Concords are the major and minor thirds and sixths, the perfect fifth, octave and prime. The discords are the M2, m7 and the tritone, a4–d5. Sharper discords are the m2 and M7. This classification should not be taken as absolute. There are instances, as we will see later, where a "concord" is discordant to the prevailing harmony and a discord sounds less dissonant in the context of a current chord. The relative stability or instability of intervals, and the harmony they imply, furnish a useful guide to their use. Concords, in varying degrees, are comparatively stable; discords are unstable, tending to move to concords. The concord of a perfect fourth often exhibits instability when moving to a third, in which circumstance it is considered a discord. The harmonic implications of intervals will be examined in Chs. 2 and 4, which deal with representing three- and four-tone chords by the two tones of an interval in two-part polyphonic music. Some intervals in such music are composed of a chord and a nonchord tone. This factor, as we will see later, has a bearing on their treatment as concord or discord.

It had been remarked that eighteenth century polyphony was subject to the influence of implied harmony moving to designated keys. Facility in writing this type of counterpoint depends in no little measure on a firm grasp of harmony and modulation. It is therefore essential to study or review some factors of elementary harmony before proceeding with the first steps in counterpoint. By and large the fundamental precepts of chordal use govern implied chords that serve as framework for contrapuntal writing. The nature of polyphonic texture, however, permits some latitude in application, specifically where the melodic line takes precedence over harmonic considerations.

12

Triads

A chord is the effect produced by three or more tones sounding together. Three-tone chords called *triads* are formed by using any scale step as *root* and adding notes which are a third and a fifth above each root. These additional notes are called *chord-third* and *chord-fifth* (Fig. 1-4). A root and notes which are a major third and perfect fifth above it constitute a *major triad*. Triads based on the first, fourth and fifth steps of major scales are major triads. These three chords—the *tonic* triad on step 1, the *subdominant* on step 4 and the *dominant* on step 5—are classified as *primary* triads because they are essential in establishing a sense of key. Roman numerals I, IV and V are used to designate these triads. The tonic triad of each key is its central chord. All other chords move or "progress" directly or indirectly to it as a stable concluding chord.

Figure 1-4

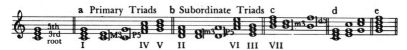

The secondary or *subordinate* triads based on steps 2, 3 and 6 are *minor triads* with notes a minor third and perfect fifth above their roots (Fig. 1-4b). These minor triads—the *supertonic* II, the *mediant* III and the *submediant* VI—provide contrast in major keys. The leading-tone triad based on step 7 is a *diminished* triad (Fig. 1-4c). Its upper notes are a minor third and a diminished fifth above the root. The VII is a form of dominant harmony which will be discussed later. A four-tone chord, the dominant seventh (Fig. 1-4e), is introduced in passing because it recurs in subsequent examples. The notes in C are G–B–D–F. It is treated fully in Chs. 3 and 4.

Exercise 5a. Write the I, IV and V triads of each major key in the manner of Fig. 1-4a; do this with II, VI and III as in Fig. 1-4b, and include the VII.

Examine the rearrangement of I chord tones in Fig. 1-4d. The triad is seen with fifth, root and third successively as top note. The term *position* denotes which chord tone is uppermost. The C triad in Fig. 1-4d is first in position of the fifth, then in root position, and lastly in position of the third.

Exercise 5b.   Add the root position and position of the third to each triad written in Ex. 5a.

Doubling

The resonance of the C triad in Fig. 1-4a is amplified by the addition of another tone, C in bass, as in Fig. 1-5a. Duplication or *doubling* of chord tones in triads furnishes a four-voice texture adapted to performance by high and low female and male voices in choral music. The highest note of such four-tone chords is the soprano note. Below successively are the alto, tenor and bass notes, seen in Fig. 1-5b. Although almost any note of a chord may be doubled, the root is most often doubled to establish chord identity. Note the doubling in Fig. 1-5b. Observe that bass and tenor take the same note in measure 2. Less often the root is tripled and the chord fifth is omitted, as in Fig. 1-5c. Excepting the third of V, thirds and fifths are doubled on occasion. The third of V is the leading tone of the key. Doubled it resolves to an octave of tonic tones, a prohibited type of voice movement that is discussed below. Where the flow of melodic lines in counterpoint runs through two leading tones heading in opposite direction, as in Fig. 1-15, measure 1, beat 4, considerations of doubling are of secondary importance.

Figure 1-5

Spacing

Compare the distribution of chord tones in the first two measures of Fig. 1-5. The tones in soprano, alto and tenor of the first chord are so closely bunched that another chord tone cannot be inserted. Tones spaced in this way are in *close harmony.* The spacing in the second measure is in *open harmony.* Har-

14

mony may be conducted in either style or in a combination of both. We will employ open style harmony in our exercises. Examine the spacing in the first two measures of Fig. 1-5d. The alto is separated by more than an octave, first from the soprano and then from the tenor. For ordinary purposes the alto should lie not more than an octave from the soprano and tenor notes. Inner melodic lines in counterpoint, particularly in instrumental music, occasionally draw away from adjacent voices by more than an octave. The wide spacing between tenor and bass like that seen in the last measure of Fig. 1-5d is permissible and almost always effective.

Exercise 6a.   Write the I of C in open harmony and in as many ways as possible. Double the root for the most part. Proceed as follows: Take the first note of Fig. 1-6a as bass with each note of Fig. 1-7a in turn as soprano. Fill in the inner voices. Do not omit a chord third. Then take the second note of Fig. 1-6a as bass again with the notes of Fig. 1-7a as soprano, excepting the low E. Follow the same procedure using the bass notes of Fig. 1-6b with the soprano notes of Fig. 1-7b. Do this also with the bass notes of Fig. 1-6c and the soprano notes of Fig. 1-7c. Observe that note stems on each staff in Fig. 1-5 are turned in opposite directions to identify each part. Follow the same practice in all four-voice writing.

Figure 1-6

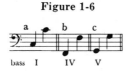

Figure 1-7

Exercise 6b.   Following the directions in Ex. 6a, write major triads on the notes D, B♭, A and E♭. Observe the upper and lower limits in the range of each voice, as shown in Fig. 1-8. These limits are extended in instrumental writing.

Figure 1-8

Voice Leading

The top tones of a series of chords form a melodic line called the *soprano voice* or *part*. The line of bass tones forms a *bass part*. Similar lines of inner tones form the *alto* and *tenor voices* or *parts*. Thus the movement or *progression* of a chord to other chords generates four melodic lines or voices. Harmony proceeding in this manner is *four-part harmony* and the process of conducting each melodic line is *voice leading*.

In strict voice leading the tones of one chord move to the closest tones of the next chord, as indicated by arrows in the I–V and I–IV in Fig. 1-9a. A tone that is common to both chords is retained in the same voice. Voice leading in V–I and IV–I is shown in Fig. 1-9b and c. Note the resolution of the leading tone in V and the downward resolution of steps 4 and 6 in IV. These active tones and step 2 are *tendency tones, i.e.,* tones that exhibit an inclination to move by step to another tone; *e.g.,* 7 to 8, 6 to 5, 4 to 3 and 2 to 1 or 3. Active tones in bass which are chord roots may skip—*e.g.,* 6–2–5 in the progression VI–II–V; 7–3 in VII–III. When these tones are not chord roots they should be led directly or indirectly to the tones indicated, particularly in soprano and bass. Exceptions are permitted in inner voices. Active tones in scale-line melody may move in a direction opposite their tendency—*e.g.,* 3–4–5; 5–6–7; 8–7–6. They may move by skip to another tone of the same chord in upper voices—*e.g.,* 7–5, 7–2 (in V), 6–4, 4–6, 4–1, 6–1 (in IV), 6–2, 4–2 (in II), etc. Such skips will not be taken in the bass part for the present.

Relative Motion

Soprano, alto and bass voices in Fig. 1-9a, measure 1, moving in the same direction are in *similar motion*. Soprano and alto move by the same kind of intervals, sixths. Similar motion by two voices in similar intervals is *parallel motion*. These two voices move in parallel sixths. The bass moves away from the stationary tenor and the other voices move toward it. Motion toward or away from a held or repeated tone is *oblique mo-*

tion. The bass and tenor in Fig. 1-9b, second unit, move away from each other in *contrary motion.* See Fig. 1-12b.

Cadences

A section of music, usually two, four or eight measures in length which comes to a partial or full close, is a *phrase.* The close of a phrase, of a period (double phrase) or of a piece of music is its *cadence.* An ending with V–I is an *authentic cadence* (Fig. 1-9b). A cadence V–I with I on the accented beat and its root in soprano and bass (Fig. 1-9b, first example) is a *perfect authentic cadence.* This type of authentic cadence is used to close a piece or a section of music. The other cadences in Fig. 1-9b are *imperfect authentic cadences.* An incomplete ending in the course of the music on V (Fig. 1-9a, first example) is a *half cadence.* Imperfect authentic cadences are also used for this purpose. The addition of IV–I after a perfect authentic cadence forms a *plagal cadence* (Fig. 1-9c, second example). The progression V–VI at a cadential point is a *deceptive cadence.*

Figure 1-9

I V I IV V I

IV I

Exercise 7a. Starting with the various positions of the C triad in Ex. 6a, write the progressions I–V–I and I–IV–I in strict voice leading. Work these progressions out in G, F, D, B♭, A and E♭.

Free Voice Leading

Voices that are not conducted to the closest tones of the next chord are in *free voice leading.* This type of melodic movement may be necessary with a wider ranging soprano and when it is advisable either to double tones other than the root or to move tendency tones irregularly. Compare the unacceptable measure 1 of Fig. 1-10a and the poor example of free voice leading shown in Fig. 1-10b with the acceptable version shown in Fig. 1-10c. A shift of chord tones is always permissible in chord repetition (Fig. 1-10d). Free voice leading provides an opportunity to make inner lines more interesting. This is subject to restrictions in voice crossing (Fig. 1-10e) where the alto falls below the tenor note; the soprano drops below the level of the previous alto note in Fig. 1-10f. Voice leading like this should be avoided because it obscures the identity of each line. Melodic lines may cross in counterpoint momentarily when the natural sweep of a line brings it across another line.

Figure 1-10

no 3rd

Parallels

Examine the parallel motion of bass and soprano indicated by arrows in Fig. 1-11a. These voices an octave apart (here a double octave) move to another octave. *Parallel octaves* in the same pair of voices have the effect of thinning down the texture momentarily to three voices, while giving the doubled tones undue prominence. Parallel octaves anywhere in two-voice counterpoint reduce the texture at that point to single line melody duplicated in the octave. The doubled leading tone of V mentioned earlier compels a resolution in parallel octaves, as seen in Fig. 1-11b.

Parallel perfect fifths are shown in Fig. 1-11c. They are perhaps less obvious in Fig. 1-11d. The perfect fifth, held as a concord in organum and yielding after some time to the preferred thirds and sixths, is a hollow sounding interval. Eighteenth century practice still regarded the perfect fifth as a concord but barred two or more in succession in the same pair of voices. Their empty effect is readily apparent in two-part counterpoint. *Do not use parallel fifths.* Both types of

18

undesirable parallels appear in Fig. 1-11e as a consequence of parallel motion in all four voices.

Figure 1-11

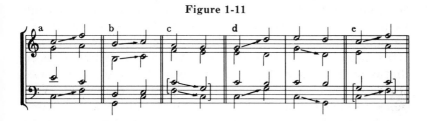

Exercise 8. Write the I–V–I and I–IV–I in free voice leading first in C, then in keys up to and including those with three sharps and flats.

Triads IV and V have no tones in common. Parallel motion in all voices (Fig. 1-12a) results in parallel fifths and octaves. These parallels are eliminated when the upper voices move contrary to the bass (Fig. 1-12b). Voice leading in *all* stepwise root movement, V–VI, I–II, etc., is treated the same way. The injunction hereafter to "avoid parallels" should be taken to mean parallel fifths or octaves.

Figure 1-12

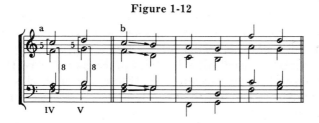

Exercise 9. Write the progression IV–V in all major keys and in three positions, as in Fig. 1-12b.

Triad Progressions in Common Practice

The strongest triad progression is V–I, dominant resolving to the harmonic center of the key, in root movement down a fifth or its equivalent, up a fourth. Similar *fifth-fall* progressions are common: II–V, VI–II, I–IV, etc. Voice leading is the same as in V–I. Progressions gravitating toward I make for tonally centered harmony and should be used frequently. Fifth-fall progressions further removed from the tonic center, such as III–VI and VII–III, decrease in dynamic drive and are less often encountered. The progression I–IV carries the harmony away from the central I. IV returns to I either directly– through V, IV–V–I or it progresses in the cycle of downward fifths, I–IV–VII–III–(VI–II–V–I). Any group of two or more chords in this order may be used freely. Those in parentheses are most common. Root movement up in fifths, except IV–I, takes the harmony in contrary direction to the normal progression toward I: V–II–VI–III, etc. Such progressions tend to return to tonic immediately, I–V–I, or in due course, I–V–II–V–I. VI–III is used on occasion for its modal character.

Stepwise root movement is next in common usage. Progressions most often employed are: IV–V, V–VI, VI–V, I–II and less often III–IV. II–I is used occasionally. Voice leading is the same as in IV–V; *i.e.*, move the upper voices contrary to the bass. Least satisfactory are II–III, III–II, IV–III, VI–VII and VII–VI. Consideration of I–VII and VII–I will be deferred.

The best progressions of chords with root movement down in thirds are: I–VI, IV–II, and VI–IV. These paired chords have two tones in common. In strict voice leading keep these tones in the same pair of voices and move the fourth voice contrary to the bass. Contrary motion in at least one part is necessary to avoid parallels in free voice leading. Similar root movement with other paired triads is weak: V–III, II–VII, and III–I. The diminished triad VII is less effective with root in bass; it may be used with V: VII–V. Except for I–III, progressions with roots ascending in thirds are, as a class, least satisfactory: II–IV, III–V, IV–VI, and VII–II; VI–I is used occasionally.

Any triad may be repeated. Chord repetition is not chord movement and therefore is not a progression. It is employed mainly with I, V, IV, VI and II. A standard pattern of progressions in common use is often called a *formula*.

Exercise 10a. Write each of the following formulae in four-part harmony in C, F and G: I–VI–II–V–I; I–I–V–VI–IV–II–V; I–IV–V–II–V–I. Rewrite these and the other formulae in Ex. 10 in free four-part harmony with a different soprano line.

Exercise 10b. Repeat the process in B♭, D and E♭ with I–III–IV–II–V–I; I–VI–V–V–II–V–I; in A, E and B with I–V–

IV–V–V–I; I–III–VI–II–II–V–I; in A♭, D♭ and G♭ with
I–V–VI–II–I–IV–I; I–III–VI–I–II–V–I.

Exercise 10c. Devise original formulae in different keys.

As a matter of regular practice we will reduce four-part
harmony to two parts, soprano and bass. These two lines, although lacking rhythmic diversity, are polyphonic since each
line is melodic. Two-part harmony will, for some time, provide
the scaffolding for melodic and rhythmic diversity.

Exercise 10d. Reduce each formula in Exs. 10a and b to a
simple bass and soprano line, as in Fig. 1-13. Intervals
between these voices will be mainly thirds (tenths), with
an occasional fifth or octave. Avoid parallels and a fifth
followed by an octave, or vice versa. Use contrary motion
wherever possible. Parallel thirds may be used in stepwise progressions: IV–V, VI–V, etc. An octave skip in
bass is permissible in chord repetition. Work out each unit
with at least two different soprano lines.

Use the treble staff for the upper line and bass staff for the
lower line in this and *all subsequent two-part exercises*. This
permits more freedom of range in instrumental writing. These
exercises form the basis for further work in Ex. 11.

Figure 1-13

I VI II V I   I IV V II V I

Nonharmonic Tones

Play each voice of Fig. 1-14 separately, noting the melodic and
rhythmic individuality of each line. Now observe the har-
monious effect of the voices in combination. While each voice
maintains its independence and melodic purpose, the chordal

framework, seen in the large note-heads, binds the texture into a generally concordant unit moving toward a projected harmonic goal. The harmonic structure may not be readily apparent because of the presence of modifying nonchordal or *nonharmonic* tones, indicated by small note-heads in the example.

Figure 1-14

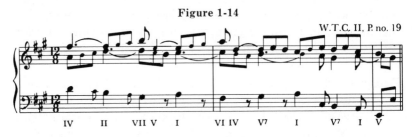

Nonharmonic tones are indispensable in writing free flowing melody and in subduing the bold harmonic framework of contrapuntal passages. They also contribute a vital admixture of dissonance to the generally consonant nature of the texture. These tones are sometimes called "nonessential tones" to distinguish them from the "essential" chord tones. This distinction is apt to be misleading in view of the substantial importance of nonharmonic tones. We will explore the resources inherent in various types of nonharmonic tones in the course of our study.

Nonharmonic tones, depending on their rhythmic placement, are discordant with the prevailing chord in varying degrees. Fig. 1-14a includes several types of nonharmonic tones. Those falling on unaccented beats and unaccented portions of a beat are least discordant. Examine Fig. 1-15 with particular attention to the starred notes. These are *unaccented passing tones*, the most common type of nonharmonic tone.

Figure 1-15

The Unaccented Passing Tone

A nonchordal tone on the unaccented beat or unaccented portion of a beat, used ordinarily to pass from one chord tone to another, is called an *unaccented passing tone*. It is almost invariably a tone of short duration and may form any interval concordant or discordant with a tone of a second voice. Tones in a melody are classified as chordal or nonchordal according to the way they are harmonized. Note the changing function of the same melody tones in different harmonizations (Fig. 1-16) ; starred tones are passing tones.

Figure 1-16

A single passing tone fills the skip of a third in the same chord (Fig. 1-17a). In the same interval, the passing tone leads to a tone of a different chord* (Fig. 1-17b). Two passing tones fill the skip of a fourth in the same chord (Fig. 1-17c). The second of these passing tones leads to a chord tone harmonized by a different chord* (Fig. 1-17d). A scalewise group of four tones consisting of a passing tone between two tones of a chord is followed by a tone of a different chord (Fig. 1-17e).

Figure 1-17

* The second chord tone is common to both chords in the first measure of these examples.

Exercise 11a. Using the simple bass and soprano lines of Ex. 10d, derived from progressions in Exs. 10a and b, fill in skips of a third and fourth in soprano with passing tones, as in Fig. 1-18a. A skip of a fifth may be treated as in Fig. 1-16, measure 1. Where there is no skip in your soprano line from one note to the next, a different chord tone may be substituted, provided that no parallels result (Fig. 1-18b). Do not change the bass. Observe the resolution of tendency tones if possible. Use rhythms similar to those in the example, and at least two different soprano versions for each formula.

Figure 1-18

Exercise 11b. Work out the formulae of Ex. 10d with passing tones in $\frac{3}{8}$, using rhythms similar to those in the model (Fig. 1-18c).

Passing tones resulted in conjunct or scalewise melody in the preceding exercise. A more interesting line includes skips from one chord tone to another, disjunct movement.

The following exercises are designed to explore various combinations of chord skips within the prevailing chord and passing tones that move from one chord tone to another. You will be amply repaid for the time devoted to these and other exercises of this type because they open up ampler melodic resources.

The model (Fig. 1-19) demonstrates various ways of moving from a chord tone on step 1 up a third, to a chord tone on step 3. Both tones may be harmonized with I or VI; IV–I is

24

possible; I–VI with the same scale tones is somewhat weak because the first interval with the bass is an octave and that for the second chord is a fifth, both hollow intervals. It is preferable that at least one of the intervals be a third. The chord-third generally appears soon after a hollow interval. Weak progressions like VI–I and V–III and those producing parallels with the bass (I–III, IV–VI) should not be used. Study the model closely. Large note-heads are chord tones. Note that the second chord tone may be approached from above or below. Read the footnotes keyed to the music.

Figure 1-19

[1] A skip of an octave with a chord tone eliminates the immediate repetition of a note.

[2] A skip from chord tone to chord tone is always possible.

[3] An occasional rest at the beginning of a beat may be used; if it follows a nonharmonic tone, the note after the rest should be a resolution of that tone.

[4] Such repeated tones should be used in moderation. They may be used when the melody continues in a similar pattern.

[5] This reaches the next chord tone too soon; avoid it.

[6] The note D is not a passing tone.

[7] Passing tones that are scale tones are *diatonic* passing tones; the D♯ is a *chromatic* passing tone. These are used sparingly in this style. Observe the combined chord skips and passing tones in $\frac{3}{8}$, Fig. 1-19b.

Exercise 12a.   Other upward skips of a third in soprano between two chord tones, and the harmonizations possible with our present means, are listed below. Using Fig. 1-19 as a model, work out similar variants. Write them in different keys, in $\frac{2}{4}$ and $\frac{3}{8}$. Two units of $\frac{2}{4}$ will be used later in $\frac{4}{4}$ and two units of $\frac{3}{8}$ in $\frac{6}{8}$.

Write the paired soprano scale steps with the bass tones first, as in Fig. 1-20a. This should eliminate parallels between these tones. Move the bass in contrary motion to the upper part wherever possible, as in Fig. 1-20b.

Scale steps	2	4;	3	5;	4	6;	5	7;
Chords	II		I		IV		V	
	V	II	I	V	II		I	V
			VI	V			III	

6	8;	7	2;
IV		V	
VI		V	II
IV	I		
IV	VI		

Permissible progressions in this and in the following exercises are fewer for some paired tones than for others; *e.g.*, V–I cannot be used for 2–5 because it results in parallels; I–VI with steps 1–3 results in successive hollow intervals, octave-fifth. A wider choice will be at our disposal when chord-thirds are used in bass (inversions) and with the introduction of four-tone chords (sevenths).

Exercise 12b. Harmonize each pair of scale tones that skip down a third: 3–1, 2–7, 1–6, etc.; then move from one chord tone to another, as in Fig. 1-19. Check your progressions with the material on pp. 19–20.

The process of working out Exs. 13 and 14 is similar to that of Ex. 12: (1) harmonize paired scale tones in soprano that are a fourth, fifth and sixth apart, in two-part harmony; (2) move from the first note of each pair to the second, either in scalewise motion of chord and passing tones or in a combination of chord skips and passing tones, as in Fig. 1-19. Write each part of these exercises in a different key.

Harmonizations are the same for paired scale tones with a skip up a fourth and the same lettered notes skipping down a fifth. This applies to skips down a fourth and up a fifth; up a third and down a sixth; and down a third and up a sixth. The wider interval skip, of course, will have different melodic treatment.

Exercise 13a. Use paired scale tones that skip up a fourth: 1–4, 2–5, etc. Avoid the parallels shown in Fig. 1-20c and, wherever possible, successive hollow intervals on the second half beat and the next beat (Fig. 1-20d). At this stage do not skip away from a "passing" tone (Fig.

1-20e) ; the starred note is a different type of nonharmonic tone.

Figure 1-20

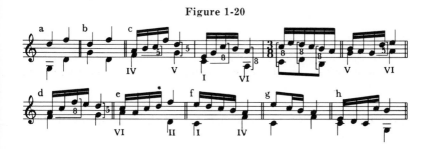

Exercise 13b.   Use the paired scale tones with a skip down a fifth: 5–1, 6–2, etc. A scalewise unit (Fig. 1-20f) or chord skip and passing tone (Fig. 1-20g) can be used. Employ the unison sparingly (Fig. 1-20h).

Exercise 13c.   Use paired scale tones with a skip down a fourth: 8–5, 7–4, 6–3, etc., and skips up a fifth: 1–5, 2–6, etc. The second note of each pair may be approached from above, as in Fig. 1-20h.

Exercise 14a.   Use paired scale tones that skip down a sixth.

Exercise 14b.   Use paired scale tones that skip up a sixth.

Where two adjacent chord tones in melody are a second apart it is impossible to insert a diatonic passing tone. The chromatic passing tone (Fig. 1-21a) may be used occasionally. Bach, with certain notable exceptions, uses chromatic passing tones sparingly. Chromatic tones in his music often indicate a chromatically altered chord or a key change.

The first scale tone may take a chord skip (Fig. 1-21b). A combination of chord skip and passing tone can be used to approach the second tone (Fig. 1-21c). Two examples of the various possibilities in $\frac{3}{8}$ are seen in Fig. 1-21d.

Figure 1-21

Exercise 15a. Harmonize each pair of ascending scale steps: 1–2, 2–3, etc., then work out as many variants of Fig. 1-21 as possible. Use different major keys in this and the next exercise.

Exercise 15b. Repeat the process with descending paired scale tones: 8–7, 7–6, etc.

Except for stepwise root movement, two triads have one or two tones in common; *e.g.*, I and IV, IV and II, etc. Clearly when common tones occur in the upper part, a passing tone cannot be interpolated. Examine Fig. 1-22. The chord tone skips to another chord tone and returns scalewise to the common tone (Fig. 1-22a). The chord skip comes at the end of the unit (Fig. 1-22b). The tones move away and return scalewise (Fig. 1-22c).

Figure 1-22a–c

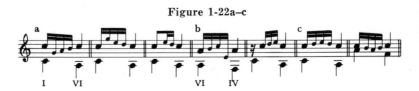

The last note of a unit is in a common tone tie (Fig. 1-22d). It is generally preferable to tie notes of equal value and to tie a longer note to a shorter one (Fig. 1-22e), than the reverse (Fig. 1-22f). Avoid tying short notes except when they run in a continuous pattern (Fig. 1-22g). A simple chord skip intervenes between common tones (Fig. 1-22h).

Figure 1-22d–h

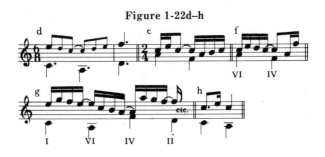

Exercise 16a. Employing the formulae of Exs. 10a and b, write an upper part* in uniform rhythm for each, as shown in the model (Fig. 1-23a), using chord skips and passing tones. Check each unit for parallels. Resolve tendency tones, except in scalewise movement and in leaps within the same chord.

Figure 1-23

Exercise 16b. Use the same harmonic material in $\frac{3}{8}$, in varied rhythm. Use common tone ties and rests as in Fig. 1-23b. Do the same thing in $\frac{4}{4}$.

* The soprano and bass in two-part writing will henceforth be called upper and lower voice (abbreviated: u.v., l.v.).

2

First Inversions; Interval Implications; Melodic Figures and Figure-Groups; Sequences

Triads in First Inversion

Progressions with roots in bass are solid in effect but the bass line is apt to be stiff and angular. A more melodious line is obtained by substituting chord-thirds for roots in some of the triads. Compare two versions of the same progressions in Fig. 2-1. The first has roots only in bass; the chord-third replaces the root of three triads in the second version. Play the bass of both, noting the smooth flowing line of the second version. A triad with its third in bass is in *first inversion;* with the fifth in bass it is in *second inversion.*

Triads in first inversion are referred to as *chords of the sixth* because their roots lie a sixth or a sixth plus one or more octaves above the bass tone. The symbol indicating first inversion is the Roman numeral representing the chord and the Arabic 6; *e.g.,* I_6 (One-six), IV_6, II_6, etc.

Figure 2-1

$$\text{I} \quad \text{V}_6 \quad \text{VI} \quad \text{II}_6 \quad \text{V} \quad \text{I}_6 \quad \text{VI}$$

Inverted triads are lighter in effect than the same chords with root in bass. They afford a moving bass in chord repetition and make available progressions that are weak or poor.

Doubling

Regulations governing doubling in uninverted triads apply in general to first inversions. Double the root preferably, or the fifth if necessary, in I_6, IV_6 and V_6. Double the root or third in II_6, VI_6 and III_6. Double the third in VII_6. Avoid doubling the third of major triads in four-part harmony unless the lines of two voices move through the doubled third in contrary motion, as in Fig. 2-2a. The linear purpose here, and in two-part counterpoint, outweighs considerations of doubling. Otherwise the root or fifth is used in soprano with a first inversion.

Progressions of Triads in First Inversion

Inversion does not alter the relative frequency with which root progressions in fifths, in thirds and by step are used. Progressions down in fifths (or up in fourths) remain strongest; e.g., V_6–I, II_6–V, I_6–IV; also V–I_6, II–V_6, I–IV_6, IV–VII_6, etc. With the exception of V_6–I_6, both of the paired triads may be inverted: I_6–IV_6, III_6–VI_6, etc. The leading tone in V_6–I_6 is improperly resolved (Fig. 2-2b). Instances of irregular resolution of the leading tone in Bach will be discussed later. The bass in II_6–V_6 should drop a diminished fifth (Fig. 2-2c) to avoid the ungainly upward leap of an augmented fourth.

Progressions up in fifths (or down in fourths) are weaker as they recede from the central I. Those that include I are most useful: I–V_6, I_6–V, I_6–V_6, IV–I_6, IV_6–I_6. V–II_6 tends to return to V. The preceding comment on II_6–V_6 applies to V_6–II_6; skip up a diminished fifth. Less common are II–VI_6, VI–III_6 and III–VII_6.

A sense of harmonic motion is maintained in progressions

CH. 2

Figure 2-2

down in thirds when the first of two such paired triads is inverted; *e.g.*, IV₆–II and I₆–VI, or when both are inverted, I₆–VI₆ and II₆–VII₆. Inverting the second triad *only* produces a common tone bass; I–VI₆, VI–IV₆ or II–VII₆. This and the single tone difference between the triads results in almost static harmony. It is inadvisable to place the second of these chords across the bar-line or across the mid-accent in $\frac{4}{4}$, from beat 2 to 3, in $\frac{6}{8}$ from beat 3 to 4 (Fig. 2-2d), unless a strong harmonic progression is not desired. Repeated bass tones representing two different chords are, however, used in counterpoint when the course of the lower melodic line requires it.

The progression V–III is weak with or without inversion. III₆–I approximates V–I; VII–V₆, VII₆–V and VII₆–V₆ may be freely employed as a variant of dominant repetition.

The inherent ineffectiveness of root progressions up in thirds is not appreciably altered by inversion. The most useful are those in dominant repetition; V–VII₆, V₆–VII and V₆–VII₆, as well as III₆–V and III₆–V₆. Progressions of VII–II; *i.e.*, VII–II₆, VII₆–II and VII₆–II₆, generally revert to dominant harmony; VII₆–II–V–I. Those with common bass tones; I₆–III, II₆–IV, III₆–V, etc., are harmonically immobile. Bach uses VI₆–I at times, as well as VI–I₆.

Practically all root movement by step up or down may be used with either or both chords of a pair inverted. Those that include the primary triads I, IV and V, inverted or uninverted, are in the main, the stronger progressions. A series of first inversions in scale order up or down is used on occasion; *e.g.*, V₆–VI₆–VII₆–I₆ or V₆–IV₆–III₆–II₆. Parallels result when all voices in these progressions move in parallel motion (Fig. 2-3a). This can be redressed by using contrary motion in an inner voice with altered doubling (Fig. 2-3b) and by an inner voice skip (Fig. 2-3c). Ordinarily the soprano as a series of roots or chord-fifths runs in parallel sixths or thirds with the bass. The soprano may, however, move independently (Fig. 2-3d).

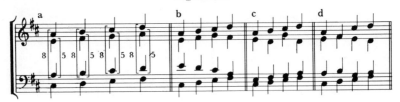

Figure 2-3

Exercise 1. Write the following progressions in four-part harmony in the keys indicated by capital letters. A dash signifies the repetition of the chord for one beat; two dashes extends it for two beats. The beat is divided between two chords in parentheses. Re-examine your work for parallels, recommended doubling and resolution of tendency tones.

C $\frac{2}{4}$ I I₆|IV I₆|II II₆|V–|I III₆|VI II₆|VII₆ V|I–||

F $\frac{3}{8}$ I I₆ VII₆|III IV IV₆|V V V₆ V|I₆ – – |IV IV₆ V₆|I–II₆|VII₆– V|I– –||

G $\frac{6}{8}$ I–III₆ VI–VI₆|II II₆ I₆ V– –|I V₆–VI–V|IV₆ V–I– –||

B♭ $\frac{2}{4}$ I VI₆|V₆ V|VII₆ V|I–|V₆ IV₆|V VI|III₆ V|I–||

D $\frac{3}{8}$ I VII₆ V₆|I IV₆ II₆|V–(VII₆V₆)|I–III₆|(IV–II₆) V₆–|I– (IV VI)| V₆ VII₆ V|I– –||

E♭ $\frac{4}{4}$ I V₆ I I₆|VI II₆ V–|I IV VII₆–|V II₆ V–|I₆ I IV₆ IV|V₆ V VI–| III IV II₆ V|V–I–||

A $\frac{2}{4}$ I (I₆ III)|IV (II VII₆)|I (VI V₆)|I V|(IV₆ V₆) I|(II I₆) II₆| V₆ (IV₆ V)|I–||

E $\frac{3}{4}$ I VI IV₆|III₆ II₆ I₆|V–V₆|VI₆ VII₆ I₆|II₆–VII₆|I₆–I|II₆ I₆ VII₆|I||

Interval Implications

Chords in a progression are easily identified when all the tones of each chord are present. In two-part counterpoint the harmonic framework merely consists of a series of intervals, each representing a complete chord. Our objective is to make this framework clear with these limited means.

We used the major third previously to denote a major triad.

34

CH. 2CH. 2

While this interval best represents such chords, it may also stand for the first inversion of a minor triad (Fig. 2-4a). Working with a rhythmically active upper part only, we must use additional chord tones to confirm the major third as representing the major or minor triad. The inclusion of the chord-fifth (Fig. 2-4b) verifies the major third as denoting the major triad; the presence of the root (Fig. 2-4c) identifies it as indicating the minor triad. Changing the bass tone from root to third, or the reverse (Fig. 2-4d), confirms the harmony.

Figure 2-4

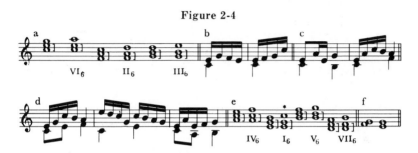

Minor thirds best imply minor triads (Fig. 2-4e).* But they are also components of major triads: IV_6, I_6, V_6. The minor third of II may also be used to imply VII_6. Subsequent melody tones or tones in the other part confirm the interval as indicative of a major, minor or diminished triad. Bach, incidentally, uses VII in both inverted and uninverted form. A preceding interval may identify the one following, as in Fig. 2-4f. Here an interval representing V^7 precedes the minor third. The normal resolution of that chord is to I, not to III. Major and minor thirds, as we will see later, are less indicative of seventh chords than other intervals.

The harmonic implications of a third at some point in a two-part contrapuntal work may be indefinite. Bach at times consciously uses intervals in equivocal manner to avoid an abrupt chord change or shift in key.

The perfect fourth will not be used at present to imply a triad, except as noted in Ex. 3 and Fig. 2-7a. Bach employs it as a harmonic interval on occasion. The minor sixth (Fig. 2-5a) represents a first inversion of a major triad; the major sixth (Fig. 2-5b) stands for the inverted minor triad as well as for VII_6. Here the chord-fifth is required in subsequent tones or in the other part to confirm its identity. The augmented

* The minor third starred in this example represents I_6 more often than III.

fourth (Fig. 2-5c), also used for V^7, will not be used in our present exercises as a harmony interval.

The root of the perfect fifth (Fig. 2-5d) usually indicates the triad. This interval is used proportionately less to imply the harmony than thirds and sixths. The chord-third (Fig. 2-5e) usually follows closely. The octave offers little indication of the harmony, except as I in the cadence or V preceding that cadence. Intervals implying seventh chords will be considered in connection with study of these chords.

Figure 2-5

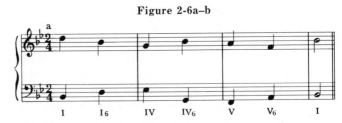

min.6 I₆ IV₆ V₆ Maj.6 II₆ VI₆   VII₆

To ignore interval implications is to invite faulty sounding contrapuntal passages that lack harmonic direction.

Exercise 2a.   Reduce each unit of Ex. 1 to two-part harmony, as in Fig. 2-6a. Note the exchange of root and third between lower and upper parts in chord repetition. Use thirds and sixths mainly, with an occasional fifth to imply the harmony. Reserve the octave for the cadence.

Exercise 2b.   Elaborate the upper part with passing tones and chord skips, in uniform rhythm, as in Fig. 2-6b. An occasional broken chord (starred) may be used. Observe the altered last note. It may be necessary to substitute a different upper chord tone for the original to improve the melodic line. Do not alter the harmony. Check your work for parallels.

Figure 2-6a–b

I   I₆   IV   IV₆   V   V₆   I

* This sixth more often represents I than III₆ in Bach. He uses other sixths freely to imply the triad only, and not its second inversion.
† The same interval is used for the second inversion of I.

Exercise 2c. Using the same two-part harmony, proceed with varied rhythm in the upper part, as in Fig. 2-6c.

Observe the similarity of the melodic units bracketed in Fig. 2-6d. Melodic writing like this unifies what would otherwise become a line of meandering tones.

Figure 2-6c–d

Exercise 3a. Employing two-part harmony, write lower parts in uniform rhythm to each unit of Ex. 2a, as in Fig. 2-6d. Check your work for parallels. The perfect fourth, hitherto used with one of its tones as passing tone, may now be used on a weak fraction of the beat as a chord interval (Figs. 2-7a and b). For the present, avoid the use of it shown in Fig. 2-7c.

Exercise 3b. Supplement the upper part of each unit in Ex. 3a with additional chord tones, as in Fig. 2-8a. This will fill in a missing chord tone in some instances. The octave may be used on the second half beat or on a weak fraction of the beat.

Figure 2-7

Figure 2-8a

Exercise 3c. Write lower parts in varied rhythm with the two-part units of Ex. 2a, as in Fig. 2-8b; do this also in $\frac{3}{8}$; add supplementary chord tones in the upper parts. Note the melodic pattern in the bass (Fig. 2-8b).

Figure 2-8b

The Motive, Figure and Figure-Group

The shortest coherent unit in melody is the motive or figure, a particle that cannot be broken down into simpler constituents. It may consist merely of two, three or four notes, as in the slurred units of Fig. 2-9a. The first unit of Fig. 2-9b illustrates a five-note motive.

In ordinary usage the terms *motive* and *figure* are synonymous. We will reserve the term *motive* for any brief unit that is extracted from a *theme* (subject) and used to generate

38

melodic passages. The five-note motive of Fig. 2-9b is the core of a fugal theme that dominates the whole fugue. Examine the whole theme.

Figure 2-9

The term *figure* will be applied here to similar melodic fragments that do not have a thematic origin. Like the motive, they will be used to develop passages of similar material. The *figure-group* is a melodic unit composed of at least two different figures. Examine Fig. 2-15a. The notes of beat 1 constitute one figure; the broken chord notes of beat 2 is another figure. This two-beat figure-group forms the pattern for the next unit. The last note of a figure is sometimes the first note of the next figure. Such elision is seen in Fig. 2-11b. The first figure consists of the tied note and the scale line to D♭; the second figure starts with D♭ as a broken chord figure. Together these figures form a figure-group.

Exercise 3d. After reviewing first inversions from the beginning of this chapter, plan several original chord series, each at least six to eight measures long; then: (1) sketch your progressions in two-part harmony; (2) write a rhythmically active upper part for each one, using figure-groups; (3) do the same with the lower part, as in Fig. 2-8b.

Harmonic Rhythm

In working out Ex. 1 you may have observed that the number of chords in a measure varies, that patterns of chord change are regular and irregular and that strong and weak progressions fall on various beats in a measure. The distribution of

---

* Reduced to two voices.

different chords in a measure or longer unit is the *harmonic rhythm* of the unit. Note the regular pattern of chord change in Fig. 1-15 and in Figs. 2-8b and 2-11a. Chord repetition in the last two examples is not considered as chord change. Compare these examples with the irregular chord distribution in Fig. 5-10b, second example.

A single chord change may occur with every measure (Fig. 2-11a), with consecutive beats (Fig. 2-11b), with consecutive half beats (Fig. 4-13d), or lesser fractions of a beat (Fig. 2-10). Regular patterns of chord change are less suited to polyphonic than to homophonic music because melodic lines that are different in length, contour and climax sweep across bar-lines and cannot be restricted to harmonization in regular harmonic rhythm.

Figure 2-10

W.T.C. II, F. no. 5

A factor that reinforces relatively regular harmonic rhythm is the presence of *harmonic accents; i.e.,* accents created by chord resolution. The tension inherent in V and V⁷ tendency tones, and released in resolution, creates a harmonic accent on I. Similar accents, though less pronounced, occur in other fifth-fall progressions with the second triad of the pair on the accented beat. The location of harmonic accents has a bearing on their effect. Observe the marked difference in this respect between the location of fifth-fall progressions in Figs. 2-11a and 2-11b. In the first example the I of V₆–I and the V of II₆–V fall on first beats. In the second example similar harmony is carried across the bar-lines. Placing these chords as indicated by the dotted bar-lines would make the harmonic accent coincide with the strong beats, a procedure that goes counter to the upper phrase slurring and Bach's intention. Play the example as if it started on beat 1 and note the difference. The notes in Fig. 2-11c are roots of the implied harmony. Examine the three preceding bass measures of this invention. This

40

should reveal the necessity for the conflict between harmonic accents and metric accents, a device that sets up exciting contrapuntal tension.

Progressions in thirds (I–VI, IV–II) are weak in harmonic accent because they share two common tones and similar functions. Harmonic accent is negligible with triads sharing the same bass tone or function. Stepwise progressions that include one or both primary triads create harmonic accents by virtue of movement in all voices to different tones.

Exercise 4. Plot the harmonic rhythm for each chord series in Ex. 1. Treat chord repetition with or without inversion as a single chord, as well as triads with the same bass tone or function, for example:

$$\begin{array}{c}\frac{3}{4}\end{array}$$ I I_6 IV | V II V_6 | I II VII$_6$ I | VI$_6$ IV II$_6$ | V$_6$ VII$_6$ V | I

Our attention has been centered so far on the use of passing and chord tones in each rhythmically active voice. As we proceed with our studies we will be more deeply concerned with various aspects of melodic structure.

The Melodic Sequence

Repetition is the fundamental means of achieving cohesion and unity in music. A figure or figure-group repeated in the same voice, but on a higher or lower level, is a *melodic sequence* (Fig. 2-11a). Slurred units in each voice are sequences of the initial units. See also the lower voice in Fig. 2-8b and the upper voice in Fig. 1-23a. The melodic sequence, apart from imitation (repetition in a different voice), is the most common form of melodic repetition in polyphonic music.

Sequences in one voice are also written without a corresponding sequence in another voice. Play the lower part of Fig. 2-11a, substituting the notes in brackets. In this instance the lower slurred unit is a *modified sequence*. (Read the paragraph on this on pp. 51–52.)

A more elaborate initial unit and its sequence in the lower part accompanies the upper part in Fig. 2-11b. Examine the alternative slurring in each part. While the initial unit may be considered as starting with the first note tied (u.v.), another phrasing that starts after the tied note is indicated by upper

Figure 2-11a

slurs. Initial units often start on an unaccented note and end on an accented note. Observe a similar choice of phrasing in the lower part. Your attention is drawn to this point because the initial unit (and its sequence) do not invariably start with the beginning of a beat. The starred notes form seventh chords; the expected G in the u.v. is altered to G♭ to provide a momentary dominant of IV.

Figure 2-11b

The lower part of Fig. 2-11b, reduced to chord roots, is seen in Fig. 2-11c. We will soon learn how to develop single chord tones so as to produce lower part sequences like that in Fig. 2-11b. Bracketed notes in the lower part of that example conclude a preceding line of thematic material. Bach otherwise would have started the lower part as in Fig. 2-11d.

Figure 2-11c–d

Melodic sequences are modified in various ways that will be examined in due course. Our immediate objective is to use sequences in conjunction with set harmonic patterns.

An initial unit and its sequence may be harmonized by single chords (Fig. 2-12a). While the progressions underlying the melodic sequences in Fig. 2-12b are acceptable, they do not follow a particular harmonic pattern like that in Fig. 2-11a.

42

Figure 2-12

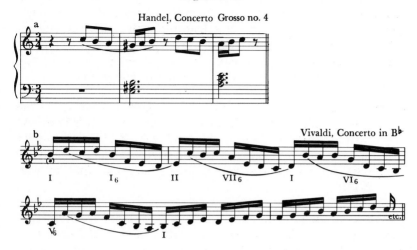

Handel, Concerto Grosso no. 4

Triads in Harmonic Sequences

Examine the implied harmony in Fig. 2-11a. Two triads with their inversions (VI–II) in fifth-fall progression are followed by a similar type of progression (V–I). The second pair of chords is a *harmonic sequence,* a similar pattern of harmonic progression but on a different level. Figure 2-13a illustrates harmonic sequences in four-part harmony of the initial unit, VI–II. The soprano moves from chord-third of VI to root of II; the same melodic pattern is followed in the sequence. Moreover, each voice in V–I is a sequence of the same voice in VI–II. Observe that the altered lower part in Fig. 2-11a would nullify the harmonic sequence.

Figure 2-13

Different initial soprano parts for the progressions of Fig. 2-13a are given in Fig. 2-13b. The melodic logic of the sequence permits irregularities in voice leading such as the movement of the leading tone, starred in the example. Harmonic sequences are important in contrapuntal passage work. Exs. 5 through 9 are the bases for later work in composition.

Exercise 5a. Write Fig. 2-13b in four-part harmony. Do the same with fifth-third, fifth-root and root-third as the initial soprano. Reduce this and Fig. 2-13a to two-part harmony. Avoid skips of consecutive fourths in the lower part, shown in Fig. 2-13c; use a bass like that in Fig. 2-13a.

While single sequences (as in Fig. 2-13a) are used, at least two sequences often follow the initial unit. Fifth-fall root movement can be carried full circle back to the first chord; *e.g.*, VI–II, V–I, IV–VII, III–VI. Observe that roots of the first chord of each pair form a descending scale line.

Exercise 5b. Continue Fig. 2-13a in four-part harmony with IV–VII, III–VI and conclude with II_6–V–I. Reduce the parts to two-part harmony. The same progressions paired differently: II–V, I–IV, VII–III, also return to VI–II, V–I.

Exercise 6. One or the other of each pair is inverted in the following harmonic sequences. Write these progressions in the given keys in four-part harmony, then reduce them to two-part harmony.

G $\frac{2}{4}$ I_6–ΙV, VII_6–ΙIII, VI_6–ΙII, V_6–ΙI;

F $\frac{2}{4}$ I–ΙIV$_6$, VII–ΙIII$_6$, VI–ΙII$_6$, V–ΙI$_6$;

B♭ $\frac{2}{4}$ VI–ΙII$_6$, V–ΙI$_6$, IV–ΙVII$_6$, conclude with V–I

D $\frac{2}{4}$ I–I$_6$–ΙIV, VII–VII$_6$–ΙIII, VI–VI$_6$–ΙII, V–V$_6$–ΙI; Use a
       rhythm of ♩♩ ♩

E♭ $\frac{3}{4}$ I_6–I–ΙIV, VII_6–VII–ΙIII, VI_6–VI–ΙII, V_6–V–ΙI;

A $\frac{3}{4}$ VI–ΙII–II$_6$, V–ΙI–I$_6$, IV–ΙVII–VII$_6$, conclude with V–ΙI;

E $\frac{3}{4}$ VI–ΙII$_6$–II, V–ΙI$_6$–I, IV–ΙVII$_6$–VII, conclude with V–ΙI;

A♭ $\frac{6}{8}$ VI–VI$_6$–ΙII, V–V$_6$–ΙI, IV–IV$_6$–ΙVII, conclude with
       V–V$_6$–ΙI; Use ♩. ♩ ♪

44   CH. 2

Exercise 7. Initial root movement down a fifth (or up a fourth) is followed by similar units on successive scale steps upward. Follow the directions given in Ex. 6.

C $\frac{2}{4}$ I–IV, II–V, III–VI, IV–VII, conclude with V–I;

F $\frac{2}{4}$ I$_6$–IV, II$_6$–V, III$_6$–VI, IV$_6$–VII, V$_6$–I

A♭ $\frac{2}{4}$ V$_6$–I, VI$_6$–II, VII$_6$–III, I$_6$–IV, conclude with V$_6$–I;

B $\frac{2}{4}$ I–IV$_6$, II–V$_6$, III–VI$_6$, IV–VII$_6$, V–I$_6$;

D♭ $\frac{3}{4}$ I–I$_6$IV, II–II$_6$V, III–III$_6$VI, IV–IV$_6$VII, V–V$_6$–I; Use

F♯ $\frac{6}{8}$ I–IV–IV$_6$, II–V–V$_6$, III–VI–VI$_6$, IV–VII–VII$_6$, V–I; Use

Exercise 8a. Three-chord initial units are used in sequence. Work out the following:

C $\frac{4}{4}$ VI–II$_6$–V‖ V–I$_6$–IV‖ IV–VII$_6$–III, conclude with II–V$_6$– I; Use

Exercise 8b. Occasionally one triad in a fifth-fall series is omitted, as in Fig. 2-14. The sequence excuses the irregular doubling of the leading tone in V$_6$. Work out the following with the omission of the triads in parentheses:

G $\frac{3}{4}$ II$_6$–V–I$_6$‖ (IV) VII$_6$–III–VI$_6$‖ (II) V$_6$–I–IV$_6$, conclude with II$_6$–V–I

Figure 2-14

Exercise 9. An initial fifth-fall progression is followed by similar progressions, each a third higher. Work out the following:

D $\frac{2}{4}$ I–IV, III–VI, V–I;

B♭ $\frac{2}{4}$ I$_6$–IV, III$_6$–VI, V$_6$–I;

A $\frac{2}{4}$ I–IV$_6$, III–VI$_6$, V–I$_6$;

Harmonic sequences employing different types of root movement will be studied later.

The Auxiliary Tone

The first tone of each group bracketed in Fig. 2-15 is a chord tone that moves by step to a nonharmonic tone. This tone then returns to the same chord tone. The middle tone of each group (starred in the example) is an *auxiliary tone*, also called a *neighboring tone*. The three-tone group is an *auxiliary figure*. Those below the chord tones are lower auxiliaries. They are used more frequently than upper auxiliaries (starred in Fig. 2-15b).

Figure 2-15a–b

Sonata no. 1 (Flute and figured bass)

Prelude, English Suite no. 3

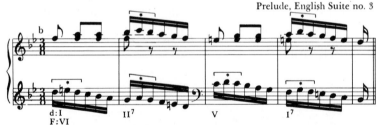

Notes starred in Fig. 2-15c are not auxiliaries. The auxiliary is a nonharmonic tone; the starred notes are harmonized.

The upper auxiliary is invariably the next scale tone above the chord tone. While later composers prefer the chromatic

Figure 2-15c

W.T.C. II, P. no. 7

half step below as lower auxiliary, Bach and his contemporaries favor the diatonic scale step below. The principal exceptions are: (1) step 4♯ is often used as lower auxiliary of step 5. Bach uses both 5–4♯–5 and 5–4–5. (See measure 1, Fig. 2-16a and the middle voice, measure 2 of the same example.) (2) The chromatic lower auxiliary is used with the root of a chord (measure 3 in this excerpt). Let this be your guide in the next exercises. Study the auxiliaries in the *Two-Part Invention, #6.*

Figure 2-16a–c

When the auxiliary returns to the chord tone in the upper part, the lower part may shift to a different tone of the same chord (Fig. 2-16b) or to a tone of a different chord (Fig. 2-16c). Less common is an auxiliary of a passing tone (Fig. 2-16d).

Figure 2-16d

Aria and 30 Variations, no. 27

Auxiliaries are tones of brief duration. For the present they will be used on an unaccented fraction of the beat. The auxiliary figure is used in rhythms such as those shown in Fig. 2-17a.

Figure 2-17

Those in $\frac{2}{4}$ are used in $\frac{3}{4}$, $\frac{4}{4}$ and $\frac{4}{8}$ as well; those in $\frac{3}{8}$ are also used in $\frac{6}{8}$, $\frac{9}{8}$ and $\frac{12}{8}$. The symbols over the notes (Fig. 2-17b) are *mordents*. The first indicates a rapid auxiliary figure with the note's upper neighbor; the second indicates its use with the note's lower neighbor.

When the chord tone following the auxiliary figure is a step higher, it is best to use the lower auxiliary note (Fig. 2-18a); use the upper auxiliary when the following chord tone is a step below. A passing tone often follows the auxiliary figure (Fig. 2-18b), continuing upward from the lower auxiliary and downward from the upper auxiliary. Avoid a passing tone like that marked x (Fig. 2-18c), unless the figure proceeds in sequence. A chord skip may precede or follow the auxiliary figure (Fig. 2-18d). Rhythm patterns in $\frac{3}{8}$ (Fig. 2-18e) may also be used in $\frac{6}{8}$, $\frac{9}{8}$ and $\frac{12}{8}$. The starred notes are unaccented passing tones that will move on to the next chord tones.

Figure 2-18

Each single beat unit (and single $\frac{3}{8}$ measure) of Fig. 2-18 may be extended by sequential repetition (Fig. 2-19a), and by combination with each other (Fig. 2-19b). Tones running scalewise or in broken chord form (Fig. 2-19c) may follow or precede the brief units of Fig. 2-18. A short passage in broken thirds is not uncommon. All these units, and many that are similar, lend themselves to sequential extension.

Exercise 10a. Start with the two-part harmony of Ex. 2a. Write an upper part for the first four formulae in a uniform rhythm of sixteenths, employing auxiliaries, passing tones and chord skips. Imitate the patterns of Figs.

48

Figure 2-19

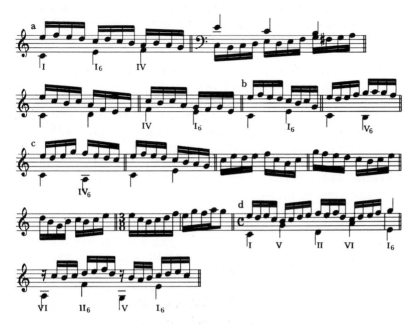

2-18 and 2-19 with patterns of your own. The lower part will consist of the given chord tones.

Exercise 10b. Write similar lower parts for the last four formulae.

Exercise 10c. With the two-part harmony of Ex. 10a, write upper parts in varied rhythms taken from Fig. 2-17a. Add whatever beats in uniform rhythm are necessary to avoid monotony. Examine the rhythm in the upper voice of the *Two-Part Invention, #7,* and the numerous examples of the auxiliary. Include changes of bass tone, as in Figs. 2-16b and c.

Exercise 10d. Write lower parts in varied rhythm, using the two-part harmony in the last four formulae of Ex. 2a.

Auxiliary tones added to chord skips and passing tones amplify our resources in creating figure-groups for sequential treatment (Fig. 2-19d).

Exercise 11a. Write sequential upper parts in uniform rhythm, employing auxiliaries, chord skips and passing tones, based on the two-part harmony of Exs. 5b and 6. Remember that upper chord tones in the sequence have the same relationship as in the initial unit (Fig. 2-13a). Use the given keys.

Exercise 11b. Write sequential lower parts in uniform rhythm, using the same progressions and keys.

Exercise 11c. Use varied rhythms in initial units and their sequences in the upper parts, based on the progressions in Exs. 7, 8 and 9. Use the given keys.

Exercise 11d. Write lower parts in varied rhythm, based on the same progressions.

Bach, Handel, Vivaldi and other eighteenth century composers used sequences both in the key and in moving to a different key to give a passage melodic coherence and harmonic purpose. Unless the sequence is employed in moderation and is modified at times, it becomes little more than a mechanical device, devoid of interest and often unduly long.

The number of sequences usually depends on the length or brevity of the initial unit. More sequences of a short figure can be used (Fig. 2-20a) than of the longer figure-group (Fig. 2-20b). Observe the general curve of this melodic line. Note the leap in the initial figure-group. Subsequent leaps in sequences, even if awkward, are permissible as continuance of an obvious pattern, particularly if the leap is from a chord tone or from the end of one unit to the beginning of the next. Two sequences appear after the initial figure-groups in Figs. 2-20b, e and h. A different figure in sequence follows the first to avoid monotony (Fig. 2-20a).

Figure 2-20a–b

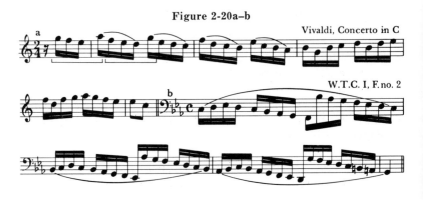

The long initial figure-group in Fig. 2-20c embodies brief sequential figures within it. The short slurs indicate these secondary figures. Note the repeated tones beginning measures 1 and 2. Unless the first note is clearly the beginning of a figure or figure-group, it is generally better to consider that the figure starts with the repeated note, after a tie at the end of the initial figure (Fig. 2-20d) or after a rest (Fig. 3-1). The up-beat is usually part of the initial figure.

Figure 2-20c–d

Exercise 12a.   Add several sequences to a figure; continue with a new figure and sequences of it that move in a direction opposite that of the first sequences.

Exercise 12b.   Write a figure-group; add two sequences.

Exercise 12c.   Write a figure-group that incorporates a figure and one or two sequences of it, as well as a second figure, also with one or two sequences; then write one or two sequences of the entire unit; see Fig. 2-20c.

Exercise 12d.   Write a figure that is not in uniform rhythm; add several sequences; continue with a nonsequential scalewise or broken chord unit in uniform rhythm.

Modified Sequences

Sequences often differ in detail from the pattern of the initial unit. Apart from the variety furnished by modified sequences, changes may be necessary to fit the immediate chord or to avoid unnecessary conflict in interval or rhythm with another voice. While the first sequence may be modified, such changes occur more often in a second or subsequent sequence (Fig. 2-20e).

These are some common modifications: (1) The last sequence may be abbreviated, as in Fig. 2-20d. (2) It may be spun out of the tag end of the initial unit, as in Fig. 2-20c, or with a related unit (Fig. 2-20e). Observe the course this melodic fragment takes. Passages in which the initial figure-group contains one or more relatively long notes wind up with a bustling close in uniform rhythm, as in this example. (3) An intervallic leap may be narrower or wider, as in measure 3, Fig. 2-20e. (4) Tones may be omitted or added, as in Fig. 2-20f, with a resultant alteration of the rhythm. Compare measures 2 and 4. Notes in brackets are the sequential counterpart of notes in measure 2.

Figure 2-20e–f

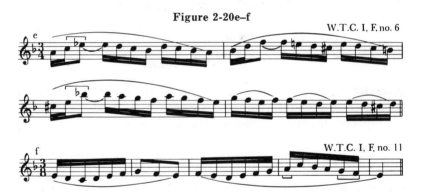

(5) Chromatic inflection of expected diatonic tones are used primarily to produce a shift in key (modulation), as in Figs. 2-20c and h. Note the abrupt ending in Fig. 2-20g, measure 3, and the tapering off in rhythm on the approach to the cadence. Observe the stepwise drop in each sequence and the rise to its high point before dropping to the cadence. Compare it with the upward surge in Fig. 2-20e to a climax on Bb in the middle of the passage, followed by the stepwise fall in fragments.

A figure-group common to music of this period pivots on a reiterated tone. It creates the illusion of two voices, an upper held tone with a moving voice below it. This is carried forward sequentially in Fig. 2-20h. The common tone in alternate repetition is also used with its auxiliary (Fig. 2-20j). Compare the original with the simplified version (Fig. 2-20k).

Figure 2-20g–k

Vivaldi, Concerto in C

Original motives and figure-groups in sequences that are variously organized and modified (as in Fig. 2-20) is the substance of Ex. 12. Repeat each exercise with a different figure or figure-group. Use different major keys. While it is not essential at this point that the ending should cadence on step 1, the last note should be a chord tone.

Exercise 12e. Start with a figure-group; add a sequence; add an abbreviated sequence.

Exercise 12f. Write a figure-group containing one or two chord skips; add a sequence, then another with a change in size of the skips.

Exercise 12g. Write a figure-group that is not in uniform rhythm; add a sequence, then an elaborated sequence.

Exercise 12h. Start with a figure-group in uniform rhythm; add a sequence, then another and simpler version.

Exercise 12j. Write a figure with an intermittently repeated note, as in Fig. 2-20h. The repeated note may also be the low note of the figure. Add two sequences.

Melody Harmonization

There is less occasion in counterpoint to think in terms of melody harmonization than in the study of harmony, since the harmonic basis of a contrapuntal passage should be planned in advance. We do not write a complete single part and then harmonize it.

Not infrequently, however, our imagination outstrips the plotted path. A novel twist in melody or the discovery of a latent thematic resource requires a readjustment of the harmonic plan or recognition of the harmony implied in an altered melodic line.

Upper voice melodies present a simple problem. At this stage the first note of each beat is a chord tone that is either root, third or fifth of some triad. In C, for instance, the note C is root of I, third of VI and fifth of IV. If I is used, I_6 is preferred to avoid the empty octave on the beat. The following table indicates the alternatives for each scale step. Those omitted produce an octave, a perfect fourth, a diminished fifth or augmented fourth on the beat. Re-read the section on interval implications.

For scale step 1	2	3	4	5	6	7
I_6	II_6	I	II	V_6	IV	V
VI	V	VI	IV_6	I_6	II	VII_6
IV	V_6	III_6	VII_6	I	II_6	III
IV_6	VII	VI_6		III		

A series of chords selected at random from the table will not necessarily produce a good progression. For instance, steps 6–7–8 harmonized with IV–III–I is poor; compare it with IV–VII_6–I_6. Review the material from the beginning of Ch. 2 to Ex. 1. The choice of chord may be determined by the succeeding tones of the beat. Are there chord skips with or without nonharmonic tones that spell out the harmony? Can a scalewise fragment be harmonized with a single chord and its inversion? Will the selected chords form a good progression?

Additional factors to consider are: Does your harmonization

54

result in fifths on successive beats? Does the lower line run smoothly, without wide and awkward leaps? Are there melodic sequences, exact or modified, that should be harmonized with harmonic sequences? Are your progressions repetitive and monotonous? Remember that a note in the middle of a beat may require a change in the lower voice from root to third, or vice versa, of the same chord. Remember also that a chord may be sustained over more than a beat. The return to the chord tone after an auxiliary may or may not involve a change of chord.

Most of the questions raised in regard to the upper line also apply to the harmonization of the lower line. As seen from the following table, there are fewer alternatives with chords at our present disposal.

	I	II	I_6	IV	V	VI	V_6
Lower voice	VI_6	VII_6	III	II_6	III_6	IV_6	VII
scale tones	1	2	3	4	5	6	7

Check the lower line for possible sequences. Have you a corresponding pattern of chord tones in the upper part? Any interval formed between nonharmonic tones in the lower voice and a chord tone in the upper voice is acceptable. The perfect fourth is admissible if it does not fall on the beginning of a beat.

Exercise 13. Upper and lower line melodies to be assigned.

Harmonic Sequences, Root Movement up in Fifths

Since sequences of triads with roots up in fifths move away from I (Fig. 2-15a), they are used less often than fifth-fall sequences. Write Exs. 14 through 16 in four-part harmony; reduce them to two parts, then develop each line of chord tones separately in active rhythm. Use auxiliaries, passing tones and chord skips.

Exercise 14a. Write these sequences in G: I–V, II–VI, III–VII, end with V–I. Use these steps in soprano: 3–2, 4–3, 5–4, 7–8.

These sequences in two-part harmony may have alternate tenths and thirds (Fig. 2-21a); despite the irregular movement of tendency tones, the harmony provides a basis for passages like that in Fig. 2-21b.

Figure 2-21

A better result is achieved by inverting either of the paired triads.

Exercise 14b. Write the following sequences in F: I–V₆, II–VI₆, III–VII₆, IV–I₆, V–II₆, end with V–I. The upper part in two-part harmony will run in tenths with the lower part. Note that each unit starts on the next scale tone up. Write in D: I₆–V, II₆–VI, III₆–VII, IV₆–I.

Paired triads, roots up in fifths, are used sequentially so that each succeeding pair starts a third below. These are also more effective when either triad is inverted.

Exercise 14c. Write in B♭: I–V, VI–III, IV–I, with three different soprano lines: 5–5, 3–3, 1–1; 3–5, 1–3, 6–1 and 3–2, 1–7, 6–5. Write in A: I–V₆, VI–III₆, IV–I₆, close with V–I. The upper part in two-part harmony moves in tenths with the lower or skips: 3–5, 1–3, etc. Write in E♭: I₆–V, VI₆–III, IV₆–I, close with V–I. A scale-line upper part, 8–7–6–5, etc., produces alternate sixths and thirds with the lower part.

Sequences in Stepwise Root Movement

Paired triads in stepwise sequential progressions are best inverted.

Exercise 15a. Write in E: I₆–VII₆, VI₆–V₆, IV₆–III₆, V–I. Start with V₆–IV₆, III₆–II₆, etc., using 5–8, 3–6, 1–4 in soprano. Write in A♭: I₆–II₆, III₆–IV₆, V₆–VI₆, VII₆–I.

Such paired triads are used in sequence, so that each unit is a third lower or higher.

Exercise 15b. Write in B: V–VI, III–IV, I–II, close with V–I. Write in D♭: V₆–VI, III₆–IV, I₆–II, V–I. Write in F♯: VI–V₆, I–VII₆, III–II₆, V–I; in two-part harmony, try a rising scale: 1–2, 3–4, etc.

Exercise 15c. Each sequence in the following is set a fourth higher. Write in G♭: VI₆–V₆, II₆–I₆, V₆–IV₆, I₆–VII₆, V–I.

Sequences, Root Movement down in Thirds

Exercise 16a. Write in C: I–VI, IV–II, VII–V, I. Write in G: I₆–VI₆, IV₆–II₆, VII₆–V₆, I. The upper part in two-part harmony runs in thirds with the lower part, and in sixths in the second series. Passages like that in Fig. 2-22a and b should not be extended for too long. Note the double passing tones, starred.

Figure 2-22a–b

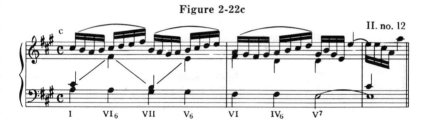

I VI IV II VII I₆ VI₆ IV₆

The initial pattern I–VI₆ is followed in sequence by units set a step down (Fig. 2-22c); the inner part is reduced to its essential harmony notes.

Figure 2-22c

II. no. 12

I VI₆ VII V₆ VI IV₆ V⁷

Exercise 16b. Write in F: I–VI₆, VII–V₆, VI–IV₆, V–I.

Root movement down in thirds is taken sequentially on successive upward scale steps in Fig. 2-22d.

Exercise 16c. Write in G: IV–II, V–III, VI–IV, VII–V, I.

Changing Tones

We described the auxiliary figure as a three-tone group, chord tone-auxiliary-chord tone. The auxiliary may leap a third to the opposite auxiliary before returning to the chord tone. Such auxiliaries are *changing tones* and each group of four tones

Figure 2-22d

Courante, French Suite no. 4

Bb: IV___II V___III VI___IV VII___V I

(bracketed in Fig. 2-23a and b) is a *changing tone figure.* This figure, which may be regarded as an embellishment of a chord tone, is often the generating motive of a passage. Either auxiliary may precede the other in the figure. The upper is first in Fig. 2-23a; the lower auxiliary is first in Fig. 2-23b.

Figure 2-23

Like any chord tone, the last tone of the figure moves by step or skip. Moving by step, it generally continues in the direction started by the preceding auxiliary; it continues upward from the lower auxiliary and downward from the upper auxiliary, as indicated by arrows in Fig. 2-23a and b. The last tone of the figure may leap to a tone at any interval up or down. A leap of a third down is seen in Fig. 2-23a, #3.

The changing tone figure is used above and below a single chord tone (Fig. 2-23a, #1 and #2). It is used with skips in the same chord in Fig. 2-24a, with a passing tone in Fig. 2-23a, #4, with a passing tone and chord skip in Fig. 2-24b and with an auxiliary figure in Fig. 2-24c.

Bear in mind that changing tones are nonharmonic. When

CH. 2

Figure 2-24

one or both are harmonized, they are not changing tones (Fig. 2-25a). (See also Fig. 2-23b, V⁷.) Groups in broken brackets (Fig. 2-23a and b, #5) are not changing tone figures. These start with a nonharmonic tone. Harmonic situations arising out of a thin two-part texture are sometimes subject to different analyses, depending on the interpretation of tones as chordal or nonharmonic. Figure 2-25b may be viewed as I–II–I₆ or simply as I–I₆ separated by a passing tone.

Figure 2-25

The changing tone figure is used in the various rhythms shown in Fig. 2-26a. Combined with other figures, it forms useful figure-groups that may be spun out sequentially or otherwise (Fig. 2-26b).

Figure 2-26

Exercise 17a. Write upper parts in active rhythm, based on several of the two-part progressions of Ex. 2a, employing

the changing tone figure. Insert an occasional passing tone in the lower part between tones of a triad and its first inversion, under the figure. (See Fig. 2-24b.) Use different major keys.

Exercise 17b. Write lower parts in active rhythm, based on the same two-part progressions. Use two tones of the same chord in the upper part over the changing tone figure. (See Fig. 2-24a.) Add an occasional passing tone in that part. We will revert to the use of changing tones in developing both parts melodically (Ex. 6b, Ch. 3).

The Anticipation

The note starred in Fig. 2-27a is an *anticipation,* a nonharmonic tone sounded prematurely to its repetition as a tone of the following chord. Anticipations are tones of short duration that fall on the unaccented parts of beats. While they may be used anywhere in the course of a composition, they frequently occur prior to the cadential tonic tone, as in Fig. 2-27b. A tone of V is also anticipated in the example.

Figure 2-27

Exercise 18. Revise the cadences of Ex. 17 by substituting anticipations: (1) of the final tonic tone, and (2) of both V and I chord cadential tones.

3

Two-part Counterpoint; Triad and Dominant Seventh Framework; Other Unaccented Nonharmonic Tones

Two-part Counterpoint

Two-part writing that consists of one melodic line associated with another, formed exclusively of chord tones, may be viewed as rudimentary two-part counterpoint. Our present objective is to develop a melody from this second line of chordal guideposts —one which is contrasted to the first in rhythm and contour, yet bound to it in harmonic sequential progressions—as in Fig. 3-1, a slightly altered version of the original. Note the harmonic sequences. Observe the contrasting lines and the harmony in Fig. 2-11a and b.

With the introduction of a melodically developed second line, it is essential to examine more closely the use of intervals

Figure 3-1

Prelude no. 3, L.P.F.

VI   II₆   V   I₆   IV   VII⁷   V

that fall on the after beat. We will continue our present practice of using chord tones on the beat, implying triads and their inversions by intervals of a third, sixth, fifth and occasional octave. It should be understood that the three-beat unit of $\frac{3}{8}$, $\frac{6}{8}$, $\frac{9}{8}$ and $\frac{12}{8}$, particularly in fast tempo, will often be considered as "the beat."

Intervals on Unaccented Fractions of the Beat

Passages in parallel thirds, sixths and a combination of both (Fig. 3-2a) are frequently used. These are often chord tones with passing tones between them.

The octave is used on a fraction of the beat as a chord interval (Fig. 3-2b) and in an exchange of chord tones (Fig. 3-2c). Note its use in the auxiliary figure (Fig. 3-2d).

Figure 3-2a–d

The octave is best approached and left by contrary motion (Fig. 3-2e). Skips to and from the octave in similar motion (Fig. 3-2f) are used infrequently. The interval appears on consecutive beats before and in the cadence (Fig. 3-2g). Parallel octaves used obliquely, as in Fig. 3-2h, are permissible. The unison (Fig. 3-2j) is encountered in voices that run too close. As a general rule it should be approached and left in contrary motion.

Figure 3-2e–j

The perfect fifth is used within the beat as a chord interval (Fig. 3-3a) and in the approach to the cadence (Fig. 3-3b). Chord tone forms a fifth with passing tone (Fig. 3-3c) and with auxiliary (Fig. 3-3d). The fifth is best approached and left by step in at least one voice. A leap to a fifth in similar motion, as in Fig. 3-3e, is rarely used. The perfect fifth moving to a diminished fifth (Fig. 3-2h) is better than the reverse. These fifths are not considered parallels. Bach also takes the diminished fifth to the perfect fifth. (See Fig. 6-22b, measures 1 and 2, soprano and alto.)

Figure 3-3

The perfect fourth is used as a harmony interval in chord repetition (Fig. 3-4a) and before the cadence with one of its tones an anticipation (Fig. 3-3b). Chord tone forms a fourth with passing tone (Fig. 3-4b) and with auxiliary (Fig. 3-4c). See Fig. 3-21 and read the paragraph preceding it.

Figure 3-4

The major second, used later as a chord interval of V^7, is a nonchordal interval at this stage. Minor seconds occur less often. Chord tone forms a second with passing tone (Fig. 3-5a), with auxiliary (Fig. 3-5b) and with changing tone (Fig. 3-5c). It is generally better to move from a second to a larger interval than to converge the tones on a unison. Seconds will occur in the occasional crossing of voices (Fig. 3-5d). Voice crossing should be used with caution, and then only for a fraction of a beat. Prolonged crossing confuses the identity of the lines.

Figure 3-5

The compound interval of a ninth occurs more often than its simple counterpart, the second, because of the usual spread of voices in two-part counterpoint. Chord tone forms a ninth with passing tone (Fig. 3-6a), with auxiliary (Fig. 3-6b) and changing tone unit (Fig. 3-6c). It is best to approach and leave this interval by contrary motion, as in this example. See, however, Fig. 3-6d. Successive ninths (Fig. 3-6e) are tones of dominant harmony; the ninth in Fig. 3-6f is formed of V^7 tones.

Figure 3-6

The minor seventh, treated later as representing V⁷, and the major seventh will be used presently as incidental discords, as passing tone between chord tones (Fig. 3-7a), with auxiliary (Fig. 3-7b). The interval often moves to a sixth or an octave. Note its movement in similar motion in Fig. 3-7c.

Figure 3-7

The tritone used within the beat is generally an interval of V⁷, VII or VII⁷ (Fig. 3-8a). It occurs occasionally between chord tone and auxiliary (Fig. 3-8b), with passing tone (Fig. 3-8c) and with anticipation (Fig. 3-8d).

Figure 3-8

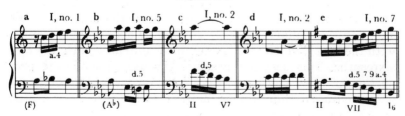

Observe the successive discords in Fig. 3-8e. This is acceptable when it serves a melodic purpose and results from lines moving in contrary direction.

Melodic Contrast

Two lines are melodically independent when their figures or figure-groups are contrasted; when one moves largely stepwise while the other moves in chordal skips; or when their over-all contours are different and they climax at different points (Fig. 3-9, the starred notes). Then, too, longer figure-groups in one voice may be set against short figures in the other. When both parts are in uniform rhythm their individuality is maintained by contrary motion. An admixture of parallel and contrary motion in longer passages (Fig. 3-9) is preferable to continuous parallel motion. These are factors to bear in mind in working out all two-part exercises.

Figure 3-9

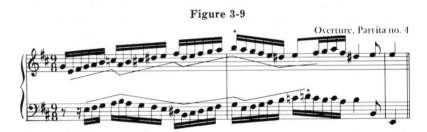

Overture, Partita no. 4

Rhythmic Independence

Melodic lines that differ appreciably in rhythm, measure against measure or for several measures, are rhythmically independent. Rests and ties help in setting off one part against the other. A rest may precede the resumption of either line. Rhythmic diversity is limited, however. It is subject to the overriding *basic rhythm* in a section of a polyphonic work or in its entirety. The basic rhythm is one of eighths when there is a preponderance in rhythm of the eighth or of the dotted eighth and sixteenth, with occasional injection of the dotted quarter and eighth. Similarly, a basic rhythm of sixteenths is set up with the beat divided into sixteenths or into an eighth and two sixteenths. This does not preclude the use, in moderate proportion, of other rhythms within a basic rhythm of eighths.

The basic rhythm may be maintained for several measures in one or both voices, or it may be transferred from voice to voice. In either case it is continuous with little interruption. A basic rhythm of eighths is seen in Fig. 3-10a. A basic rhythm of sixteenths is pursued in one voice in Fig. 2-23a. Both voices, differing in rhythm, sustain the flow of sixteenths in Fig. 3-10b. It is maintained in similar rhythm, from voice to voice, in Fig. 3-1.

Figure 3-10

The following are common rhythms in a basic motion of eighths in $\frac{2}{4}$, $\frac{3}{4}$ and $\frac{4}{4}$:

as well as

An occasional rhythm of

may be used; avoid

unless these are characteristic of a theme in later use. These rhythms set up a basic motion of eighths in $\frac{3}{8}$, $\frac{6}{8}$, $\frac{9}{8}$ and $\frac{12}{8}$:

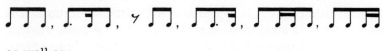

as well as:

The presence in undue proportion of rhythms like

transforms the basic motion to one of sixteenths.

Common rhythms in a basic motion of sixteenths are:

as well as the tied rhythms:

Avoid short ties,

unless this is a continuing pattern; avoid the short note tied to a longer one,

Use rests,

and an occasional syncopation,

Rhythms of the basic motion in eighths can also be used in that part which is not maintaining the basic motion in sixteenths.

Avoid simultaneous ties and rests in two-part counterpoint:

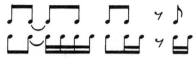

Except for uniform rhythm in both parts, as in Fig. 3-9, avoid similar rhythms in both parts at the same time; *e.g.*,

Do not use a triplet in one part against the beat divided in half in the other, or the triplet against the beat divided in quarters. The harmonic implications of notes on the after beat in such situations are often unclear.

Exercise 1a.   Work out a number of four-measure units *in rhythm only*, that maintain a basic motion of sixteenths between the parts, as in this example:

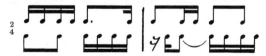

Exercise 1b.   Do the same to maintain a basic motion of eighths in $\frac{2}{4}$ and $\frac{3}{8}$.

Sequences in Two-part Counterpoint

We had written sequential melody based on harmonic sequences in Ex. 11, Ch. 2. The harmony in this exercise was outlined by one or two chord tones in the other part. Our present aim is the evolvement of contrapuntal passages like Fig. 3-11d, in which *both* lines are melodically developed. Motives extracted from themes are frequently used sequentially in development sections (episodes) of inventions and fugues.

The model (Fig. 3-11) demonstrates the progressive steps taken in developing a simple scale figure in sequence (Fig. 3-11b), based on the skeletal harmonic outline (Fig. 3-11a), into: (1) a figure-group in sequence (Fig. 3-11c) and then (2) the production of a sequential *second* line evolved from the chord tones of the lower part (Fig. 3-11d).

Figure 3-11

Note the contrasting lower line in Fig. 3-11d, #1, chord skip against scale line. Observe also the modified sequence (starred) and the close with both parts rhythmically active. The second version of Fig. 3-11d has an auxiliary figure in the figure-group. These examples are but two of many alternatives. We will later use such sequences in modulation by chromatically altering some of the notes.

The previous example starts with an initial unit of two triads in fifth-fall progression. A single inverted triad is the basis for sequences in stepwise progressions (Fig. 3-12). A figure-group composed of broken chord and scale-line figures (Fig. 3-12b) is developed from the upper chord tones of Fig.

3-12a. The chord tones of the lower line furnish the basis for the sequential figures in Fig. 3-12c. Changes in measures 3 and 4 are designed to eliminate a mechanically repetitious sequence. Such alterations should be made subsequent to working through the original pattern.

Figure 3-12

Exercise 2a.　Employing several sequential progressions from Exs. 5–9, Ch. 2, write melodic sequences in both parts, following the procedure described in working out Figs. 3-11 and 3-12. Note that the order of chord tones in Fig. 3-11a (third–third in the upper part and root–third–root in the lower) is maintained in the sequences.

Exercise 2b.　Repeat the process with progressions taken from Exs. 14, 15 and 16 of that chapter.

Exercise 2c.　Rewrite several of the upper and lower parts of Ex. 11, Ch. 2, substituting melodic lines in sequence for those parts in simple chord tones.

The rest takes the place of the chord tone in Fig. 3-12c.

The Dominant Seventh Chord

We used scale step 4 in previous exercises as a passing tone in the progression V–I (Fig. 3-13a). This usage and the retention of this step in moving from II or IV to V (Fig. 3-13b) were the means whereby the chord-seventh was originally introduced and the combined four tones accepted as a distinct chord, the *dominant seventh* (Fig. 3-13c).

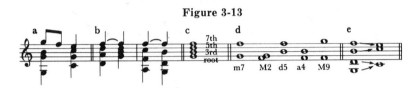

Figure 3-13

The dominant seventh, represented by the symbol V⁷ (Five-seven), is a four-tone chord composed of the V triad with a superimposed third, seven scale tones above the root. It is the *primary* seventh chord as distinguished from *secondary* sevenths that are based on other scale steps—such as II⁷, VI⁷, etc.—and was used with greater frequency in eighteenth century polyphony than any other chord.

Harmonic Discord

Our experience with discord so far has been confined to melodic dissonance incurred by incidental nonharmonic tones in one voice against chord tones in the other. The interval of a minor seventh, root to chord-seventh which is integral to V⁷, is a *harmonic discord*. This interval and intervallic discords formed by other combinations of V⁷ chord tones—the major second, major ninth and the tritones of a diminished fifth and augmented fourth (Fig. 3-13d)—provided seventeenth century composers with an expressive foil to harmonic concords of thirds, sixths, fifths and octaves.

Early practice required both *preparation* of the chord-seventh—meaning the use of that tone in the preceding chord in the same voice—and its stepwise resolution down (Fig. 3-13e). Composers later exercised greater freedom in this regard, melodic necessity taking precedence over normal resolution.

We had previously seen V as a dynamic triad requiring resolution to I. V⁷ with three tendency tones—steps 7, 2 and 4—

is a more dynamic chord, one which provides a stronger cadence: V⁷–I. Step 5, as root, has a fifth-fall harmonic tendency to the root of I. The normal resolution of V⁷ tendency tones to tones of I is seen in Fig. 3-13e. Step 2 may also move to step 3.

Two other chords of the dominant class, treated more fully later, may be mentioned here to understand the presence of step 6 in dominant harmony. These are the dominant ninth, V⁹ (Five-nine) and the VII⁷. The V⁹ (Fig. 3-14a) has the tones G–B–D–F–A in C; it is used less often than VII⁷ (Fig. 3-14b). The VII⁷ (Seven-seven), also called V⁹ incomplete, is a V⁹ minus its root. Note the V⁹ in Fig. 3-10a.

Figure 3-14

Doubling in V⁷

Doubling any tone of a four-tone chord in four-part harmony is obviously impossible and seemingly unnecessary. The correct resolution of V⁷ chord tones, however, results in a I minus its fifth (Fig. 3-15a). While this resolution is acceptable, a complete I is obtained by omitting the V⁷ chord-fifth, its least

Figure 3-15

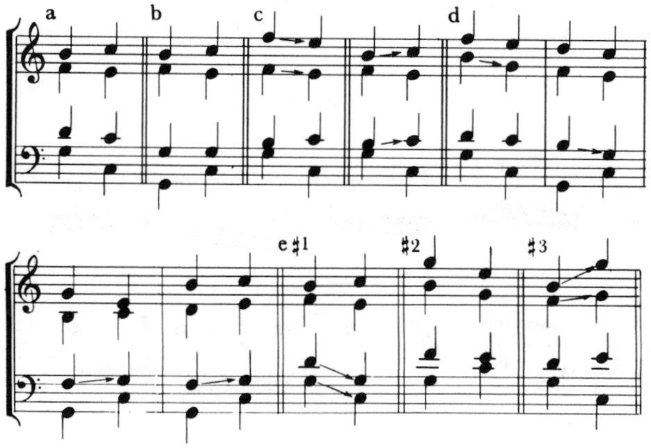

essential tone, and doubling its root (Fig. 3-15b). Any other doubling (Fig. 3-15c) results not only in an incomplete I, but in parallel octaves as well (Fig. 3-15c). Permissible, though less satisfactory, is the irregular movement of the leading tone or chord-seventh in any inner voice (Fig. 3-15d). Avoid parallel fifths in free voice leading (Fig. 3-15e, #1). The second example, with its irregular resolution of the leading tone and the doubling of the third in I, is preferable to the third example.

The Approach to V^7

Any triad, either with root in bass or in first inversion, may precede V^7; *e.g.*, I or I_6–V^7; V or V_6–V^7; II or II_6–V^7; IV or IV_6–V^7; VII_6–V^7 and VI–V^7. III and III_6–V^7 are infrequently used. Move two voices in contrary motion to the bass in IV–V^7, keeping the common tone in the same voice. Use contrary motion in VI–V^7. A perfect fifth moving to a diminished fifth, or vice versa (Fig. 3-17, meas. 9, 10, inner voices) is acceptable.

Continuous activity, a characteristic of Baroque music, is evident in harmonic motion as well as in constant rhythmic motion. Frequent use of V^7–I tends to break the harmonic flow into brief discrete harmonic units. Progressions of dominant harmony to chords other than I and lighter cadences on I_6 provide more fluid harmony.

Other Progressions of V^7

Progressions frequently used are those that postpone the resolution of V^7 by interposition of subdominant and supertonic harmony: V^7–IV_6–V^7; V^7–II (or II_6)–V^7. The secondary seventh, II^7, often replaces II in this progression (Fig. 3-16). The second inversion of I also delays resolution of V^7: V^7–I_4^6–V^7–I.

Figure 3-16

I, no. 5

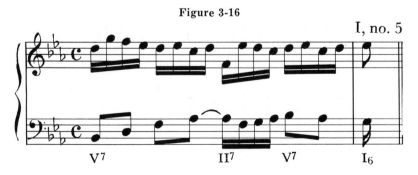

V^7 II^7 V^7 I_6

Resolution of V⁷ may be delayed by repeating the chord in inverted form. The progression V⁷–I₆ is used more often than the heavier cadential V⁷–I. The approach to and resolution of V⁷ is shown in Fig. 3-17. When the V⁷ resolves to VI at a cadential point, the cadence is called a *deceptive cadence*. This sometimes occurs several measures before the final cadence. See the *Two-Part Invention*, no. 4, four measures prior to the close. Used at other points, the progression is simply a deceptive resolution of V⁷ (Fig. 3-10a, measure 2).

Figure 3-17

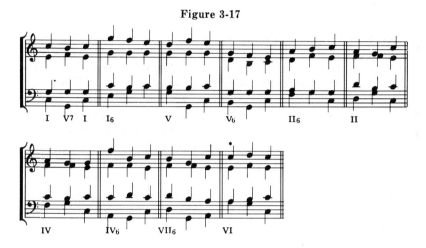

Exercise 3a. Write the progression in the first measure of Fig. 3-17 starting with I in position of the third and fifth. Write each succeeding measure starting with another position of the first chord.

Exercise 3b. Add the progressions you have written to those in Fig. 3-17, then rewrite the whole in the keys of F, G, D, B♭, A and E♭. Play these progressions.

Exercise 3c. Reduce this material to two-part harmony, using the *first* interval only of Fig. 3-13d to represent V⁷.

Exercise 3d. Using several progressions of Ex. 3c—which should be at least two measures long: (1) write rhythmically active upper parts to each of these; (2) do the same with the lower parts; (3) write two-part counterpoint based on the same progressions, contrasting the lines in rhythm and contour.

Triads in Second Inversion

A triad with its chord-fifth in bass is in *second inversion*. The root is a fourth and the chord-third is a sixth above the bass tone. Triads in this inversion are therefore designated as *six-four* chords. It should be understood that the upper notes of a six-four chord may be a fourth and sixth plus one or more octaves above the bass tone. Triads in second inversion are symbolized by the figures $^6_4$ following the Roman numeral for the triad; *e.g.*, I^6_4, V^6_4, etc.

The Tonic Six-Four Chord

The I in second inversion, more commonly used than other triads so inverted, is an unstable form of the chord. The upper tones tend to move stepwise down to tones of V, which has the same bass tone. Some theorists are therefore prone to regard I^6_4 as V with two nonharmonic tones, particularly since it is common practice to double the bass tone of I^6_4. This inversion is most often used in the approach to the cadence: I^6_4–V (or V^7)–I. While the cadential I^6_4 ordinarily falls on a strong beat in homophonic style music, it usually appears a beat or two before the cadence in polyphonic music (Fig. 3-18). (See also Fig. 2-27a.)

Figure 3-18

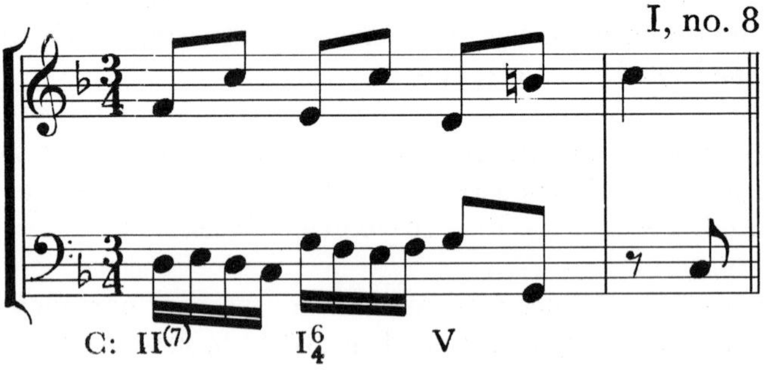

I, no. 8

C: $II^{(7)}$ I^6_4 V

Approach to I^6_4

Chords that precede V or V^7 also precede I^6_4 (Fig. 3-19a). Triads most often used are those with a bass tone that is a scale step above or below the bass of I^6_4: II_6–I^6_4, IV–I^6_4, IV_6–I^6_4 and VI–I^6_4. Skips to its bass tone are also used: II–I^6_4 (later

$II^7-I_4^6$) and I or $I_6-I_4^6$, to maintain tonic harmony. As previously noted, I_4^6 is used to delay the resolution of dominant harmony: $V-I_4^6-V-I$ or $V^7-I_4^6-V^7-I$, progressions which share the same bass tone (Fig. 3-19b).

Progressions of I_4^6

The normal resolution of I_4^6 is to dominant harmony. Its resolution may be delayed by repetition of the chord or by interposition of IV or II before repetition: $I_4^6-IV_6-I_4^6$; $I_4^6-II-I_4^6$ or $I_4^6-II_6-I_4^6$ (Fig. 3-19c).

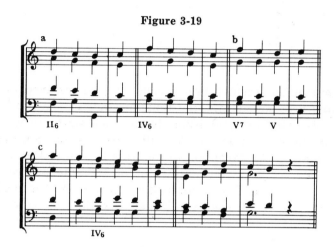

Figure 3-19

The I_4^6 is used on an unaccented beat or unaccented fraction of a beat as a "passing" chord between two chords. The bass in this progression will be three stepwise tones up or down (Fig. 3-20a, measure 1). The upper part is generally the bass line in reverse order.

Other Triads in Second Inversion

Six-four chords other than I_4^6 are most often used as "passing six-fours." These progressions, outlined on a single staff in two-part harmony (Fig. 3-20a), are arranged in order of their frequency in use. (See Fig. 5-18e.)

Second inversions are also used on unaccented beats with triads sharing the same bass tone. The bass of such progressions is given in Fig. 3-20b. VII is not used in second inversion.

As a general rule, avoid the use of any six-four other than

Figure 3-20

the tonic on an accented beat because V_4^6, for instance, on the accented beat sounds like the tonic six-four of the dominant key. It is therefore inadvisable to use such six-fours when a key change is not intended. Actually this is a common means of modulating. An exception to this rule is seen in Fig. 3-20c, where IV_4^6 serves as embellishment of I in the progression V^7–I. Since the six-four is an unstable inversion of a triad, it is not permissible to use two different six-fours in succession, such as I_4^6–IV_4^6, etc.

Exercise 4a. Write Fig. 3-19a and b with a different soprano.

Exercise 4b. Write Fig. 3-20 in four-part harmony in several major keys.

Exercise 4c. Write the following progressions in four-part harmony in the keys indicated; employ the anticipation in the next to last chord.

F II_6–I_4^6–V^7–I; IV_6–I_4^6–V–I; V–I_4^6–V–I.

G   IV–I_4^6–II_6–V; VI–I_4^6–V^7–I; V^7–I_4^6–V^7–I.

B♭   II–I_4^6–IV_6–V; I–I_6–I_4^6–V^7–I; I_4^6–II_6–I_4^6–V.

D   I–V_4^6–I_6–IV; I–IV_4^6–I–V.

E♭   V–I_4^6–IV_6–V_6–I; I–V–IV_4^6–VII_6–V^7–I.

A   V–I_4^6–V–V^7–I; I–V–II_4^6–V_6–I.

CH. 3

E   II–VI$_4^6$–II$_6$–V^7–I ; I–VI–II$_4^6$–VI–V^7–I.

A♭ I–VII$_6$–III–VI$_4^6$–III–IV–V$_6$–I.

Interval Implications of Six-Fours

Exceptional use of the fourth to imply a six-four is seen in
Figs. 3-21a and b. In the first example this interval is used in a
measure of the same chord. The fourth in the second example
is a brief chord tone followed by the chord-third. The whole
measure may, however, be regarded as V^7 with the notes in
brackets as a changing tone figure. The fourth may be freely
used as a chord interval on a weak fraction of the beat (Fig.
3-21c). Note the cadential I$_4^6$. The sixth, used previously to
imply first inversions, also serves to imply a six-four, as in this
example. Bach sometimes employs a six-four when that form
of a triad is most convenient to the melodic line (Fig. 3-21d).

Figure 3-21

Exercise 5a.   Reduce the progressions in Ex. 4c to two-part
harmony. Do not use the fourth to imply a six-four; use
the sixth.

Exercise 5b. With the two-part harmony of the previous exercise, write: (1) a rhythmically active upper part; (2) a rhythmically active lower part; (3) two lines contrasted melodically and rhythmically, as in Fig. 3-21c and d.

Other Unaccented Nonharmonic Tones

The Turn

A five-note figure with auxiliary tones pivoting around a chord tone is called a *turn*. These notes are: (1) the chord tone, (2) the auxiliary, (3) return to the chord tone, (4) the opposite auxiliary and (5) the original chord tone (Fig. 3-22a). The first auxiliary may be either upper or lower auxiliary. Except for the rapid turn which is concluded within a beat or less and indicated by the ~ sign over a note, the last chord tone runs over into the next beat. The figure may be harmonized with a single chord tone, with a change in bass of the same chord (Fig. 3-22a), or a different chord may be used with the last chord tone (Fig. 3-22b). Note the rhythm of the turn in $\frac{9}{8}$ (Fig. 3-22c). The same rhythm can be used in $\frac{6}{8}$ and $\frac{6}{8}$. The rhythm in Fig. 3-22a may also be used in $\frac{3}{4}$ and $\frac{4}{4}$. The turn, appearing at times in parallel sixths or thirds (Fig. 3-22d), may be used against any figure in the other part; it is used against an auxiliary figure in Fig. 3-22e.

Figure 3-22

(F)

The turn may move on to any other figure to form a figure-group, to a changing tone figure, to a chord skip and to passing tones, to an auxiliary figure or (as in Fig. 3-22c) to another turn. Examine the use of the turn in #13 of the *Three-Part Inventions* and Fugues #1 and #14 of the *Well-Tempered Clavier*.

The Cambiata

Changing tones that do not return to or start from the original chord tone are seen in Fig. 3-23. The groups bracketed are *cambiata figures;* the starred note, *cambiata*—a changing note which moves to a different chord tone after the skip. It is used continually in the Bach Fugue #11, Book II of the *Well-Tempered Clavier*. The cambiata figure also takes the form seen in Fig. 3-23b. Some writers regard the second of these two changing tones as the cambiata note. The cambiata note is often accented.

Figure 3-23

Exercise 6a. Employ the turn and cambiata in ways suggested by Figs. 3-22 and 3-23, basing the parts on several brief progressions in two-part harmony. Use different major keys.

Changing Tones in Two-part Counterpoint

We previously used the changing tone figure in a single part against chord tones in the other part (Fig. 3-24a) and a passing tone between chord tones in that part (Fig. 3-24b). The auxiliary figure is used against the changing tone figure in Fig. 3-24c, and the figure is used in both parts in several ways in Fig. 3-24d. Note the parallel motion in the Bach excerpt (Fig. 3-24e). The leading tone, starred, need not resolve normally. As a rule, do not extend such parallelism for more than a beat.

Figure 3-24

W.T.C. II, F. no. 1

Exercise 6b.   Use the changing tone figure in sequential two-part counterpoint based on several of the harmonic sequences of Exs. 5–9 and 14–16, Ch. 2. Refer to Fig. 3-24 when using the figure on beats with rhythmic activity in both parts.

4

Dominant Seventh Inversions; The Minor Mode; Imitation

Inversions of V⁷

The dominant seventh and other four-tone chords have three inversions, which are symbolized by Roman numerals denoting their roots and Arabic numerals indicating the intervallic distance of chord-seventh and root above the bass tone. The first inversion of V⁷ is written as V$^6_5$ (Five, six-five), the second inversion as V$^4_3$ (Five, four-three). Since the chord-seventh is in bass in the third inversion, the symbol V₂ simply indicates the location of the root (Fig. 4-1a).

Figure 4-1

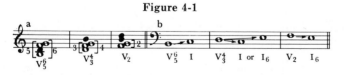

All bass tones of the inverted V⁷ are tendency tones. The strong tendencies of leading tone and chord-seventh in V$^6_5$ and

83

V_2 make these inversions more dynamic than V_3^4, which is often used as a passing chord between I and I_6. The normal resolution of the inverted V^7 is to I or I_6 (Fig. 4-1b).

These inversions provide a smooth bass line, particularly when repetition of V^7–I is required. Compare Fig. 4-2a with the bass of the same chords uninverted in Fig. 4-2b. Inversions of V^7 supply a better bass when it is necessary to maintain dominant harmony (Fig. 4-2c). These may be taken in any order with the proviso that the last inversion is properly resolved. See Fig. 4-3a; note also the free exchange of chord tones in such repetition. Passing tones between inversions (Fig. 4-2d) make for a melodious bass line.

Figure 4-2

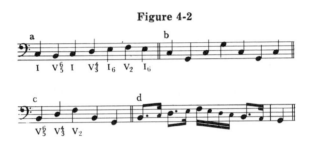

Unlike V^7 with root in bass, tones are neither omitted nor doubled in inversions of the chord. A note in bass therefore should not appear in an upper voice. Resolutions of each inversion are shown in Fig. 4-3b, c and d. The interval of a diminished fifth (Fig. 4-3b) contracts in resolution to a third; the augmented fourth (Fig. 4-3c) expands to a sixth.

Figure 4-3a–d

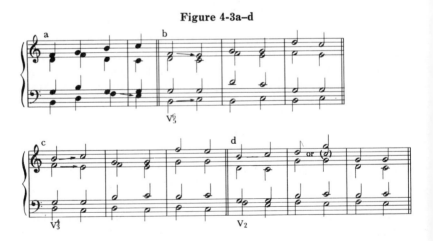

84

Although V^4_3 resolves to both I and I_6 (Fig. 4-1b), this inversion of V^7 is taken to I in Fig. 4-3c to avoid a doubled chord-third in I_6, as in Fig. 4-3e. Melodic lines in contrary motion, as in the next measure, admit such doubling. The chord-seventh in soprano will occasionally move contrary to its normal resolution when bass and soprano move up in parallel tenths (Fig. 4-3f). The bass tone of V^6_5 may move stepwise down when approached from above, as in the next measure.

Figure 4-3e–f

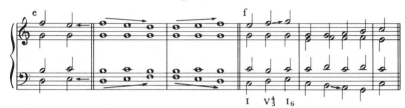

I V^4_3 I_6

Triads in first and second inversion are used as passing chords between inversions of V^7 and between V^7 and V^6_5 in Fig. 4-4. The soprano in these progressions runs contrary to the bass or with it in parallel sixths and thirds (tenths).

Figure 4-4

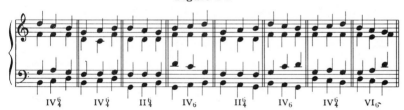

IV$^6_4$ IV$^6_4$ II$^6_4$ IV$_6$ II$^6_4$ IV$_6$ IV$^6_4$ VI$_6$

Exercise 1a. Write the following progressions in four-part harmony in the given keys:

F $\frac{2}{4}$ I–V$^6_5$–| I–I$_6$–| IV–V$_2$–| I$_6$––| V$^4_3$–I–| IV$_6$–II$_6$–| V$^6_5$–V^7–| I ‖

G $\frac{2}{4}$ I–IV$_6$–| V$^6_5$–V^7–| I–II$_6$–| V––| IV$_6$–V$^6_5$–| I–II$_6$–| V$_2$–V$^6_5$ –| I ‖

B♭ $\frac{3}{4}$ I––V$^4_3$–| I$_6$––II$_6$–| I$^6_4$–IV$_6$––| V––––| V$_2$–V$^4_3$––| I$_6$––I–| V$^6_5$––V^7–| I ‖

D $\frac{2}{4}$ I–| V$_6$–V$^6_5$–| I–VII$_6$–| V$^4_3$–V–| I$_6$–I–| V$^6_5$–IV$_6$–| V^7–I–| I$^6_4$ –V^7–| I ‖

Eb $\frac{2}{4}$ I–V$^6_5$–| IV$^6_4$–V$^4_3$–| I$_6$–IV–| V– –| V^7–II$^6_4$–| V$^6_5$
    –I–| IV$_6$–V^7–| I ‖

A $\frac{3}{4}$ I–IV–V$_2$–| I$_6$–V$^4_3$–I–| V$^6_5$–II$^6_4$–V^7–| I– – – –I$_6$–|
    V$^4_3$–VI$_6$–V$^6_5$–| I–II$_6$–V$_2$–| I$_6$–I$^6_4$–V^7–| I ‖

E $\frac{3}{4}$ I–| V$^6_5$–IV$_6$–V^7–| I–II–V$^4_3$–| I$_6$–I–IV$_6$–| I$^6_4$– –V–| V^7–IV$_6$–
    V$^6_5$–| I–IV$^6_4$–I–| V^7–I$^6_4$–V^7–| I ‖

Exercise 1b. Reduce these progressions and those of Fig. 4-4 to two-part harmony.

Interval Implications of V⁷

Root and seventh as minor seventh, major second and major ninth imply V^7. The tritone, an interval of VII, more often implies V^7 (Fig. 4-5a). These five intervals are used on any beat, any part of a beat and for several beats in succession. Other intervals of V^7 (Fig. 4-5b) are less indicative of the chord. They can also be intervals of II, II$_6$, V, V$_6$ and VII, and must be interpreted as such when their missing chord-fifth follows or is present in either part. When any interval of Fig. 4-5b is succeeded by an interval of Fig. 4-5a, the whole implies V^7 (Fig. 4-5c). An interval implying V is often followed by another implying V^7 (Fig. 4-5d). Examine the Bach excerpt (Fig. 4-5e). A fourth alone does not imply V^7; see Fig. 4-9d.

Figure 4-5

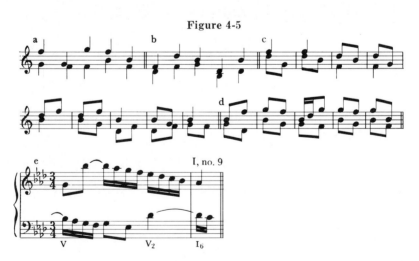

Normal resolutions of V^7 intervals in two-part harmony are shown in Fig. 4-6a. The chord-seventh moves stepwise down and the leading tone stepwise up. Examine the resolutions of

these intervals in Fig. 4-8. Resolution to the doubled third of
I and the irregular resolution of the chord-seventh (Fig. 4-6b)
should be avoided if possible. See, however, Fig. 4-9a. The last
intervals in Fig. 4-6b, V^7–I^6_4, are usually followed by an interval of V^7.

Figure 4-6

A few units taken from Fig. 4-5c and d are resolved in Fig.
4-7a. The seventh (Fig. 4-7b) and the leading tone (Fig. 4-7c)
often move to the root before resolving indirectly. One of these
tones frequently moves to the other, which then resolves normally (Fig. 4-7d). Irregular resolutions are necessary at
times (Fig. 4-7e), the last example occurring occasionally in
cadences.

Figure 4-7

The following excerpts from the *Two-Part Inventions* illustrate Bach's practice in the use of V^7. Examine them carefully.
Direct resolution of seventh and leading tone are seen in Fig.
4-8a. The fifths on alternate unaccented fractions of the beat
in this example are not considered parallels. Indirect resolutions are shown in Fig. 4-8b. Other indirect resolutions are
shown in Fig. 4-8c. The resolution of V^7 tones is transferred to
the other voice in Fig. 4-8d.

Figure 4-8

It is inadvisable at this point to resolve the tritone irregularly (Fig. 4-9a), as well as the leading tone or seventh (Fig. 4-9b), except in the approach to cadences. Doubling the leading tone is occasionally necessary (Fig. 4-9c). Unless other tones of V^7 are present, avoid the fourth to imply V^7 (Fig. 4-9d).

Figure 4-9a–d

We previously referred to the means employed to maintain an unbroken flow of harmony. Bach uses chord repetition (Fig. 4-8d) and interposing subdominant, supertonic or I_4^6 (Fig. 4-9e) between inversions of V^7.

Figure 4-9e

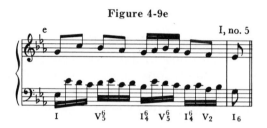

Frequent use of VII^7 in place of V^7 requires attention to this chord. Its nondominant function is explained in Ch. 6. This four-tone chord, based on the leading tone, has an implied root on the dominant (Fig. 4-10a). It is variously symbolized as VII^7 and $V^{9°}$ (Five-nine, incomplete). Like V^7, it moves directly or indirectly to I: $VII^7–V^7–I$. The leading tone moves up, fifth and seventh move down by step (Fig. 4-10b). Fifths are evaded by the doubling in I (Fig. 4-10b) or by indirect resolution in the first measure (Fig. 4-10c). Another indirect resolution is seen in the last measure: $VII^7–IV_4^6–I$. The chord is preceded by any chord used to precede V^7 (Fig. 4-10d). It is

Figure 4-10

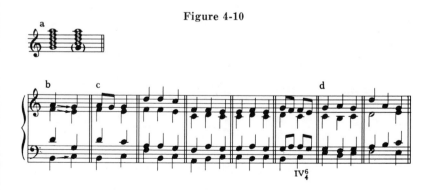

used in all inversions but preferably in those with seventh above the root. Omission and doubling of tones is not permitted.

Dominant harmony functions in the key both as primary and secondary dominants and in modulation. It appears with greater frequency than any other class of chords. Tones of V^7 and its inversions are used in the following exercises with a variety of nonharmonic tones, in figures that are characteristic of melody in polyphonic texture. The importance of these exercises should therefore be evident.

Exercise 2a. Write the intervals in Fig. 4-5a in the keys of F, G, B♭, D, A and E♭ major.

Exercise 2b. Using the intervals of Fig. 4-5a and b: (1) add another V^7 chord tone to the upper note and (2) another V^7 chord tone to the lower note, as in Fig. 4-5c; (3) add another V^7 tone to both upper and lower notes, as in Fig. 4-5d; (4) do this in the keys of the previous exercise. Write these on two staves.

Exercise 2c. Resolve these intervals to tones of I.

Exercise 2d. Try this procedure with tones of VII^7.

Figure 4-11a

Exercise 3a. Passing tones between V^7 chord tones are used in the upper parts of Fig. 4-11a, #1; they are similarly used in the lower parts of #2; each unit of #3 is resolved to I. Invent similar units in the keys listed in Ex. 2a. There are many possibilities besides those presented in the example. Work systematically. Start with two V⁷ tones in the lower part, adding each combination of two tones in the upper part. Do this with a different pair of V⁷ tones below and above. The fifths in #3 are not considered parallels because the second fifth is not a harmony interval; it consists of a chord tone and passing tone. The doubled leading tone in #2 (†) may be used on an unaccented fraction of the beat. The starred notes are passing tones sounded with chord tones on the half beat. Accented passing tones, treated more fully later, may be used occasionally here.

Exercise 3b.   Both parts are rhythmically activated in Fig. 4-11b in figures using V⁷ chord tones and passing tones. Successive discords appear in the starred examples. This is permissible in contrary motion and, at our present stage, when the figure ends on a chordal interval. Invent similar units, combining them with those of Fig. 4-11a. Write on two staves and in the previously given keys.

Figure 4-11b

Auxiliary tones, chord skips and passing tones are used in the upper part, #1, in each single measure of Fig. 4-11c, in the lower part, #2, and in both parts, #3.

Double Auxiliaries

Auxiliary figures in both parts are seen in the first three measures of Fig. 4-11c, #4. These are in parallel motion. They are in contrary motion in the rest of #4. Double auxiliaries are used in parallel thirds and sixths; they are best in contrary motion when proceeding from a third (tenth) or sixth. Those in the last measure of #4 are also used.

Figure 4-11c

Exercise 3c. Work out units similar to those in Fig. 4-11c, first in C and then in several other major keys. Write on two staves.

The changing tone figure, passing and V^7 chord tones are used in the upper part, #1, in Fig. 4-11d, in the lower part, #2, and in both parts, #3.

Figure 4-11d

Exercise 3d.   Write figure-groups based on V⁷ similar to those in Fig. 4-11d, following the procedure shown in the example. Use different major keys.

Ex. 3 consists of one- and two-measure fragments in two-part counterpoint centered on V⁷ and used with nonharmonic tones. These are extended in the next set of exercises.

Exercise 4a.   Write a rhythmically active upper part to several of the progressions in Ex. 1b. Use various types of nonharmonic tones in the figure-groups; use chord tones only in the lower parts; write in the indicated keys.

Exercise 4b.   Using other progressions from the same source, write rhythmically active lower parts.

Exercise 4c.   Fill out the lower parts of Ex. 4a with contrasting lines; do the same with the upper parts of Ex. 4b.

Scale Passages in Contrary Motion

Passages like those in Fig. 4-12a and b, based on tonic and dominant harmony, are used in many instances to bring the passage to a climax or to a theme announcement. At times the passage is based almost entirely on V⁷. Note the series of discords in the first example.

Figure 4-12

Exercise 5a.   Using two staves, start with each interval of Fig. 4-5a and b in turn in contrary motion for one beat, terminating on beat 2. Use a sixteenth rhythm. Do this

for two beats, as in Fig. 4-12c; use $\frac{3}{8}$ for some of these exercises and use different major keys. This is an experimental exercise to discover starting intervals that produce the best results.

Exercise 5b. Run the lines away from and toward each other, as in Fig. 4-12d. Run the lines away from each other for two beats before they converge, as in Fig. 4-12b.

Exercise 5c. Start with intervals of a third and sixth of I and repeat the preceding process.

The Échappee

Unaccented auxiliaries that move by leap instead of returning stepwise to the chord tone are *échappées* or *escape tones,* starred in Fig. 4-13a. The escape tone, which may appear at any point in melody, is often used in the approach to the cadence, as in Fig. 4-13b. Such tones, used less often in the lower line (Fig. 4-13c), are brief in duration and generally skip a third in the opposite direction. Although the upper auxiliary as escape tone usually skips down, and the lower auxiliary skips up, these tones may skip in any direction and with a leap wider than a third.

A figure that is seemingly a changing tone figure must be differently interpreted at times. The first "changing tone" starred in Fig. 4-13d is an escape tone, since it leaps to the second "changing tone" which is really a chord tone. The last

Figure 4-13a–d

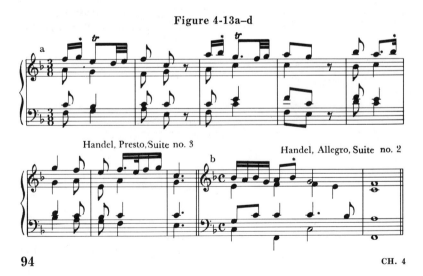

Handel, Presto, Suite no. 3

Handel, Allegro, Suite no. 2

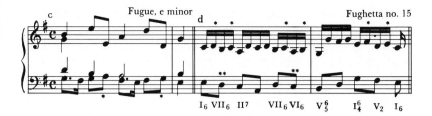

tone of the figure therefore becomes nonharmonic, leaping as escape tone to a chord tone. Interpreted otherwise, the double-starred tones may be regarded as passing tones. Escape tones that skip to nonharmonic tones will be treated later.

Examples of the échappée for use in Ex. 6 are shown in Fig. 4-13e. The second of the bracketed tones in the last example is not an échappée; it is a V^7 chord tone.

Figure 4-13e

Exercise 6a.   Employing one of the progressions of Ex. 1, Ch. 2, write an upper part in active rhythm using escape tones.

Exercise 6b.   Introduce escape tones in a rhythmically active lower part based on another progression from the same source.

The Minor Mode

A composition, or any section of it, in which tones of a minor scale are consistently used, is in a *minor key. Harmonic minor* and *melodic minor* are the names for two differently con-structed forms of minor scales in each minor key (Fig. 4-14). The first of these is called the *harmonic minor scale* because the basic minor chords are constructed from its tones. It in-cludes the wide gap of a step and a half between steps 6 and

7–an augmented second. This awkward leap is reduced to a whole step in the melodic minor in both its ascending and descending form. This alteration produces a smoother line in melody and accounts for the name of the scale. The ascending form, with exceptions noted later, is used for scale-line melody rising from the dominant to the tonic tone; the descending form is sometimes called the *natural minor*. Note that the first five tones of the harmonic and melodic minor scales are identical. Study the structure of both scales.

Figure 4-14

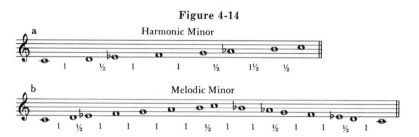

Exercise 7a.   Following the pattern of Fig. 4-14a, write the harmonic minor scales starting with these notes: D, A, E, B, G, F♯, F, C♯, B♭, G♯, E♭ and D♯. Insert the required accidentals, as in Fig. 4-14a.

Exercise 7b.   Write melodic minor scales ascending and descending in the same manner, starting with the same notes.

Each minor key has a close relationship to two major keys. Major and minor keys sharing the same tonic tone—*e.g.*, C major and c minor*—have a *tonic* relationship; *i.e.*, c minor is the tonic minor of C major. Major and minor keys sharing the most scale tones—*e.g.*, E-flat major and c minor—are in *relative* affiliation. The key of c minor is the relative minor of E-flat major. The third step of any minor scale is the tonic tone of its relative major key; the sixth step of any major scale is the tonic tone of its relative minor key. Minor keys have the same signature as their relative major keys—*e.g.*, c minor and E-flat major both use a key signature of three flats.

Exercise 7c.   Write the minor key signature for each scale in Ex. 7a.

---

* Lower case type will be used to indicate minor keys.

Step 7 of the harmonic minor and steps 6 and 7 of the melodic minor differ from the ordinary minor key signature. These tones must therefore be raised by an accidental sharp or natural when they are used in minor melody and chords.

Exercise 7d.   Using the minor key signatures of Ex. 7c, rewrite the harmonic and melodic minor scales, altering step 7 of the first scale and steps 6 and 7 of the second scale.

Triads and V⁷ in Minor

Lowered steps 3 and 6 of the harmonic minor and the lowered leading tone of the descending melodic minor control the structure of the basic triads except V. I and IV are minor triads; II is a diminished triad; VI and III are major triads (Fig. 4-15a). The augmented form of III, in c minor (E♭–G–B), is infrequently used. Except for V⁹ and VII⁷, dominant chords are the same as in major. The leading tone in these chords must be raised, since the key signature automatically lowers it (Fig. 4-15b). The lowered leading tone is used occasionally in VII (Fig. 4-15c) and V (Fig. 4-15d). V⁹ and VII⁷ have the lowered sixth step (Fig. 4-15b and Fig. 4-16a). Step 6 is sometimes raised in IV (Fig. 4-16b) to avoid the leap of an augmented second.

Figure 4-15

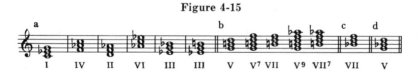

Diatonic chords in minor are those formed from tones that do not conflict with the key signature; *i.e.*, tones of the descending melodic minor. By definition, dominants like that in Fig. 4-16a and the IV in Fig. 4-16b are *chromatic*. Bach occa-

Figure 4-16

sionally reverts to a modal feeling by using V with lowered leading tone (Fig. 4-16c).

Triad Progressions, Doubling in Minor

Progressions in minor are similar, with a few exceptions, to those in major. The diminished triads II and VII are more effective in first inversion. Fifth-fall progressions should therefore include II$_6$ and VII$_6$, rather than the uninverted forms. This applies to stepwise progressions. The best progressions down in thirds are: I–VI, II$_6$–VII$_6$, IV–II$_6$, VI–IV and VII$_6$–V. Double the root preferably or the fifth in I, IV and V; double the root or third in II, VI and III; double the third in VII. Avoid, if possible, the skip of an augmented second in two-part writing. The tones of this interval inverted —a diminished seventh—are almost always good.

Exercise 8a. Write each formula in Ex. 10a, Ch. 1, in minor, changing II to II$_6$. Use a variety of minor keys.

Exercise 8b. Convert the progressions of Ex. 1, Ch. 2, to minor. Where possible, avoid the augmented second in bass in progressions like IV$_6$–V$_6$. Use the diminished seventh. In IV–V$_6$ and II$_6$–V$_6$ skip down a diminished fifth in bass in preference to skipping up an augmented fourth.

Interval Implications in Minor

Intervals of a third and sixth, root and chord-third, best represent triads in minor. The fifth is also serviceable and must be used for the augmented III. Interval implications of V^7 are the same as in major; the dominant ninth is implied by a minor ninth (Fig. 4-17a); the VII^7, a diminished seventh chord in minor, by an interval of a diminished seventh or an augmented second (Fig. 4-17b). Chord skips in V^9 (Fig. 4-16a) and in VII^7 (Fig. 4-17c), are, of course, clear indications of the harmony.

Figure 4-17

Exercise 8c. Reduce the progressions in Ex. 8a and b to two-part harmony.

Passing Tones in Minor

Minor scale steps 1–5 in either direction, used as passing tones, conform to their use in major. The minor *upper tetrachord* (upper four tones) presents a special problem. These tones are ordinarily used as previously described and illustrated in the bass of Fig. 4-18a. Steps 6–7 and 7–6 of the harmonic minor are rarely used as passing tones. When they appear so (Fig. 4-18b) they are actually chord tones of VII⁷ or V⁹.

The raised leading tone as chord tone, except in chord skips, is generally preceded or followed by the raised step 6 (Fig. 4-17a and Fig. 4-18a) and does not appear simultaneously

Figure 4-18

with the lowered step 7 in another part. Note how differently this step is used in the bracketed tetrachords of Fig. 4-18c. The first conforms to the coming chord tone of VI; the second cannot conflict with the tone of V in the lower voice. The lowered step 6 of IV, II and VI must be preceded by the lowered step 7 as passing tone. Observe the descending form of the tetrachord used in upward direction with I in Fig. 4-18d, and to avoid conflict with a lower voice passing tone in Fig. 4-18e. Raised and lowered steps 6 and 7 move downward in Fig. 4-18f: #1 in I, #2 to a tone of IV.

The raised and lowered leading tones may follow each other in rapid succession (Fig. 4-18a), particularly if one is a chord tone and the other a passing tone. This applies to the raised and lowered step 6.

Exercise 9a.   Convert Figs. 1-19, 1-20, and 1-22 to c minor.

Exercise 9b.   Starting with the two-part harmony of Ex. 8c, write several upper parts in active rhythm; do this with several of the lower parts.

Auxiliary Tones in Minor

The upper auxiliary is the next higher step of each scale step from step 7 up to step 5. The upper neighbor of step 5 is step 6 of the harmonic minor (Fig. 4-19a, the notes in brackets).

Figure 4-19

Note the close proximity of the raised 6 as passing tone and the lowered 6 as auxiliary. The upper auxiliary of the lowered step 6 is the lowered step 7.

The lower auxiliary of scale step 1 is the raised leading tone. From step 2 to 6 it is the next minor scale step below. There are two possible exceptions. The lower auxiliary of step 4 may be a half step below, step 3 of the major (Figs. 4-17b, and 4-18c, lower voice). The lower auxiliary of step 5 is variable. Both step 4 and 4♯ are used (Fig. 4-19b). The lower auxiliary of the raised leading tone is raised step 6 (Fig. 4-19c).

Auxiliaries used in minor changing tone figures, in the turn and as escape tones, are governed by the practice described above. Note the changing tones in Fig. 4-19d.

Exercise 10a. Convert Fig. 2-19 to c minor; do the same with Fig. 3-24 and Fig. 4-11.

Exercise 10b. Using the two-part progressions of Ex. 8c, write several upper parts in active rhythm in figures that include auxiliaries, changing tones and échappées. Do the same with several lower parts.

Sequences in both voices in minor based on a series of first inversions are shown in Fig. 4-20. Starred notes are non-harmonic tones that will be treated later. While the initial melodic units in both parts may start on the same beat, a better sense of melodic independence is obtained by starting one sequential line before the other, as in this example. See also Figs. 3-12c and 7-9b. In sequences like VI₆–II, V₆–I, IV₆–VII, base one line on VI₆–II, etc.; start the other on II–V₆; etc.

Figure 4-20

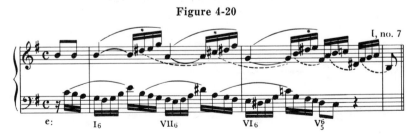

Exercise 10c. Write several brief passages in minor with melodic sequences in both parts, based on any sequential harmony derived from Exs. 5–9, Ch. 2.

Imitation

Melodic units, varying in length from a brief figure or motive to the longer figure-group and fugal subject, are transferred from voice to voice in various types of polyphonic music. The repetition of a melodic unit in another voice is an *imitation* of that unit (Fig. 4-21a). *Strict imitation* is an exact copy of the unit, reproduced: (1) on the same level, (2) with the notes in a higher or lower octave—as in the example, or (3) on any other level—as in Fig. 4-21b. The imitation, in these instances, is a literal copy of the note-to-note melodic movement. For instance, a step of a minor second or a skip of a major sixth in the initial unit is duplicated in the same intervals in the imitation. Strict imitation is applied mainly to imitations at the beginning of a fugue, with exceptions noted later, and to certain types of canon.

Free imitation is a modified copy of the initial unit in another voice, one that conforms in general to the rhythm and melodic line of the original unit. Compare the theme in Fig. 4-21c, #1, with the first and subsequent free imitations, noting the deviations in rhythm, in skips and in the added notes. This type of imitation is used in developmental passages and will be employed in most of the following exercises. In some instances only the rhythm is transferred from voice to voice, as in Fig. 4-21d, in figures that differ. This is called *rhythmic imitation*.

Figure 4-21

#4

#5

#6　　Prelude no. 6, L.P.F.　d

W. F. Bach, Fugue

Imitation of themes and of thematically related motives unify a polyphonic work, equalizing the lines in importance as each imitation draws attention to the voice carrying it. This device is used not only in fugues, inventions and canons, but in the lighter dance forms of the suite. Ex. 11 and subsequent exercises deal with imitation in preparation for later work in the composition of inventions and canons.

Various types of figures and figure-groups, similar to motives extracted from themes and used in developmental sections (episodes), are treated in free imitation in the following exercises. These are brief passages in which each imitation is adjusted to a preset harmony which does not necessarily begin or end on I.

Proceed as follows: (1) Start with progressions of a few chords in two-part harmony (Fig. 4-22a), using those from previous exercises. (2) Write some strict or free imitations of the given initial figure or figure-group, as in Fig. 4-22a, adjusting the imitation to fit the harmony and the chord tones to an upper or lower octave. In some instances a better imitation is obtained by starting with a different chord tone of the preset harmony. (3) Use a single chord tone in the part against the imitation, and then amplify the part with additional chord tones and/or nonharmonic tones, as in Fig. 4-22b. These parts need not be similar; otherwise the passages are canonic, a mode of continuous imitation treated in Ch. 7.

Each beat or measure of counterpoint against the imitations should be in contrasting melodic outline and rhythm, if possible. The melodic line should, for instance, run scalewise against broken chord figure-groups. Where the rhythm is similar, run the line in contrary motion, wholly or in part. Use different major keys for each unit. After completing it check it for parallels such as those in Fig. 4-22c; then play each line alone, eliminating awkward skips, poor articulation from measure to measure or eccentric rhythm. Start with the initial melodic unit in either upper or lower voice.

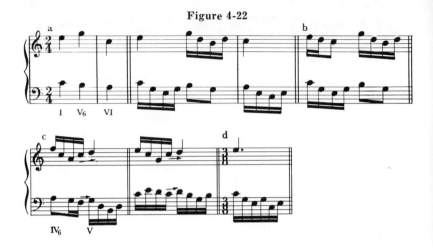

Figure 4-22

Exercise 11a. Write single-beat broken chord figures in imitation in $\frac{2}{4}$ and single measure units in $\frac{3}{8}$, as in Fig. 4-22d, adding the counterpoint in the manner described above.

The initial figure is a two-beat broken chord unit in Fig. 4-23a. A passing tone is used between tones of the broken chord in Fig. 4-23b. The other alternate parts have an added chord tone. An auxiliary figure is the initial unit in Fig. 4-23c. It is used for two beats in the same part in $\frac{2}{4}$ and for a measure of $\frac{6}{8}$ in Fig. 4-23d. The auxiliary figure is combined with a chord skip in Fig. 4-23e, and is expanded to two beats in $\frac{2}{4}$ and to a measure of $\frac{6}{8}$ in Fig. 4-23f.

Figure 4-23

Exercise 11b. Write imitative passages in different major keys modelled on those in Fig. 4-23, adding the counterpoint as before.

Exercise 11c. Write initial units that include changing tones, then treat these in free imitation.

Inversion

A melodic unit that follows the line of an initial unit in the opposite direction is an *inversion* of that unit. The initial unit of Fig. 4-23f is imitated in contrary direction in Fig. 4-23g. Each scalewise step up in the initial unit is correspondingly taken down by a step in the inversion; each skip in the first unit is countered by a similar skip in the opposite direction.

The inversion of a theme is placed after its original form in Fig. 4-24a, a fairly *strict inversion* of it. More often the inversion is free in quality and size of interval. *Free inversion* may start from any note. An inversion in which scale step 5 corresponds to scale step 1 of the uninverted unit (Fig. 4-24b) tends to retain the basic harmony of the key. Note the implied harmony in the last measure of #2.

Figure 4-24a–b

Exercise 12a. Write strict and free inversions of the following themes from the two- and three-part inventions: I, nos. 7 and 13, the first half measure; II, nos. 4, 8 and 14, the first measure; I, nos. 3, 4 and 15, and II, no. 10, the first two measures. (In some instances the last note of the theme extends into the next measure.)

Imitation by Contrary Motion

A voice may respond with an imitation by *contrary motion* to an initial unit in another voice, as in Fig. 4-24c. Since the rhythm is the same and distinctive lines or skips are comparable, the ear recognizes the relationship. Imitation by contrary motion, continued sequentially for several beats or measures, can be written with ease over fifth-fall progressions, as in Fig. 4-24d.

Figure 4-24c–d

Exercise 12b. Write the themes of Ex. 12a in the upper voice, then start the lower voice with inversions of them at a level that will provide good harmony. Continue the upper voice in counterpoint to the inversion.

Exercise 12c. Write several passages in different keys using various brief motives sequentially that are imitated in contrary motion, as in Fig. 4-24d. Do not allow the inversion to overlap the end of the initial unit.

5

Secondary Dominants; Accented Nonharmonic Tones and Suspensions in Two-part Counterpoint

Secondary Dominants

All chords rooted on step 5, as well as those with an implied dominant root, are classified as *primary dominants*. The chords of this group—V, V⁷, V⁹, VII and VII⁷—normally resolve to I. Similar dominant groups, based on the other scale tones, precede the other triads of the key and stand in the same relation to their triads as the primary dominants to tonic. These *secondary dominants,* also called *antecedent* or *embellishing* dominants, are based on a root or implied root that lies a fourth below the root of the associated triad (Fig. 5-1). The symbols Vof, V⁷of, etc., are used to distinguish this category of chords from primary dominants. For instance, secondary dominants of II are: VofII (Five of Two), V⁷ofII (Five-seven of Two), etc.

All forms of secondary dominant related to each triad are shown in Fig. 5-1 to facilitate recognition in analysis. Our attention will be confined to the starred chords, V⁷of and VII⁷of, because they are used with greater frequency than others of this class.

Figure 5-1

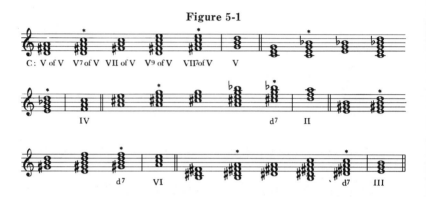

Except for their nontonic resolutions, secondary dominants do not differ in use from primary dominants. They are treated as if they were primary dominants of a "tonic" represented by the associated triad to which, with few exceptions, they resolve. Note the influence of the minor triads II, VI and III on the lowered ninth of V⁹of and lowered seventh of VII⁷of for these triads. The VII⁷ofII, of VI and of III is therefore a *diminished seventh* chord: d⁷. The interval from root to seventh is a diminished seventh. Structurally the chord is composed of superimposed minor thirds. It may be freely inverted. Secondary dominants are not ordinarily used to precede the diminished triads VII, II in minor or the augmented triad III in minor. Secondary dominants of triads in minor are shown in Fig. 5-2. The starred chords may be used in diminished seventh form by lowering the seventh a half step.

Figure 5-2

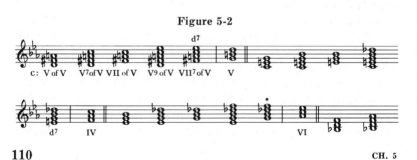

110

Secondary dominants are used to enrich a diatonic texture, to precede triads in harmonic sequences and as stepping stones in modulation. The coupled secondary dominant-triad is, however, too transitory an effect to set up a new key feeling (Fig. 5-3). Read the section on modulation in Ch. 6.

Figure 5-3

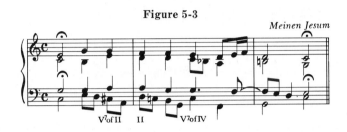

Exercise 1a. Resolve the starred secondary dominants in Fig. 5-1 to their respective triads in open-style harmony. Do this in all major keys.

Exercise 1b. Do this with V⁷of and VII⁷of and their triads in each minor key.

Doubling and voice leading in four-part harmony is exactly like that for V⁷; if necessary, double the root and omit the fifth. Resolve the third up and the seventh down by step. Each triad in C is preceded by its secondary dominant in Fig. 5-4a.

Cross-Relations

Chromatic tones in secondary dominants require special attention in voice leading. The note F in the alto of Fig. 5-4b is followed by F♯ in a different voice. This manner of voice leading, called *cross-relations*, should be avoided. In consecutive chords, the chromatic note should be in the same voice as the preceding diatonic note with the same letter (Fig. 5-4c and measures 2 and 5, Fig. 5-4a). Cross-relations are sometimes unavoidable in chromatic harmony and in counterpoint. This practice is permissible when one or both tones are nonharmonic (Fig. 5-4d).

Figure 5-4a–d

Approach to Secondary Dominants

These chords may be interpolated between any two triads in normal progressions; *e.g.*, II–V, II–V⁷ofV–V; VI–IV, VI–V⁷ofIV–IV, etc. Secondary dominants may follow a triad on the same root as in Fig. 5-4a (the starred chords). Progressions that are weak or poor, like V–IV, become available when the second triad is preceded by its secondary dominant: V–V⁷ofIV–IV. Progressions up in fifths or thirds (Fig. 5-4e) become similarly useful.

Figure 5-4e

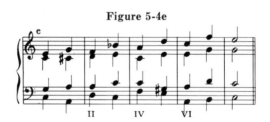

Progressions of Secondary Dominants

These chords normally progress to their associated triads. V⁷ofV often moves to I⁶₄ before V, or to V⁷. A deceptive resolution of V⁷ofVI to IV is not uncommon (Fig. 5-8b). Less often V⁷ofIII moves to I. In minor, V⁷ofV occasionally moves to III.

The progressions in Exs. 2 and 3 will be written in four-part harmony in the keys assigned.

Exercise 2a. Write the following in C, G, F, D and B♭ (triads in fifth-fall progressions): III–V⁷ofVI–VI, V⁷ofII–II, V⁷ofV–V, V⁷–I, V⁷ofIV–IV, V⁷–I. Write in C, A and E♭ (triads up in fifths): I–V⁷ofIV–IV, V⁷–I, V⁷ofV–V, V⁷ofII–II, V⁷ofVI–VI, V⁷ofIII–III, V⁷–I.

Exercise 2b. Write the following in C, E, A♭ and B (progressions down in thirds): I–V⁷ofVI–VI, V⁷ofIV–IV, V⁷ofII–II, V⁷ofV–I⁶₄–V⁷–I. Write the progressions of Fig. 5-4e in G, F and D.

Exercise 2c. Write the following in C, G, F, D and B♭ (progressions up in seconds): I–V⁷ofII–II, V⁷ofIII–III, V⁷ofIV–IV, V⁷ofV–V, V⁷ofVI–VI, V–V⁷–I.

Exercise 2d. Write the following in C, A, E♭ and B (progressions down in seconds): I–V⁷ofVI–VI, V⁷ofV–V, V⁷ofIV–IV, V⁷of III–III, V⁷ofII–II, V⁷–I.

Inversions of Secondary Dominants

The inversions of these chords are similar to V⁷ inversions and are treated the same way. The bass of the first inversion resolves up and the third inversion down by step. Inversion symbols are the same; e.g., V⁶₅ofV, V⁴₃ofV and V₂ofV represent the first, second and third inversions of the chord. For practical reasons inversion symbols are omitted from the Bach examples. Inversions like those in Fig. 5-5a provide a smoother bass line.

Figure 5-5

Exercise 3a.   Write the following in C, G, F, D and B♭: *I$_6$–V$_2$ofVI–VI$_6$, V$_5^6$ofII–II, V$_2$ofV–V$_6$, V^7–I, V$_2$ofIV–IV$_6$, V^7–I. Using the same bass as in Fig. 5-5a, substitute the VII^7 form for each secondary dominant. Write in C, A and E♭: I–V$_3^4$ofVI–VI, V$_2$ofII–II$_6$, V$_5^6$ofV–V, V$_2$ofII–II$_6$, V$_5^6$ofV–V, V$_2$–I$_6$, V$_5^6$ofIV–IV, V$_5^6$ofV–I$_4^6$, V^7–I. Write in A♭, E and B: I, V$_5^6$ofVI–VI, V$_3^4$ofII–II$_6$, V$_3^4$ofV–V, V$_5^6$–I, V$_5^6$ofIV–IV, V$_3^4$–I. Use a melodic sequence starting with steps 3–2–1.

Write in A♭, F♯ and D♭: *I–V$_2$ofIV–IV$_6$, V$_5^6$ofII–II, V$_2$ofV–V$_6$–V$_5^6$ofIII; III–V$_2$ofVI–VI$_6$–V$_5^6$–I. The sequential series may start with the second chord, V$_2$.

Exercise 3b.   Write in C, F and G: *I–V$_3^4$, V$_5^6$ofIV–IV, V$_3^4$–I$_6$, V$_5^6$ofV–V, V$_3^4$ofII–II$_6$, V$_5^6$ofVI–VI, II$_6$–V–V^7–I. Raise the third of II$_6$ in bass to avoid the augmented second and to preserve the sequence.

Exercise 3c.   Write in C, D, B♭ and A: *I, V$_3^4$ofVI–VI–V$_3^4$of-IV–IV–V$_3^4$ofII–II, V^{7}ofV–I$_4^6$–V^7–I. Use a soprano in tenths with the bass.

Write in C, E♭ and A♭: *I$_6$, V$_5^6$ofII–II, V$_5^6$ofIV–IV; skip down a diminished seventh in bass to V$_5^6$ofVI–VI, V$_5^6$–I; skip down a diminished fifth to V$_3^4$ofIII–III$_6$, V$_3^4$ofV–V$_6$, V^7–I.

Exercise 3d.   Write in C, E and D♭: *I–V$_5^6$ofII–II, V$_5^6$ofIII–III, V$_5^6$ofIV–IV, V$_5^6$ofV–V, V$_5^6$ofVI–VI, V$_5^6$–I. Write in C and B: *I–V$_3^4$ofII–II, V$_3^4$ofIII–III, V$_3^4$ofIV–IV, V$_3^4$ofV–V, V$_3^4$ofVI–VI, V$_3^4$–I. Write in C and G: *I$_6$, V$_2$ofII–II$_6$, V$_2$ofIII–III$_6$, V$_2$ofIV–IV$_6$, V$_2$ofV–V$_6$, V$_2$ofVI–VI$_6$, V$_5^6$–I. Write in C and F: *I$_6$, V$_5^6$ofVI–VI, V$_5^6$ofV–V, V$_5^6$ofIV–IV, V$_5^6$ofIII–III, V$_5^6$ofII–II, V$_5^6$–I. Write in C and D: *I, V$_3^4$ofVI–VI$_6$, V$_3^4$ofV–V$_6$, V$_3^4$ofIV–IV$_6$, V$_3^4$ofIII–III$_6$, V$_3^4$ofII–II$_6$, V$_3^4$–I$_6$.

Harmonic Progressions between Secondary Dominants

Any secondary dominant may move to another in the same key. In such progressions move to the closest tones of the second chord, avoiding cross-relations if possible. Progressions from V^{7}ofIV to other secondary dominants are shown in Fig. 5-6a; those from VII^{7}ofIV are seen in Fig. 5-6b. A series of

* Starred progressions are in harmonic sequences.

secondary dominants in fifth-fall order (Fig. 5-6c) are called *chain dominants*. All or any part of the series is used. Counting dominants back from V^7 will identify the first of the series. The substitution of V^7ofIV for the last chord may drive the progression to the subdominant key, a device used in modulation.

Figure 5-6

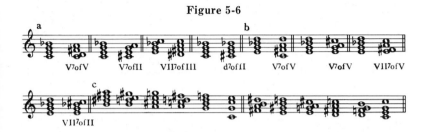

Exercise 4a.   Write the progressions of Fig. 5-6a and b in open-style harmony. Experiment with progressions from each secondary dominant, both $V^7$of and $VII^7$of, to every other secondary dominant, as in Fig. 5-6a and b.

Exercise 4b.   Write the chain dominants of Fig. 5-6c in open-style harmony. Do this with chain dominants in the keys of D, B♭, A and E♭.

Secondary Dominants in Two-Part Harmony

Intervals implying these chords are the same as those for the primary V^7. Review Figs. 4-5, 4-6 and 4-7. Note the two-part harmony in Fig. 5-5b of this chapter. Review intervals in minor that imply V^9 and VII^7.

Exercise 5.   Convert several progressions selected from Ex. 3 to two-part harmony: (1) with single intervals representing each chord, (2) with two or three chord tones, first in the upper part only, then in the lower part, and (3) with two or three chord tones in both parts.

Nonharmonic Tones with Secondary Dominants

Passing tones in secondary dominant triad progressions are written as if the progressions were a momentary new key and chromaticized accordingly. Passing tones in secondary dominants of minor triads conform to the minor character of the triad. Note the VII⁷ secondary dominants used in Fig. 5-7. This is a clear example of a single tonality enriched with secondary dominant harmony.

Figure 5-7

Auxiliaries are treated like those used in dominant–tonic of a major or minor key. Lower auxiliaries of the roots of secondary dominants and their associated triads are often a half step below. Auxiliaries of V⁷ofII, V⁷ofVI and V⁷ofIII are generally treated as if the following associated triads were tonic chords in minor, preceded by their dominants. Upper auxiliaries are a half step above the roots of V⁷ofII, V⁷ofVI and V⁷ofIII. This also applies to upper auxiliaries of the fifths of their triads. Review the section on auxiliaries in minor. Auxiliaries in changing tones, the turn and the cambiata are treated similarly.

Examine the two-part examples of secondary dominants in major (Fig. 5-8). These precede IV and II in Fig. 5-8a. The deceptive resolution of V⁷ofVI to IV is seen in Fig. 5-8b. Chain dominants are used in Fig. 5-8c.

Figure 5-8

Prelude, English Suite no. 2

Exercise 6a. Write upper parts in uniform rhythm, as in Fig. 5-8a, based on the progressions in two-part harmony, Ex. 5. Use chord tones in the lower parts. Upper parts should be melodically sequential in the starred progressions taken from Ex. 3.

Exercise 6b. Do the same with lower parts based on other two-part progressions taken from Ex. 5.

Exercise 6c. Write several passages like that of Fig. 5-7, in which rhythmic activity is shifted from voice to voice. These will be based on the same two-part progressions.

Exercise 6d. Write several passages based on chain dominants in free imitations like those in Fig. 5-8c.

Exercise 6e. Add passing, auxiliary and, where possible, changing tones to those parts formed of chord tones in Exs. 6a, b and c.

Secondary Dominants in Minor Keys

Triads III, IV, V, VI and VII with lowered leading tone are preceded by secondary dominants in minor. (See Fig. 5-2.) V⁹ofV is used in Fig. 5-9a; V⁷ofIV and V⁷ofIII are used in Fig. 5-9b. Sequences in fifth-fall progression cannot include V⁷ofII, since II is a diminished triad. They may include V⁷ofVII, as in Fig. 5-9c. Note, in this example, that V⁷ofIII is based on the lowered leading tone.

Figure 5-9a–b

The Neapolitan Sixth

A secondary dominant will sometimes precede an altered II chord that commonly appears before a cadence. This II, a major triad whose root is a half step above the tonic tone, is called a *Neapolitan sixth* (N6), starred in Fig. 5-9c. It is used mainly in first inversion and moves to I$^6_4$ or V^7. The chord as used in two-part counterpoint is seen in Fig. 5-9d. (Also see Fig. 7-21d.)

Figure 5-9c–d

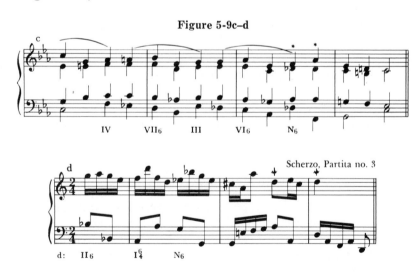

Exercise 7a.   Write each part of Ex. 7 in four-part harmony in the keys indicated. Write in c, d and a minor:

118

I_6, V^7ofV–V–V_2–I_6, V^6_5ofIV–IV–V_2ofVII–VII_6, V^7ofIII–III–V_2ofVI–VI_6, V^6_5–I. Use melodic sequences.

Exercise 7b. Write in e, g and b minor: IV–V_2ofVII–VII_6–V_2ofV–V_6–V^7ofIII, III–V^4_3–I–V^4_3ofVI–VI–V^4_3ofIV, $N6$–I^6_4–V^7–I.

A fifth-fall progression is produced by stepwise triad progression, each triad of which is preceded by its secondary dominant.

Exercise 7c. Write in f and c♯ minor: V^7ofVI–VI, V^7ofV–V, V^7ofIV–IV, V^7ofIII–III, II_6–V^7–I. Use a sequential soprano.

Exercise 7d. Rewrite several of the preceding exercises, substituting VII^7of for V^7of.

Exercise 8a. Reduce the progressions of Ex. 7 to two-part harmony.

Exercise 8b. Use these two-part progressions in the manner employed in Ex. 6.

Melodic Discord, Accented Nonharmonic Tones

Harmonic discords are intervals that are inherent in the structure of dominants and other seventh chords. In V^7 and secondary dominants, these are the seventh, second, ninth and the tritone. Melodic lines pursuing independent courses may, and often do, clash at some points, producing intervals that are *melodically discordant*. Our experience with such discord has been limited, so far, to nonharmonic tones clashing with chord tones at rhythmically inconspicuous points, on *unaccented* fractions of the beat.

Melodic discords at rhythmically prominent points sharpen the difference in melodic purpose of each line. Passing, auxiliary and other types of nonharmonic tones occurring at such points are called *accented nonharmonic tones*. They are in direct discord with chord tones or other nonharmonic tones in a different part. Such tones invest melodic lines with greater freedom in movement. Chordal intervals normally on the beat or on the accented fraction of a beat are shunted to unaccented beats or unaccented fractions of the beat.

Accented Passing Tones

Play Fig. 5-10a, with particular attention to the notes marked ('). These are *accented passing tones*. They appear in the lower voice in Fig. 5-13a. Accented passing tones on a weak beat in $\frac{3}{8}$ (or $\frac{6}{8}$ and $\frac{9}{8}$) (Fig. 5-10b), except in slow tempo, and on the second half beat in $\frac{2}{4}$, $\frac{3}{4}$ and $\frac{4}{4}$ in a rhythm of sixteenths are rhythmically less prominent. Discords in these examples are formed between accented passing tones and chord tones.

Figure 5-10a–c

Problems in analysis will occasionally arise when an accented passing tone occurs with a passing tone in another voice. The function of the tones on beat 4 in Fig. 5-10c is clear. It is less so in Fig. 5-10d. The passing tone A in the upper voice may be viewed as a chord tone of I; the first passing tone of the lower voice may be considered a tone of IV. The most reasonable analysis is indicated by the chord symbols and accent marks, as well as by the skip in I in the upper voice. Scalewise tones in the lower voice may be viewed as passing tones or as tones of a passing chord (Fig. 5-10e), the first of two examples from the *Goldberg Variations*. The measure may be regarded as I with passing tone in the lower part, or as passing II with accented passing tone as marked in the upper

120

voice. At times the accented passing tone will form a concordant interval with a passing tone in the upper voice, as marked in the second example.

Any discord of which the accented passing tone is a component is acceptable (Fig. 5-10f).

Figure 5-10d–f

Accented passing tones are used with secondary dominants in Fig. 5-11.

Figure 5-11

The following exercises employ accented passing tones in conjunction with chords at our present disposal. Figure 5-12

Figure 5-12

demonstrates the process of shifting unaccented passing tones so that they are rhythmically accented. Compare #1 with #2; #3 with #4; #5 with #6. The last tone of the auxiliary figure becomes an accented passing tone.

Each part of Ex. 9 relates to upper parts only. Employ accented passing tones where possible; use chord tones in the lower parts.

Exercise 9a.   Use a uniform rhythm of eighths in passages based on two-part harmony taken from Ex. 1, Ch. 2. Use an eighth and two sixteenths to fill a skip of a fourth. Use a uniform rhythm of sixteenths in some of the progressions, including those in $\frac{3}{8}$. Write a few in varied rhythm.

Exercise 9b.   Repeat the process above with progressions in minor taken from Ex. 8c, Ch. 4.

Exercise 9c.   Use the two-part V⁷ progressions of Ex. 1b, Ch. 4, as the basis for passages in a uniform rhythm of sixteenths and in varied rhythm. Do this also in minor.

Exercise 9d.   Write several passages based on the secondary dominant harmony of Ex. 5 of this chapter. Use the rhythm of the preceding exercise.

Exercise 10.   Reverse the process of Ex. 9 by making the lower parts of these progressions rhythmically active in the manner prescribed in those exercises.

Exercise 11.   Elaborate the parts of several passages from Exs. 9 and 10 that consist of chord tones, with passing and other nonharmonic tones.

The accented passing tone, used in the upper voice figure (Fig. 5-13a), is used subsequently in free imitation. A scalewise figure including an accented passing tone is imitated in Fig. 5-13b.

Figure 5-13

Gigue, French Suite no. 3

Exercise 12a. Devise several brief passages in different keys and meters, employing accented passing tones in imitative figures or figure-groups, as in Fig. 5-13b.

Exercise 12b. Write similar passages based on secondary dominant and triad harmony.

Accented Auxiliary Tones

Auxiliary tones rhythmically located like accented passing tones are *accented auxiliaries*. Chord skip and auxiliary figure occupy the beat in the first example (Fig. 5-14a). Accented auxiliaries on the second half beat are more common than those on the beat, as in the second example. Accented auxiliaries are shown in the lower part of Fig. 5-14b. Auxiliaries on the accent are not always discordant. One is used with a passing tone in the lower voice (Fig. 5-14c). The accented auxil-

Figure 5-14

iary often proceeds from a passing tone (Fig. 5-14d) and occurs with a change of chord.

Single measure units (Fig. 5-15) illustrate the manner of using accented auxiliaries in Ex. 13. These may be written in sixteenths in quadruple, triple and duple meters. Accented auxiliaries follow passing tones and chord skips in Fig. 5-15a and are effective as discords in a change of chord. The other part may move by chord skip or passing tone (Fig. 5-15b). Consecutive discords are permissible; accented auxiliaries are used in the lower voice in Fig. 5-15c.

Figure 5-15

Exercise 13a. Employing two-part harmony based on the progressions of Ex. 1, Ch. 2 or your own progressions, incorporate accented auxiliaries as shown in Fig. 5-15— first in the upper parts, then in the lower parts. Use different major and minor keys.

Exercise 13b. Repeat the process with some of the harmonic sequences of Exs. 5–9, Ch. 2.

Accented auxiliaries are used with secondary dominants in Fig. 5-16. Play this example, omitting the inner voice.

Figure 5-16

124

Exercise 13c. Use accented auxiliaries in two-part contrapuntal passages based on some of the progressions of Ex. 5.

Accented Auxiliaries in Changing Tones and the Turn

Upper changing tones fall on the beat (Fig. 5-17a). Note the change in harmony on the last tone of the figure in measures 3 and 5. Chord tones in the turn ordinarily occur on the accented beat or accented fraction of a beat. Auxiliaries in the turn may fall on accented fractions of the beat or on the beat when the first tone of the figure appears before the beat (Fig. 5-17b).

Figure 5-17

Fantasia, Partita no. 3

(VI   V9   VI7   IV   V7   VI7   IV6   II6

W.T.C. II, P. no. 24

Exercise 13d. Employ accented changing tones and accented auxiliaries in the turn in brief two-part contrapuntal passages based on your own progressions.

The Appoggiatura

The term *appoggiatura* traditionally was applied to all accented nonharmonic tones which "leaned on" and resolved down to the next stepwise tone. A sharper and less general definition of the term, evolving from precise classification of nonharmonic tones according to the manner of approach to and departure from chord tones, is now generally accepted. The appoggiatura, accordingly, is an accented auxiliary *approached by leap* (Fig. 5-18a) and, like any nonharmonic tone, is discordant in the prevailing chord. While it may be a tone of short duration, its rhythmic prominence and dynamic value is enhanced when it is longer than the tones immediately before and after it. A similar passage in Fig. 5-18b has a running counterpoint against the part with appoggiaturas. The harmony of Fig. 5-18c becomes clear in Fig. 5-18d with the omission of the appoggiaturas. (Notes in parentheses are missing chord tones.)

Scale steps 1, 3 and 5, which are normally static, become active as appoggiaturas and require resolution. A chord tone on the accented beat or fraction of a beat, approached by leap, is converted to an appoggiatura in Fig. 5-18e, with a chord change in the lower voice.

Figure 5-18

The leap to the appoggiatura, generally from a chord tone, is made in either direction. The upper auxiliary as appoggiatura is usually approached from below, the lower auxiliary by skip from above. The tones then normally resolve by step in the opposite direction. Appoggiaturas resolving in the direction from which the leap was made can also occur.

Appoggiaturas will sometimes resolve indirectly by first skipping to the opposite auxiliary, as in Fig. 5-19. When this occurs the other part may move to a different tone of the chord or to a different chord.

Some theorists refer to unaccented auxiliaries approached by leap as *unaccented appoggiaturas*. These (starred in Fig.

126

Figure 5-19

5-20) are fairly common. They move stepwise to a chord tone or to an accented passing tone.

Figure 5-20

Various ways of using appoggiaturas in two-part counterpoint are shown in Fig. 5-21 and will be applied in Ex. 14. (Read the footnotes that refer to each example. Note that the lower appoggiatura is often a half step below its resolution.)

Figure 5-21

[1] Simple approach and resolution.
[2] The beat includes an accented passing tone.

Exercise 14a. Write brief units that are one or two beats long which incorporate each use of the appoggiatura shown in Fig. 5-21. Try it with chords other than those in the examples, including secondary dominants. Do this in minor as well.

Exercise 14b. Write several brief free imitative passages like that of Fig. 5-18e, with appoggiaturas as a characteristic feature.

Exercise 14c. Write several sequential passages based on harmonic sequences. Use the appoggiatura in the initial unit.

The Suspension

Examine Fig. 5-22a, with particular attention to the starred notes. The notes preceding these are chord tones and are called *preparation* tones (p). Held over while the harmony changes, they become accented nonharmonic tones. These discordant tied tones, or *suspensions* (S), move by step to tones of the following chord as *resolution* tones (r). The resolution often supplies a tone missing in the second chord. Suspensions are used less often in bass (Fig. 5-22b) but frequently from voice to voice, as in Fig. 5-22c. Tied tones that are common to two chords are not suspensions.

Suspensions that do not resolve immediately, accompanied by shifting harmony and resolution tones imbedded in unexpected chords, provide further resources for pliant melody and harmonic interest. Delayed resolutions of the suspension are treated in Ch. 6.

Play Fig. 5-22a, omitting the ties. The repeated notes in soprano having the characteristics of suspensions are known as *untied suspensions*.

---

³ Indirect resolution without change in the other part.
⁴ Indirect resolution, change to a different tone of the same chord in the other voice.
⁵ Change in that part to a different chord on resolution.
⁶ Used with secondary dominants.
⁷ Escape tone to appoggiatura.
⁸ The unaccented appoggiatura.
⁹ Unaccented appoggiatura; the other part moves to a different chord.
¹⁰ Appoggiatura moves to an accented passing tone.

Figure 5-22

Any tone of a chord may be suspended except one common to the next chord. The best suspended tones, unlike those in Fig. 5-22d, fill in a missing chord tone and do not clash with the resolution tone in the other voice (Fig. 5-22e). Except in cadences (Fig. 5-22e), it is inadvisable to suspend the leading tone into I with root in bass.

Most suspensions resolve down by step, particularly those with normal downward tendencies—steps 4, 6 and 2, as well as the sevenths and ninths of secondary dominants. The suspended leading tone resolves up, as well as tones functioning as "leading tones" in secondary dominants, the third in V^7of and V^9of, and the root in $VIIof$ and VII^7of. The leading tone suspended into IV or II_6 usually resolves down. Steps 1, 3 and 5 as suspended tones resolve up or down in accordance with the following harmony.

While the resolution tone may be relatively brief, the suspension is usually as long as, if not longer than, the tone to which it is tied. The suspended tone may be repeated before resolving, as in Fig. 5-23a. An auxiliary may be inserted between a chord tone and the untied suspension (Fig. 5-23b). When chord change takes place under a dotted note (Fig. 5-23c)

Figure 5-23

or under the long note of a syncopation (Fig. 5-23d), these notes change in function from chord tones to suspensions.

Exercise 15a. Using Fig. 5-22a as model, employ suspensions in soprano parts of several progressions in Ex. 1a, Ch. 4. Bear in mind that the resolution tone must be a step from the suspension. Where necessary rearrange the voices in exercises from this source. The beat with the suspension should be divided. A fruitful preliminary exercise is to suspend each tone of every triad and of the V⁷ into a second chord. Avoid oblique fifths and octaves (Fig. 5-23e).

Exercise 15b. Rewrite several of these progressions using the suspension in bass, as in Fig. 5-22b.

Exercise 15c. Transfer the suspension from voice to voice, as in Fig. 5-22c, using the same progressions. Look for chord tones in any voice that are a step apart and suspend the first tone.

Exercise 15d. Use suspensions in minor with the progressions cited in Exs. 8a and b, Ch. 4.

Suspensions are used with secondary dominants and their triads in Fig. 5-24.

Figure 5-24

V⁷of VI   V⁷of II   V⁷of V   V⁷of IV

Exercise 15e. Use suspensions with secondary dominants in progressions taken from Ex. 3.

The bass of the underlying harmony may change with the resolution in a simple exchange of chord tones (Fig. 5-25a); the harmony shifts to a different chord in Fig. 5-25b.

Exercise 16a. In several original progressions change the bass of the same chord with the tone of resolution, as in Fig. 5-25a.

130

Exercise 16b. Write several brief progressions with chord changes on the suspension, before the resolution, as in Fig. 5-25b.

Each tone of resolution becomes in turn a suspension in Fig. 5-25c. These are called *continuous* or *chain suspensions*. Although they may be employed with any chord series, they are often used in a line of first inversions, particularly in three-part counterpoint.

Figure 5-25

Exercise 16c. Write several brief four-part progressions in major and minor employing chain suspensions. Use different keys. Watch for parallels, particularly in a series of first inversions.

Suspensions in Two-part Harmony

Suspensions appear with considerable frequency in polyphonic music. They contribute to rhythmic diversity as one voice moves against the suspended tone. Since chord-tone resolutions are shifted off the accent, suspensions are useful in emancipating the texture from four-square harmony and adding the tang of discord to it.

The Preparation

The preparation is generally a concordant interval representing the first chord. Each measure of Fig. 5-26 starts with a preparatory interval. One tone is suspended, forming various discordant intervals. (See Fig. 5-26, #1–#5.) Although the minor seventh and tritone of V⁷ and secondary dominants are harmonic discords, the preparation tone may be in one of these intervals (Fig. 5-26, #6).

The Suspension

The suspension over or under a tone of the second chord almost invariably forms a discordant interval, preferably a second, fourth, seventh or ninth. The fifth, discordant to the harmony of resolution, is less common (#3 and measures 2 and 3, #6).

The Resolution

The second resolves to a third (measures 2 and 3, #1). It is better in two-part writing to avoid a resolution to a unison (measure 5, #1). The fourth resolves to a third. Note the examples and the irregular resolution (#9). When the chord of resolution is dominant, the suspension may resolve to a tritone (measure 4, #1; see #3). The seventh usually resolves to a sixth (measure 1, #2, and #4). Note the other examples. When the chord tone leaps, as in #8, the interval of a seventh may represent either secondary dominant or secondary seventh (Ch. 6). In that case the tied note is not a suspension. The suspended major seventh moves to an octave in measure 9, #1.

The suspended minor seventh resolves to an octave in contrary motion (measures 2 and 3, #2). The ninth moves to a tenth (measures 6 and 8, #1; measures 1 and 4, #5). It moves to the octave in contrary motion (measure 10, #1). The fifth resolves to the sixth (measures 1 and 4, #3, and measures 2 and 3, #6). On occasion it moves to the augmented fourth (measures 2 and 3, #3). A rest takes the place of a tied note that would form a discord with the note in the second voice, giving the effect of a suspension (#7). Two successive tones of the next chord lie over the suspension in #10. The irregular resolution is admissible.

Figure 5-26

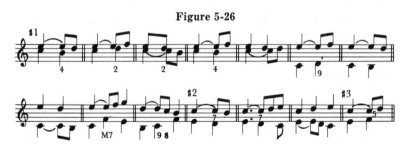

Chord tones in the voice without suspension move by step or skip; motion by skip highlights the suspension in measure 1, #6. The tone of resolution may be embellished with an auxiliary, as in #11. The resolution, as described in the next chapter, may be delayed.

Exercise 17a. With two-part harmony based on several progressions from Ex. 1b, Ch. 4, write several passages centered on the use of suspensions, first in the upper parts, then in the lower parts.

Exercise 17b. Write similar passages based on the secondary dominant harmony of Exs. 5 and 8.

Suspensions in Two-Part Counterpoint

The foregoing material applies basically to the use of suspensions in counterpoint. Melodic movement over or under suspensions may result in a resolution interval different from the one expected (Fig. 5-27a). While suspensions are used in the simple rhythm of Figs. 5-26 and 5-27b, they occur frequently in the active context of Fig. 5-27a. Inner tones of Fig. 5-27b are omitted.

Syncopated suspended tones in two-part counterpoint are

Figure 5-27

Fantasia, Partita no. 3

seen in Fig. 5-28a; these are used as chain suspensions in Fig. 5-28b.

Figure 5-28

Figure 5-29 demonstrates several ways of elaborating the simple first measure of Fig. 5-26 in two-part counterpoint. In #1 a chord tone of the lower part is embellished with an auxiliary figure; in #2 an auxiliary is used with the resolution; in #3 a changing tone figure is used with the preparation; in #4 a skip in the same chord is taken with the resolution; in #5 a chord skip and an appoggiatura are used against the preparation.

Figure 5-29

Exercise 17c. Elaborate each measure of Fig. 5-26 in ways similar to those shown in Fig. 5-29.

Chain suspensions of tones in thirds and sixths moving step-wise (Fig. 5-30a) are less useful in two- than in three-part counterpoint, where the third voice counteracts the parallel motion. Such parallelism may be interrupted by chord skips, as in Fig. 5-30b. A third between sixths suspended (Fig. 5-30c) relieves the monotony of the original (Fig. 5-30a).

Figure 5-30

Exercise 17d. Write several brief passages in major and minor similar to those in Fig. 5-30b and c.

Exercise 18a. Write several brief passages employing the suspension in sequences, starting with units similar to those in Fig. 5-29. See #6.

Exercise 18b. Employ the suspension in brief free imitative passages, as in Fig. 5-29, #7.

6

Secondary Sevenths; Delayed Resolutions of Suspensions; Closely Related Modulations

Secondary Seventh Chords

Four-tone chords based on scale steps other than 5 are classed as *secondary seventh* chords to distinguish them from the primary seventh, V^7. One of these chords, the VII^7, functions both as dominant (Fig. 4-10) and as secondary seventh. Secondary sevenths (Fig. 6-1) differ in structure and function from V^7 and, in many instances, from each other. In major keys II^7, VI^7 and III^7 are minor triads with an added minor seventh. These are minor seventh chords. Major triads with a major seventh, IV^7 and I^7, are major seventh chords. The VII^7, composed of a diminished triad with added minor seventh, is a half diminished seventh chord.

The structure of secondary sevenths in minor (Fig. 6-1b) is determined by minor scale tones. The variable steps 6 and 7 provide two forms of the same chord in some instances. IV^7

Figure 6-1

and I⁷ are minor triads with added minor sevenths. III⁷ and VI⁷ are major triads with added major sevenths. VI⁷ with raised root and II⁷ are diminished triads with added minor sevenths. The II⁷ with raised fifth is a minor triad with minor seventh. This chord, and the altered VI⁷, in addition to V⁷ofV, is used mainly in harmonizing step 6 of the rising upper tetrachord in the melodic minor. The starred chords, III⁷ and I⁷, with raised leading tone, are infrequently used.

Secondary seventh chords amplify our resources while introducing a degree of harmonic duality, since the same chord may have one function in a given key and another in a different key. They are constantly used in sequences and are highly effective in modulation. The chord-seventh often has the effect of a passing tone, as in Fig. 6-2a, measure 4.

Marked degrees of discord differentiate one group from another in this class of chords. Secondary sevenths in major keys, composed of a minor triad and minor seventh—the II⁷, VI⁷, III⁷ and the IV⁷ and I⁷ in minor—are least discordant. Seventh chords formed from a diminished triad and minor seventh—VII⁷ in major keys, II⁷ and altered VI⁷ in minor keys—as well as the diminished seventh chord, VII⁷, are less discordant than the IV⁷, I⁷ in major and III⁷ in minor which include a major seventh interval. These dissonant chords, however, can be effective as contrast to consonant and less discordant chords. By simple chromatic change secondary sevenths move to secondary dominants: II⁷–V⁷ofV, VI⁷–V⁷ofII, etc.

Exercise 1. Write the secondary seventh chords shown in Fig. 6-1 in all major and minor keys.

Secondary Seventh Chords in Major, the II⁷

The supertonic seventh, II⁷, is used with greater frequency than any other chord of this class. It may be viewed as a composite of II and IV, taking the place of either in chord progressions. Like these triads, II⁷ progresses to any form of dominant (V, V₆, V⁷ and its inversions), to VII₆, VII⁷ and to

V⁹ (Fig. 6-2a). The chord-seventh, originally introduced as suspension from I, has the same effect in the progression I–II⁷–V. Play Fig. 6-2a, observing this in the repeated and tied chord-seventh. II⁷ also moves to I, I₆ and I⁶₄ in the approach to cadences. The chord-seventh normally resolves down by step but on occasion moves irregularly.

Figure 6-2

In fifth-fall progression, II⁷ is preceded by VI and VI⁷. It is also approached by IV, IV₆, II, II₆, IV⁷ and by I and I₆. The chord is used to delay the resolution of dominant harmony (V–II⁷–V, V⁷–II⁷–V⁷) and to delay the resolution of I⁶₄ (I⁶₄–II⁷–V). It is used in all inversions. Symbols for these are similar to V⁷ inversions: II⁶₅, II⁴₃, II₂. The chord-fifth is the least essential tone. Double the root and omit the fifth, when necessary, in the uninverted chord. Do not omit or double tones in the inverted chord.

Unaccented nonharmonic tones will often form a secondary seventh chord more in appearance than in aural effect. It is inadvisable to draw too fine a line in the analysis of examples like those in Fig. 6-2b. #1 is a simple passing tone in IV; there are double passing tones in V⁷, #2; an unaccented appoggiatura in IV is used in #3. The rhythmic value and location of such tones has a bearing on their interpretation, as in #4.

The Submediant Seventh, VI⁷

VI⁷ normally resolves in fifth-fall progression to II and II⁷, moving less often to IV and to dominant harmony or I⁶₄. It is best preceded by III, III⁷, I and VI. The chord may be used in any inversion and as a passing chord in dominant harmony (measure 6, Fig. 6-3). Double the root and omit the fifth, when necessary, in the uninverted chord.

Figure 6-3

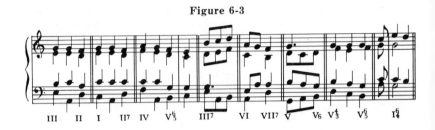

III   II   I   II⁷   IV   V⅞   III⁷   VI   VII⁷   V   V₆   V⅘   V⁶₅   I⁶₄

The Mediant Seventh, III⁷

The III⁷, except in fifth-fall sequences, is infrequently used. It progresses to VI, VI⁷ and occasionally to IV. Passing I and I₆ chords are seen in measures 3 and 4 of Fig. 6-4. The chord is preceded by VII⁷, I and III. All inversions are used. Doubling is similar to that in II⁷ and VI⁷.

Figure 6-4

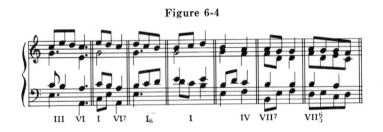

III   VI   I   VI⁷   I₆   I   IV   VII⁷   VII⁶₅

The Subdominant Seventh, IV⁷

The harsh discord of a major seventh in IV⁷ limits its use mainly to the fifth-fall progression, IV⁷–VII⁷, and to II⁷. IV⁷ moves to other dominant harmony: V, VII and V⁷. The seventh has the effect of an anticipation in the progression IV⁷–I⁶₄. Preceded by I, VI or VI⁷, its seventh as common tone has the effect of a suspension. Preceded by IV, the seventh often sounds like a passing tone. As in I⁷, the discord of the major seventh is lessened by locating the root a seventh plus an octave below the chord-seventh. In instances where the discord is desirable the tones are brought closer together or the seventh is placed immediately below the root, as in measure 7, Fig. 6-5.

140

Figure 6-5

I   VI   VI⁷   I$^6_4$ III⁷

The Tonic Seventh, Iᵀ

The tonic triad, as the harmonic center of the key, is a chord
for which no seventh chord can be a satisfactory substitute. Iᵀ
is an unstable form of tonic harmony that is used mainly in
fifth-fall sequences: Vᵀ–Iᵀ, etc. The chord is usually preceded
by dominant harmony and resolves to IV or IVᵀ. Occasionally
it moves to VIᵀ or IIᵀ and is often replaced with VᵀofIV in
harmonic sequences (Fig. 6-8d).

Figure 6-6

IV   IV⁷   VI⁷   II⁷

The Leading Tone Seventh, VIIᵀ

We had dealt earlier with VIIᵀ as a form of dominant preceded
by any chord and resolving to I, or indirectly to it: VIIᵀ–Vᵀ–I.
(See Fig. 4-10.) A similarly constructed chord—VIIᵀofV—
serves as substitute for VᵀofV.

VIIᵀ, preceded by IV or IVᵀ (Fig. 6-7), also functions as a

Figure 6-7

secondary seventh in fifth-fall progressions. It resolves to III or III⁷. (Also see Fig. 6-11d.) The chord is used in all inversions. Its fifth and seventh, tendency tones, normally resolve down by step. The leading tone root may be doubled. It skips up a fourth or down a fifth in bass. (See Fig. 6-8a.)

Exercise 2a. Write an eight-measure unit in four-part harmony centered on the use of II⁷ in major. Use inversions of the chord. Reread the textual material describing the approach to and resolution of II⁷.

Exercise 2b. Do this in different major keys with each seventh chord in turn.*

Secondary Sevenths in Harmonic Sequences

Fifth-fall progressions of seventh chords, and triads alternating with them, are the harmonic bases of many passages uninterrupted by cadential harmony in Baroque polyphonic music. Such passages either evade the cadence with V⁷–I⁷, with V⁷ofIV for the expected I or they move to a new key through the last seventh chord.

Harmonic sequences of seventh chords alternating with triads are used in Fig. 6-8a. Triads move to sevenths on the same root via a passing seventh in Fig. 6-8b. (See the starred notes in Fig. 7-17a.) Passing sevenths alternate in soprano

Figure 6-8

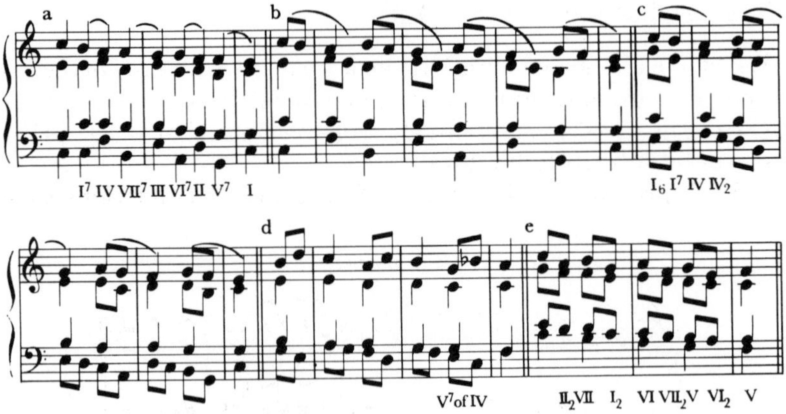

*While V⁷ and secondary dominants are also seventh chords, secondary seventh chords, except in captions, will be referred to hereafter as seventh chords for the sake of brevity.

142

and bass in Fig. 6-8c. The triad moves to the seventh by skip in alternate chords (Fig. 6-8d). Triads move to the third inversion of the following seventh chords in Fig. 6-8e. It should be understood that these sequences may start with any triad or seventh chord.

Harmonic sequences of seventh chords in fifth-fall progression are used in Fig. 6-9a. The soprano and tenor voices in Fig. 6-9b sound like untied suspensions in similar progressions. Alternate sevenths are inverted in Fig. 6-9c. The initial unit in Fig. 6-9d is a three-chord progression that is repeated in harmonic sequences.

Figure 6-9

Exercise 3a. Write sequential progressions similar to those in Figs. 6-8 and 6-9 in different major keys. Bear in mind that irregular resolution of tendency tones, awkward skips and poor doubling are excused when the initial unit is correct.

Exercise 3b. Each unit of the following moves sequentially up by step: I–IV⁷, II–V⁷, III–VI⁷, IV–VII⁷, I. Write this in C, G and F, in four-part harmony.

Exercise 3c. Root movement of the initial three-chord unit is down in thirds in the following: IV₂–II⁷–VII⁶₅, III₂–I⁷–VI⁶₅, II₂–VII⁷–V⁶₅, I. The following is a four-chord initial unit which includes a secondary dominant: III₆–V⁶₅ofVI–VI–VI₂, II₆–V⁶₅ofV–V–V₂, I₆–V⁶₅ofIV–IV–IV₂, VII₆–V⁶₅ofIII–III–III₂, VI₆–V⁶₅ofII–II–II₂, V⁶₅–V⁷–I. Write all of these sequential progressions in several major keys.

Secondary Seventh Chords in Two-Part Writing

There are fewer intervals available to imply secondary sevenths than there are for V^7, which has the characteristic tritone, in addition to the minor seventh, the major second and major ninth. Seventh chords are implied by the last three. While a leap of a seventh in melody may indicate this type of chord, it may also imply a secondary dominant. The tied note in Fig. .6-10a may be regarded as a suspension in I. Arpeggiated seventh chords, as in the upper and lower parts of Fig. 6-10b, give clear indication of the chords. II^7 is more clearly spelled out in Fig. 6-10c than is VI^7 with passing seventh. This excerpt is reduced from three to two parts, with slight alteration. In many instances the chord-seventh, missing in one part, is supplied in another. Note the use of II^7 to delay the resolution of dominant harmony (Fig. 6-10d).

Figure 6-10

Seventh chord and triad alternate in the harmonic sequence of Fig. 6-11a. Sevenths follow triads on the same root in the sequences of Fig. 6-11b. Each whole measure may, however, be regarded as a single chord: VII^7–VI^7–V^7. An initial two-chord unit is followed by seventh chord sequences in Fig. 6-11c. The melodic leap of a seventh in lower and upper parts here is clearly indicative of seventh chords. Observe that secondary dominants may resolve to secondary sevenths on the same root as the expected triad. Note how the chord-third of each triad (Fig. 6-11d) becomes the seventh of the next chord in a suspension effect. Play the excerpt, omitting the inner voice.

Figure 6-11

Bourrée, English Suite no. 1

I₆ VI⁷   II   V⁷   I   IV₆ I₆ II₆ V

I, no. 10

II₆   VII₆   VII⁷   I₆   VI   VI   VII₆   V₆   V⁷

Fughetta no. 13, L.P.F.

V⁷   V⁷ of IV   IV⁷   VII⁷   III⁷   VI⁷   II⁷   V⁷   I

Prelude no. 13, L.P.F.

I   IV⁷   VII⁷   III⁷   VI⁷   II⁷   V⁷

Exercise 4a. Convert the progressions of Ex. 2 to two-part harmony.

Exercise 4b. Using the same progressions, add another chord tone or two, first to the upper parts, then to the lower parts.

Exercise 4c.   Write passages in different major keys in two-part counterpoint, based on the harmony of the preceding exercise.

Review modified sequences, Ch. 2, before proceeding with Ex. 5. Melodic modifications, without altering the harmony, may be made with the first or subsequent sequences. A figure at the tail end of a long initial melodic unit can be used sequentially to extend a passage, or a new figure can be used for the same purpose. Developing sequences in these ways is more interesting than using mechanically repetitive sequences.

Exercise 5.   Write a number of sequential passages in two-part counterpoint, based on the harmony of Figs. 6-8 and 6-9. Use different major keys.

Secondary Seventh Chords in Minor

Secondary sevenths in minor (Fig. 6-1b) progress, in general, like those in major. The best fifth-fall progressions lie between VI^7 and VII^7. Commonly used progressions down in thirds are VI^7–IV^7 and IV^7–II^7; VII^7–V^7 is dominant repetition. Stepwise movement and both forms of VI^7 and III^7 require careful handling. Raised steps 6 and 7 in these chords (Fig. 6-12a) move up stepwise. Explore the effect of moving each seventh chord in minor to triads and other sevenths.

Seventh chords in minor are particularly effective in the typical Baroque-style approach to half cadences (Fig. 6-12b).

Figure 6-12

146

Exercise 6a. Write the following in four-part harmony in the given minor keys (the raised notes in VI⁷ and III⁷ are indicated by sharps) :

a $\quad$ I–VI⁷–II$_3^4$–V⁷–I–IV⁷–II$_6$–V–I ;

d $\quad$ I–II$_2$–V$_5^6$–I–III⁷–I⁷–IV–IV$_5^6$–V ;

e $\quad$ I–II$_5^6$–III⁷♯–VI–VI⁷–IV–II$_5^6$–V$_6$–I ;

g $\quad$ I–II$_2$–VII⁷–V⁷–I–III$_6$–VI⁷♯–VII$_6$–I$_6$;

b $\quad$ I–VI⁷–V–VI⁷♯–V$_6$–II$_5^6$–I$_4^6$–V ;

c $\quad$ I–VII$_5^6$–IV⁷–V$_2$–I$_6$–III–VI⁷–IV–II⁷–V–I ;

f♯ $\quad$ I–III⁷–I$_6$–I⁷–IV–VI⁷–VII$_2$–V⁷–I.

Exercise 6b. Reduce these progressions to two-part harmony, adding chord tones to each part, as in Ex. 4b.

Employing secondary sevenths in minor in two-part writing presents, as in major, the problem of defining the harmony with limited means. Broken and arpeggiated chords is one solution (Figs. 6-13a and 6-15b). Chord skips in both parts predominate in the invention from which Fig. 6-13a is taken, producing a harmonic rather than a contrapuntal effect. It is better, as a general practice, to counter skips in the chord with

Figure 6-13

a smoother line in the other part, as in Fig. 6-13b and c. A simple scale-line bass is used in Fig. 6-13d. Note how the pattern and the starred common tones hold the passage together.

Exercise 6c. Develop passages in two-part counterpoint from the progressions of Ex. 6b.

Exercise 6d. Write brief original progressions ending on the half cadences of Fig. 6-12b; reduce these to two parts, then develop them in two-part counterpoint.

Seventh chords in fifth-fall sequences in minor, that include VII⁷ and III⁷ with lowered leading tone and VI⁷ with lowered step 6, proceed as in major (Fig. 6-14a). (See also Fig. 6-15b.) VII⁷, in that case, is actually V⁷ofIII. (See Fig. 6-15a.) Less easily handled is the augmented second when III⁷ with raised leading tone goes to VI⁷ (Fig. 6-14b). The upper tones in these progressions sound like double suspensions. The initial unit of sevenths down in thirds is followed sequentially in Fig. 6-14c. Stepwise motion of seventh to triad is similarly sequential in Fig. 6-14d, where VI⁷♯ to VII with lowered leading tone is equivalent to secondary dominant–triad: VII⁷ofVII–VII. Note the deceptive resolution in minor: V⁷–VI.

Figure 6-14

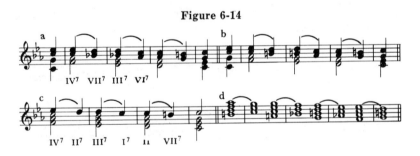

IV⁷ VII⁷ III⁷ VI⁷

IV⁷ II⁷ III⁷ I⁷ II VII⁷

Exercise 6e. Write Fig. 6-14 in four-part open harmony, reduce it to two parts, then write sequential passages in two-part counterpoint based on these progressions.

Harmonic Fusion

The term *harmonic fusion* is used to describe progressions of two or three chords with common tones that overlap or fuse, obscuring the harmony. Bach (as in Fig. 6-15b) frequently resorts to dovetailing chords in this manner to keep the harmony flexible and forward moving. (See the reference to harmonic fusion on p. 239.)

Secondary sevenths, sharing many tones with triads, seventh and secondary dominant chords lend themselves readily to harmonic fusion. For instance, II^7 has three tones in common with IV, II, VII^7, IV^7 and $V^7$of$V$; two tones with VI, VII, V^7 and VI^7, and one in common with I, III^7 and I^7. Various chords may be fused with the other sevenths. Bear in mind, when analyzing inventions later, that the harmonic ambiguity is conscious and purposeful even though it makes precise harmonic analysis difficult and, at times, impossible.

Figure 6-15

Imitations, both strict and free, are based at times on fifth-fall progressions of seventh–triad and seventh–seventh. These progressions, using thematic fragments in development passages, generally move to a different key with the last seventh chord. Each imitating figure in Fig. 6-16a starts with the chord-fifth and, after the leap, ends on the third of the next seventh chord. Structural differences between sevenths preclude strict imitation. Note the change of interval skip at the starred note. This, and the following excerpt, is a reduction of the original to two parts. For the present, do not start the imitation before the conclusion of the initial figure or figure-group. When material such as the eighth notes in Fig. 6-16b is also imitated, it results in canonic imitation, which is treated in Ch. 7.

Figure 6-16a–b

Exercise 7a. Write brief imitative passages in different keys based on fifth-fall progressions of seventh–triad, as in Fig. 6-16c, filling in the blank parts with nonimitative material. Note that each unit starts on the chord-seventh and then continues to the root of the following triad. Adhere to the pattern of the initial unit in the imitations, regardless of whether the first tone is root, third, fifth or seventh.

Exercise 7b. Write imitative passages based on the same progressions, using accented nonharmonic tones and/or suspensions, as in Fig. 6-16d. Bear in mind that a missing chord-seventh in the initial figure can be placed in the other part.

Exercise 7c. Write brief imitative passages based on fifth-fall seventh progressions, as in Fig. 6-16e and longer units as in Fig. 6-16f. Include appoggiaturas, then add nonimitative counterpoint to each unit.

Figure 6-16c–f

III⁷ VI⁷ III⁷ VI⁷ II⁷ V⁷

Delayed Resolutions of Suspensions

Interposing tones between a suspension and its resolution is a common practice in the music of Bach and his contemporaries. Delayed resolutions contribute to melodic plasticity, subordinate the harmony and cushion the impact of cadences when necessary. The term *ornamental resolution*, applied by some writers, refers more properly to an auxiliary embellishment of the resolution tone. *Delayed resolutions* involve the intervention of chord and nonharmonic tones *before* the resolution. In some instances the resolution itself is transformed to a nonharmonic tone. Read the explanatory notes as each example in Fig. 6-17 is examined, then play the *corresponding* examples taken from Bach (Fig. 6-18). Suspension and resolution are abbreviated: S, R.

Figure 6-17

---

[1] This is a simple ornamental resolution. Technically the first note B is the R; rhythmically the second B is felt as the R.

[2] The S leaps to an unaccented appoggiatura before the R; note parallel first inversions in the corresponding example (Fig. 6-18) and the method of sustaining a sixteenth-note rhythm.

[3] The S leaps to a chord tone before R.

[4] The S is repeated before leaping to the chord tone; the R follows.

Figure 6-18

Exercise 8a. Write progressions in four-part harmony that are one or two measures long, incorporating each way of

---

[5] Compare this with no. 5 in Fig. 6-18, where the starred notes are chord tones and technically a R. It is felt, however, as an échappée with the following note. The excerpt is transposed from F♯.

[6] An échappée leaps to an unaccented appoggiatura before R.

[7] A changing tone figure around the S; note the seventh-chord effect of the S.

[8] A leap from the S returns to the S before R.

[9] The chord change on the last half beat converts the R to an appoggiatura.

[10] A leap from S moves scalewise to R.

152

using the delayed resolution shown in Fig. 6-17. Use different keys and try some of them in parts other than the soprano.

Exercise 8b.   Write brief passages in two-part counterpoint in various major and minor keys, employing the delayed resolutions illustrated in Fig. 6-18.

The suspension and its delayed resolution is used over a single chord tone or over two tones of the same chord in the other part in many of the preceding examples. Melodic or harmonic movement in the other part, prior to or with the resolution, is seen in several examples in Fig. 6-18. Tones in the other part may alter the function of notes interposed between suspension and resolution. Examine Fig. 6-19 in preparation for the following exercise. Passing tones are used in Fig. 6-19a. The chord changes from triad to seventh in Fig. 6-19b. A different chord, VofV, is inserted before the resolution (Fig. 6-19c). Chord changes take place with the resolution (Fig. 6-19d).

Figure 6-19

Exercise 8c.   Reduce each unit of Fig. 6-17 to soprano and bass, then introduce changes in the bass part similar to those in Fig. 6-19.

Modulation

The process of shifting from one clearly established key to another in a manner that confirms the feeling of arrival at a different tonality is called *modulation*. This sense of arrival is produced by progressions moving to a firm cadence in the new key, or with progressions after a new-key cadence that establish that key. While any type of good chord progression is used to lead to its cadence, sufficient repetition of the new dominant-tonic or the relatively long duration of dominant or tonic will consummate a modulation.

Modulations are essential to the design of a contrapuntal work, in marking the close of one section or highlighting the beginning of another through key contrast. The eighteenth century composer was occupied not only with the creation of themes and their development, but also with the key scheme of his material. He planned each point of arrival in the broad context of the whole composition, working from key to key before concluding it in the original tonality. In this comprehensive key scheme the secondary dominant–triad combination falls into place as an incidental progression in the key or as a step en route to a new key. Observe the difference between the simple V⁷ofVI–VI and the key change felt at the cadence in Fig. 6-20.*

Figure 6-20

V⁷ofVI VI

Keys Closely Related to Major Keys

The modulation in the example above is a simple one, from C major to a, its relative minor. Key shifts from major to relative minor, from minor to relative major and modulations to keys involving a signature change of only one sharp or flat, are *modulations* to *closely related keys*. All others are *distant modulations*. Our present study is an examination of the process of modulation to closely related keys. While there is some relationship, however tenuous, between any two keys, in the interest of brevity we will refer to closely related keys as *related keys*.

Five keys are related to each major key. For instance, the keys related to G major are: (1) e, its relative minor; (2) D, the dominant key, and (3) b, *its* relative minor; (4) C, the subdominant key, and (5) a, *its* relative minor. Similarly, in flat keys, the keys related to F are: (1) d, its relative minor;

* Most of the nonharmonic tones are omitted from this and other chorale examples.

(2) C, the dominant key, and (3) a, *its* relative minor; (4) B♭, the subdominant key, and (5) g, *its* relative minor. The tonic chords of the related keys are also triads of the original key; *e.g.*, g–ii, a–iii, B♭–IV, C–V and d–vi. This makes it easy to remember the keys related to any major key. Think of the ii, iii, IV, V and vi triads of the original key. Note that major related keys are in capital letters and numerals. We will refer to these modulations as: to the supertonic, to the mediant, to the subdominant, to the dominant and to the submediant keys.

Since each major key and its tonic minor key share the same tonic tone, the same V, V⁷ and other chords, the tonic minor is generally accepted as a related key.

Exercise 9a.   List the keys related to each major key.

Keys Closely Related to Minor Keys

The keys related to a minor key are its relative major and keys differing in signature by one sharp or flat. For instance, the keys related to a minor are: (1) C, its relative major; (2) e, the dominant minor, and (3) G, its relative major; (4) d, the subdominant, and (5) F, its relative major. The tonic chords of these keys are triads rooted on tones of the descending melodic minor scale: G–VII, F–VI, e–v, d–iv and C–III. We will therefore speak of these as: modulations to the leading tone key, to the submediant, to the dominant minor, to the subdominant and to the mediant keys.

Two additional major keys may be considered as related— the dominant major and the tonic major. The first, although distant in signature, affords a simple return to the I of the original minor key. The second offers an entrance to the sub-dominant key near the close of a piece. Some minor compositions end with a major I instead of the expected minor tonic. The major third in that chord is called a *Tierce de Picardie*.

Exercise 9b.   List the keys related to each minor key.

Various processes are involved in effecting a modulation and linking one key with another. These are described below and in Ch. 7.

Modulation by Direct Entry

Modulations of this type start abruptly (1) with I of the first key to I of the new key (as in Fig. 6-21a), or from V of the first key to I of the new key (Fig. 6-21b). The new tonic may make a conspicuous entrance, as in the first example, or enter on a weak beat, as in the second. Entry in this manner requires subsequent chords confirming the key.

Figure 6-21a–b

(2) A forthright entry with dominant-tonic of the new key starts the modulation in Fig. 6-21c. Chords that follow and the cadence confirm the key. (3) The dominant of the first key moves to the dominant, in any form, of the second key, as in the next to last measure of Fig. 6-20. (4) The I of the first key is chromatically altered to become the dominant of the subdominant key (Fig. 6-21d). Bach resorts to this mode of entry fairly often. Later we will encounter other triads similarly "dominantized."

Figure 6-21c–d

Exercise 10a. Starting with any major key other than C, write a brief progression that ends with I, V or V^7. Then move to each related key in turn with V^7–I of the new key. Follow this with confirmatory chords and a cadence in the new key. Do the same thing, starting with one or two other major keys.

Exercise 10b. Repeat the process, starting with a minor key.

Exercise 10c. Write brief modulatory passages in two-part counterpoint, based on the harmony of Ex. 10a and b.

Direct entry is less common than entry through pivotal chords, *i.e.,* chords common to both keys.

Pivot Chord Modulation

Play Fig. 6-22a, noting particularly the chords with a double symbol. The upper numerals indicate their function in the first key; the lower ones signal their role in the coming key. These preparatory chords, called *pivot chords,* conduct the harmony in a natural manner to the cadence of the new key. In a modulation from C to e, C:I to e:V⁷–I is less smooth than C:I–vi/iv–e:V⁷–I.

Figure 6-22a

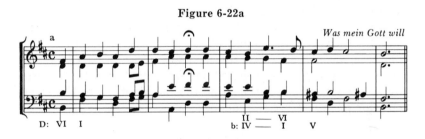

Any triad of the first key other than I, preceding a modulation, is usually a pivot chord. I closing a key is simply felt as tonic of the key. Used in progressions toward a different center, as in Fig. 6-22b, it is a pivot chord. Roots of the preparatory chords, in parenthesis, illustrate a common fifth-fall "march to the cadence."

Figure 6-22b

The I as pivotal chord appears in a transient modulation between a and F: a–C–F, starred in Fig. 6-22c. An intermediant modulation between the cadence of one key and that of another is considered a *transient modulation*. It usually has no strong authentic cadence.

Figure 6-22c

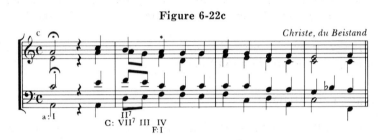

Observe the chords after the one starred. Prior to the cadence, they may be interpreted as chords of either C or F. The indeterminate nature of pivot chords makes it difficult to pinpoint the departure to the new key. Single pivot chords or several in succession are used. Those with supertonic and subdominant function in the new key move naturally to V^7 or I_4^6–V of that key. Some modulations cadence on V, a chord the ear accepts as foreshadowing the tonic. Bach frequently converts the cadential I, particularly in minor, to a diatonic seventh chord of the next key (Fig. 6-22d), the seventh having a passing tone effect. Any triad may be followed by a seventh chord on the same root as pivot. Note the interposition of IV_6 before the cadence.

Figure 6-22d

Pivot chords are either diatonic in both keys, diatonic in one key and chromatic in the other, or chromatic in both keys. Such chords are triads, seventh chords or chords with chromatic alteration. Diatonic triad and seventh pivot chords, used in modulation from a major key to related keys, are shown in Fig. 6-23a. Double starred chords, mainly subdominant and

158   CH. 6

supertonic of the new key, are most useful. Unstarred chords, particularly those remote from I of the new key, generally require additional pivot chords.

Figure 6-23a

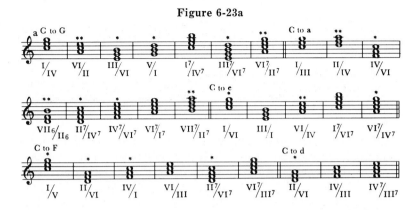

Diatonic pivot chords of a minor key, used in modulation to related keys, are seen in Fig. 6-23b. Those with raised step 6 are treated in the following chapter. Note that there are relatively few pivots in the modulations to the dominant minor, a–e, and to the subdominant, a–d. Chromatic pivot chords furnish alternatives.

Figure 6-23b

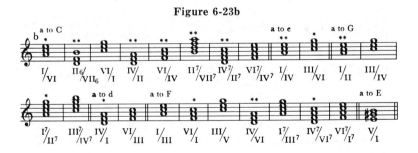

Compare the chords in Fig. 6-23a and b. You will find the same chord functioning differently in different keys. For example, the chord D–F–A–C is II⁷ in C, IV⁷ in a and VI⁷ in F. This offers a clue to the various modulatory possibilities of a particular pivot chord. The last of a series of secondary sevenths in fifth-fall progression (Fig. 6-24) is VII⁷ in G and II⁷ in e. The same chord can be used to modulate to a (VI⁷ with raised root) and to C (VII⁷ofV). Fifth-fall progressions of secondary sevenths with the last seventh or two used as pivots

is a common modulatory device. Note the sequences in each
line of Fig. 6-24.

Figure 6-24

The harmonic conditions validating a pivot chord modulation are: (1) a series of key-defining chords sufficient to establish the first key; (2) one or more pivot chords culminating in
(3) a definite half or authentic cadence. The first key is fixed
either by a similar cadence, by re-iteration of dominant-tonic
harmony or by the inclusion of subdominant or supertonic
harmony: IV, IV⁷, II, II⁷ and, at times, VI. A long drawn-out
dominant like that in Fig. 6-25 is sufficient to establish the
new key, the dominant minor. The I may be similarly extended.
(See measures 16–18, *Two-Part Invention no. 8.*)

Figure 6-25

The cadential dominant or I⁶₄ of the new key is often preceded by its secondary dominant, V⁷ofV, VII⁷ofV (Fig. 6-26).
Diatonic chords, similar to these secondary dominants except
for the chromatic alteration, provide the smoothest transition
to the secondary dominants. See measure 2 (VI–V⁷ofII) and
other measures.

Figure 6-26

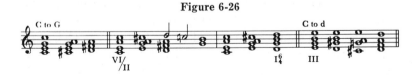

Exercise 11a. Write five progressions in four-part harmony, each establishing a different major key. Modulate from each progression to the five related keys, using pivot chords similar to those in Fig. 6-23a. Include cadences like those in Fig. 6-26 in some of them.

Exercise 11b. Repeat the process of the preceding exercise, starting with progressions in five minor keys. Use pivots like those in Fig. 6-23b and minor cadences like those in Fig. 6-26.

Pivot Chord Modulation in Two-part Counterpoint

Several examples of diatonic pivot chord modulation are shown in Fig. 6-27. Read the explanatory notes as you examine each one.

Figure 6-27

Bourrée, Suite no. 2

Bourrée, English Suite no. 5

e:I

II/V$_5^6$

G: I$_6$

IV/VI

Figure 6-28

I$_6$ IV II^7 V$_6$ I/IV III^7/VI VI/II V I$_6$ V$_6$ I

---

¹ The pivot moves to I$^6_4$ of the new key. Note the delayed resolution of the six-four chord.

² The pivot is a diatonic seventh chord.

³ I of the first key with added seventh becomes II^7 of the new key.

⁴ On the repeat the descending melodic minor tetrachord fits both II of e and V^7 of G, the second ending.

⁵ The starred auxiliary in the pivot chord becomes the leading tone before the cadence.

CH. 6

The passages in the following exercises can be worked out in one of several ways: (1) Both parts may be written from beat to beat at the same time. This is not recommended at this stage, since it is apt to produce a poor melodic line in each voice. (2) The whole upper or lower line may be written first, and a counterpoint anchored to the chord tones then added. In this case a better result will ensue if each part is unified by sequences or by the use of similar melodic material. (3) One line may be partially written, and then the other, a process demonstrated in Fig. 6-28. Figures from the first part can then be used in the second without necessarily making the second line completely imitative.

Exercise 12. Convert the modulatory progressions of Ex. 11 to passages in two-part counterpoint. Proceed as suggested by Fig. 6-28. It is permissible to substitute a different note of the set chord in the upper line or to shift lower chord tones up or down an octave to achieve a better line.

A passage modulating to a related key may return to the original key, as in Fig. 6-29, or move on to other keys before concluding in the original key. Continuous related key changes are easily managed, since each I of the related keys is a triad of the original key.

Figure 6-29

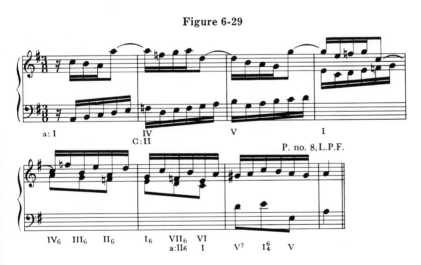

Exercise 13. Continue the passages written in Ex. 12 with a return to the first key, using both direct entry and pivot chords.

Some key schemes in a series of modulations feel more natural than others. This occurs when I of an intermediate modulation is II, IV or VI of the next key; *e.g.*, C–a–G; C–a–e; C–d–F. In a series of modulations it is generally better to reserve a shift to the subdominant key for the last phrase or section of a piece. The return to the original key should not come too close to the final cadence, lest it sound like V of the subdominant key. Measures 3 and 2 before the end of the *Two-Part Invention no. 5* come close to leaving that impression.

Examine the following modulations from the *Two-Part Inventions:* no. 2, measure 5 (c) to measure 7 (E♭) to measure 11 (g); no. 4, measure 7 (d) to measure 10 (F) to measures 18–23 (g); no. 7, measure 3 (e) to measure 4 (G) to measures 8–9 (D).

Exercise 14a.   Write passages in two-part counterpoint that modulate as follows: F–d–C; G–b–D; B♭–c–E♭; D–G–e; E♭–f–c–B♭; A–f♯–c♯–E. The cadences may be half or authentic.

Exercise 14b.   Write similar passages starting with the minor keys a, d, e, g and b and modulate to the following keys: a–d–C; d–a–C; e–C–a; g–F–d; b–e–G.

164

7

Shaping the Melodic Line; Modulation (cont.); Augmented Sixth Chords; Distant Modulations; The Simple Two-part Canon

Shaping the Melodic Line

The single line in eighteenth century polyphony is subject to various controls that limit its freedom. Unlike melody in homophonic texture, the contour, direction and rhythm of a line is conditioned to some extent by the nature of a concurrent line. In addition, it generally operates within a preset harmonic scheme, supplying essential chord tones missing in the other part. Practical considerations may restrict its range. Nor does one line remain prominent throughout a work. Its importance is submerged at various points by another line that carries a theme announcement, an imitation or vital thematic material.

Stylistic differences apart, melody in homophonic and eighteenth century polyphonic music is structurally dissimilar. The line in inventions and fugues is not patterned in symmetrical phrases terminating invariably in well-defined cadences. Salient melodic segments, that can start and end on any beat of the measure, frequently extend to an uneven number of measures, ending inconclusively or with a fleeting cadence. Phrase-structured melody may occur in lighter polyphonic forms, such as in the dances of the eighteenth century suite; e.g., Fig. 6-27, #4. Motivic play, sequential extension and imitation are means by which a continuous melodic and rhythmic flow is maintained. Continuous motion, a characteristic of Baroque music, is unfavorable to the formation of balanced phrases. Repetition of half phrases and phrases, frequently employed in homophonic music, is also foreign to the nature of the single line in the invention and fugue. Long notes do not necessarily fall on the metric accent.

These, then, are some of the factors governing linear writing in polyphony. Having acquired sufficient background in harmony, modulation and two-part writing, it is essential, as we approach the point of composing canons and inventions, to consider various aspects of the single line, molding it in ways that give it variety and interest. It should be understood that references to the melodic line pertain to salient segments of melody only, since no single line is continuously of prime importance.

Generally stated, the features of a well-designed line include a fairly clear profile, motion in a definite direction, well-planned high and low points, a coherent pattern and subtle nuances in detail that deviate from mechanical regularity. *Examine each cited reference carefully.*

The General Profile

A line should have some sense of direction. It should not proceed in aimless, meandering fashion nor return constantly to the same note. Compare Fig. 7-1a with the original (Fig. 7-1b). The first rotates monotonously around the note A. The Bach theme, after winding up around the tonic, takes off in an energetic upward direction, though anchored on the dominant in measure 2. The injunction against rotating around a note does not apply here or in passages like Fig. 2-20j. (See the upper part, Fig. 6-13c.) The line in Fig. 7-1c hovers around the notes A and C♯ before rising to its high point at the end. As a general practice, avoid this sort of line. The undulating line in Fig. 7-1d, gravitating at its center around the note B, has an over-all downward direction, indicated by the slurred scale fragments, before a slight rise at the close. A constant return to the note G, in Fig. 7-1e, has the saving grace in the placement of its high notes.

Figure 7-1

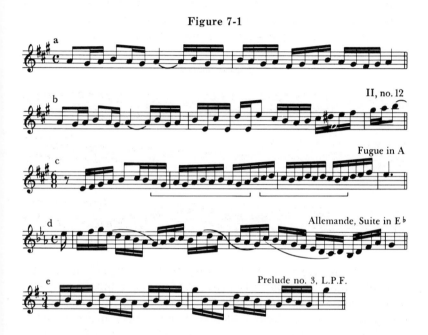

Scale-line Contour

A straight scale line in either direction, or one moving up and down like a gable roof (Fig. 7-2a), is definite in direction but uninteresting, except in meaningful context. This excerpt serves as climax to the preceding measure, before the cadence. Breaking the line in some way is preferable to the straight scale line. The drop of a third as the scale climbs to a high point in the upper part of Fig. 3-9, and the upward skip of a third (Fig. 5-10b, last example) improve the line. (See also Fig. 6-29, the lower part.) Auxiliaries embellish the scale in Fig. 7-2b. The long downward scale of over two octaves in Fig. 2-15b is interrupted intermittently by an auxiliary. The auxiliary is used in a rising scale line (Fig. 2-16d). Intervening notes between two descending scales (Fig. 7-1d) provide a better line. The injected figure on beat 3 (Fig. 6-24) improves the bass-line profile.

The longer scale line that gives way to scale fragments, or short bits of scale culminating in a longer scale line, is superior to scale runs of equal length. The scale may serve as a snap ending to a passage (Fig. 3-2a). A skip breaks the gable-type scale line in Fig. 7-2c. The sequence of the last figure (in brackets) and the broken chords provide an interesting contour. Observe the skips breaking the scale line in Fig. 5-7. A skip and a tie improve scale-line melody in Fig. 5-11.

Figure 7-2a–c

An octave skip is often necessary to avoid repeating a note, to evade voice crossing or to prevent too wide a spread between lines. Note how low the bass in Fig. 2-11b would fall except for the octave leaps. A leap wider than an octave precedes each downward scale that starts progressively lower in Fig. 2-20b. The curve on each first beat rounds off an otherwise uninteresting series of scale sequences. A similar example is seen in Fig. 4-18c.

A rising scale line in an inverted gable-scale profile (Fig. 7-2d), seen in the added eighth note stems, is disguised by the broken thirds. Chord tones of a sequential changing tone figure (Fig. 7-2e) often move along a scale line. (See also Fig. 2-23a.) Sequences of simple figures as in Fig. 7-2e and Fig. 7-2b become tedious if extended. They are justified as sequential splinters of a preceding larger unit or in leading to an extended unit.

The contour of a line will often be anchored to rising or falling scale tones (indicated by darts in Fig. 7-3a and b). This

Figure 7-2d–e

Figure 7-2d–e

is particularly true in sequential extension. The low and high points may both be scalewise (Fig. 7-3c). A subtle use of scalewise motion is seen in the suspensions and indirect resolutions of Fig. 6-18, #1. Observe the scale line formed by the quarter notes (Fig. 4-20, upper part).

Figure 7-3

Undulating or wavelike motion that is mainly stepwise will usually take a general direction up or down, as in Fig. 7-4a and b. An initial figure-group that has a clear up and down movement in sequences will impart an undulating character to the whole line. (See Figs. 7-1c and 2-22c.) Scale fragments in sequence (Fig. 2-20c) create a wavelike profile. A stepwise scale is less exciting than one with an admixture of skips.

Figure 7-4

Chord Line Contour

We used chord tones previously against stepwise motion in brief passages. Apart from considerations of contrast, the chord line, with its bold contour, may energize a passage. Arpeggiated chord tones extending over an octave are infrequently used. This device is employed mainly to climax a passage or a sequential series. Chord tone figures, particularly those in a coherent pattern and clear direction (Fig. 7-5a), are more frequently used. Note the descending line in the high tones of each unit and the abbreviated units in measures 4 and 5. Figures of this sort and those in Fig. 7-5b must, in themselves, form good chord progressions. They generally move against a stepwise line (Fig. 6-11c.) Figurated harmony in both parts has little in common with polyphonic texture. Chord figuration often debouches into stepwise motion, as in Fig. 7-5a. Instances are common of a stepwise line leading to broken chord figures (Fig. 7-5c). Note the energetic character of the line in Fig. 7-5d.

Figure 7-5a–d

Various means are employed to modify the jagged profile of a chord-figurated line. The injection of broken thirds and a scale-line (Fig. 7-5e) or passing and auxiliary tones (Fig. 7-5f) tempers an incisive outline. Note the passing tones in Fig.˙ 6-11b and the gentler curves in Fig. 7-5g. The first tied note in this example skips a ninth, a refreshing departure from the expected stepwise movement to B. Observe that melodic interest may reside in the slurred tones (Fig. 7-5h), rather than in the high broken thirds.

Figure 7-5e–h

A modified gable-type line of arpeggiated chord tones is used in Fig. 7-6a. The skips in Fig. 7-6b, alternating in direction, provide the skeletal frame of the melody in Fig. 7-6c. In more instances than are readily apparent, a single specific interval governs the contour of a line. The fourth (Fig. 7-6d) is the scaffolding for the theme (Fig. 7-6e). Note a similar function of the sixth (Fig. 7-5h) and the importance of the octave (Fig. 7-8c).

Figure 7-6

Examine Fig. 7-7a. This answering or echoing effect between two voices is called *antiphony*. It is used at times in pseudo-antiphonal manner in the *single line* that alternately leaps from one level to another (Fig. 7-7b). Examine also the upper line (Figs. 3-1 and 5-20). On occasion Bach writes a passage for the single line and, in the same work, a similar passage for two voices, in the manner of Fig. 7-7c and d.

Figure 7-7

High and Low Points of the Line

The specific direction of a line or the nature of its contour generally determines the location of high and low points. These may occur anywhere along the line. A high point situated at or near the end of a rising line has a climactic effect (Figs. 7-1b and 7-2d). High points may be approached directly by scale line (Fig. 7-1b), by an arpeggiated chord (Fig. 7-5f) or by a skip (Fig. 7-6c). A wide skip, as in Fig. 7-8d, throws the climactic note into bold relief. The approach is intensified when the rhythm of the notes preceding the climax is quickened, as in this example. The device of a rhythmic pause (on the dotted E of Fig. 7-2e) or the arpeggiated chord before the close (Fig. 7-6e) heightens the subsequent climax. Meandering and undulating lines may conclude on a high level without establishing a sense of climax. The vague ascent of Fig. 7-1c is less effective than upward curvature (Fig. 7-8a).

The high point appears in the middle of the line in Fig. 7-8b. Note the gable-type contour and the widening leaps in measure 1. Some lines have two high points. These are better when

Figure 7-8a–d

they are located on different levels, as marked by arrows in Fig. 7-8c. The climax in wide-ranging melody is often preceded by a line of secondary high points, indicated by darts in Fig. 7-8b and c. Secondary high points, in these examples, drop down to gather momentum for a further drive to climax.

Just as an upward line to climax is subconsciously associated with the effort required to attain a high elevation, so does the descent suggest motion toward a point of repose. From an initial high point the line may drop step by step, as in Fig. 7-3. It may take a curvilinear route (Fig. 7-1d) or plunge precipitously (Fig. 7-2a). A descending line accompanied by slackening rhythm (Fig. 7-8e) is effective in producing a sense of relaxation or anticlimax.

Figure 7-8e

We pointed, in passing, to various changes in detail in several examples, changes that circumvent banality and uniformity. Observe the interpolated notes in the sequence (Fig. 7-8a) and the altered rhythm in the sequential motives (measures 4–6, Fig. 7-8d). Note the change in direction of the figure (bracketed, in Fig. 7-3a) and the rhythmic change from the tied quarter notes in the sequences (Fig. 7-3b, measure 3). Compare the sequences in measure 1 (Fig. 7-4b) as altered in measure 2. Note the sequence of half of the preceding sequence in Fig. 7-2c.

Motivic Play

The melodic line, as seen in the examples above, may be developed from several figures or generated from a brief motive. Long lines of both types are employed in the invention and fugue. The motive, extended by various means, frequently forms the line in *allegro* movements of the concerto grosso. A motive, repeated in mechanical sequences, as in Figs. 7-2b, e, and 7-7b, results in a monotonous line. More variety and interest is obtained with *motivic play*, a term describing its alteration, extension and fusion with other motives (Fig. 7-8f).

The opening motive in Fig. 7-8f is an auxiliary figure (#1). This motive, used in a turn on beat 3, measure 2, is preceded

174

Figure 7-8f

Brandenburg Concerto no. 3

by a scale-tone motive (#2). The skips on the last beat of the measure (#3)—inversions of the initial skip—are now combined with the turn in measure 3 and with the first motive in measure 4. The pattern is continued in the next measure, running into measure 6.

The scale-tone motive (#2) appears first as a row of lower tones, then as a row of upper tones in the continued skips. These scale tones are indicated by added eighth-note stems. Make it your practice to analyze sections of Bach melody in the same manner.

Secondary Dominants in Modulation

Secondary dominants contribute an element of harmonic interest to progressions en route to a new key. Those starred in Fig. 7-9a precede pivot chords in modulations to g and B♭. Some theorists draw no distinction between the secondary dominant-triad combination and a key change. They regard both as modulations. A modulation to the subdominant key in Fig. 7-9b is preceded by V⁷ofIV–IV and V⁷ofIII.

Figure 7-9a–b

O Mensch, bewein'

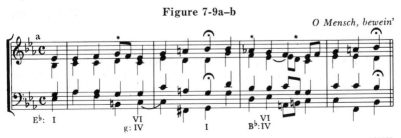

E♭: I   VI
        g: IV   I   B♭:IV

c: V⁷   a: V⁷of IV   IV   V⁷of III III

After a cadence, a common way of reaching a new key is to begin with fifth-fall progressions that are some distance away from I; *i.e.*, V⁷ofVI–VI, etc. These reach I or V of the new key or go as far as V⁷ofIV–IV before cadencing in the new key (Fig. 7-9c).

Figure 7-9c

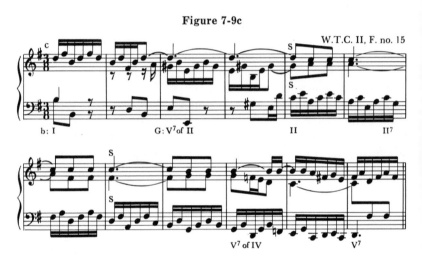

W.T.C. II, F. no. 15

b: I   G: V⁷of II   II   II⁷

V⁷ of IV   V⁷

Exercise 1a. Secondary dominant-triad units move by fifth-fall progressions to the subdominant key in Fig. 7-10a. Each two-measure unit of Fig. 7-10b, leading to the other related keys, is a substitute for the last two measures of Fig. 7-10a. Write four-measure units in four-part harmony, starting first with the key of D, then with B♭. Lead them to all related keys, in the manner of Figs. 7-10a and b.

Exercise 1b. These modulatory progressions lend themselves to sequential melody. Write passages in two-part counterpoint, based on the progressions of Figs. 7-10a and b, as shown in the model (Fig. 7-10c).

176

Figure 7-10a–c

The diatonic sequence of a melodic unit is frequently in-flected chromatically to produce a secondary dominant-triad of a new key, as in Fig. 7-10d. Modulations to the other related keys by similar means are shown in Fig. 7-10e, substitutes for measures 2 and 3 of Fig. 7-10d.

Figure 7-10d–e

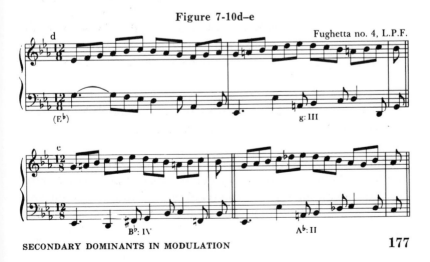

f: IV   c: IV₆   V

Exercise 1c. Write a one-measure unit in major, then take it sequentially to the related keys, as in Figs. 7-10d and e. Do the same starting with a minor key.

The same type of modulatory progressions often form the basis for imitation, as in Fig. 7-10f.

Figure 7-10f

W.T.C. II, F. no. 19

c♯:   A: V⁷of II   II   V⁷

Exercise 1d. Starting with the key of A, write brief two-part imitative passages that modulate to each related key in turn, employing imitation.

We previously employed a series of secondary dominants in the key—these are known as *chain dominants* (Ch. 5). Such a series is frequently used to carry a passage to a new key, since any dominant in the series can become V⁷ of the new key, or the series may move beyond V⁷ofIV to a distant key. Chain dominants, starting with V⁷ofVI, are carried to IV as pivot of d minor (Fig. 7-11a) and, by the same means, to other related keys (Fig. 7-11b), substitutes for measure 2, Fig. 7-11a.

Exercise 2. Starting with a key other than C, write five passages in two-part counterpoint that modulate to each related key by means of chain dominants.

The V⁷, as we have seen, resolves to I of both a major key and its tonic minor. Secondary dominants of major triads also move to the minor form of the triad to facilitate a modulation. For instance, in C, V⁷ofV can move to a minor g triad, which

178

Figure 7-11

then serves as pivot ii of F, iv of d or vi of B♭. In measure 3 of Fig. 7-12a, the normally expected triad is a major F triad as I of the related key. The f minor triad functions as II of the coming key, E♭. The note D♭ in the preceding dominant is necessary as preparation for the pivotal minor ii triad.

Figure 7-12a

A deceptive resolution of the dominant may lead directly to I of the new key, as seen in two instances in Fig. 7-12b. A secondary dominant of the first key, in a similar type of progression, moves to a major triad rooted a half step above the root of that dominant, or to a minor triad a step above its root. The resultant triad may then be any pivotal chord of the new key (Fig. 7-12c). The first triad may be VI of G or, in a distant modulation, IV of b. The numbered triads may be used as N6ths. These, in first inversion, move to $I^6_4-V^7$ or directly to V^7 of d, a, e and, in no. 4, to b minor.

Figure 7-12b–c

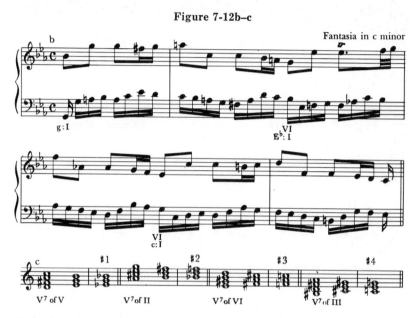

Exercise 3. Using keys other than C, write brief modulatory progressions in four-part harmony, employing the pivotal progressions shown in Fig. 7-12c.

Augmented Sixth Chords

Chromatically altered chords that contain the interval of an augmented sixth *when inverted* are *augmented sixth chords*. For reasons that are obscure the triad in Fig. 7-13a, #1, is called an *Italian sixth;* the seventh chord, #2, is a *French sixth* and the last, #3, is a *German sixth*. Note that this chord is spelled in two ways.

Italian sixths are used in first inversion with doubled fifth, as in Fig. 7-13a, #1. French and German sixths are most effective in second inversion. Their tones are neither doubled nor omitted.

The interval of an augmented sixth usually resolves to an octave. These octave tones are either roots of a triad, the doubled fifth of a six-four chord or the roots of a dominant

180

seventh (Fig. 7-13b). While other chords may precede an augmented sixth chord, the best approach to their chromatic tones is by half steps from the preceding chord (Fig. 7-13c).

Augmented sixth chords based on other scale steps are shown in Fig. 7-13d. Re-arrange the tones in thirds to determine their pivotal function. Those in Fig. 7-13d resolve to triads in the key, to secondary dominants, to I, I$_4^6$ or V^7 of related or distant keys. The starred chords may resolve to I.

Augmented sixth chords are used as chromatic chords in the key and as pivot chords in modulation. Eighteenth century composers used them chiefly in the approach to cadences (Fig. 7-13e). Italian and French sixths are often used as substitutes for V^{7}ofV before the cadential V of the original or new key.

Figure 7-13

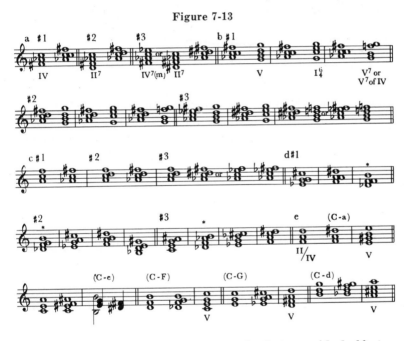

Exercise 4a. Using antecedent chords that provide half step voice leading to the chromatic tones, resolve each augmented sixth of Fig. 7-13d, #1, to a triad, a six-four chord and a dominant seventh. Do this in four-part harmony.

Exercise 4b. Starting with the keys of D, B♭ and A, write brief progressions in four-part harmony, using a6 chords in modulations to each related key, as shown in Fig. 7-13e. Take the a6 to I$_4^6$–V of the new key in some instances.

The Italian sixth (starred in Fig. 7-14a) is VIIofV in the
key. Examples of the French and German sixths, taken from
The Art of Fugue, are shown in Fig. 7-14b and c.

Figure 7-14a–c

Exercise 4c. Modulations from c minor to V or I_4^6 of all
related keys are shown in Fig. 7-14d. Write these progressions in four-part open harmony; write similar modulations starting from the keys of a, g and f minor, using
a6ths.

Figure 7-14d

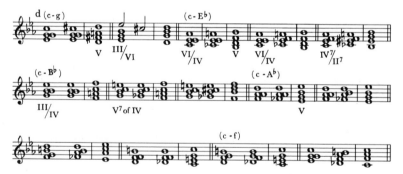

The presence of all three tones of the Italian sixth and four
tones of the other a6 chords is generally necessary to produce
their full effect. This is done best in three- and four-voice
counterpoint where the chromatic notes are resolved by half
step. Imply these chords in two-part counterpoint by dividing
the augmented sixth interval between both parts.

182

Distant Modulations

Modulations to other than related keys are *distant modulations*. Unlike those common in the nineteenth century, such key changes in the preceding century are generally neither abrupt nor to remote keys—like a modulation from E to G♭. The most common distant modulations in Bach are:

(1) *Progressive modulation,* a shift to a distant key through intermediate modulations, each progressively one sharp or flat more or less in signature than the preceding key, as in Fig. 7-15a. Those that move up in flats and down in sharps are often similar to chain dominants but lead to a distant key.

Figure 7-15a

(2) *Modulation by change of mode;* the expected major tonic of a related key is changed to minor, as in Fig. 7-15b. The reverse, a major I substituted for the expected minor I of the new key, has the effect of a Picardy third. This major ending often serves as pivotal V of the next key.

Figure 7-15b

c : VII⁷

c : VII^7

(3) *Stepwise modulation;* one or more modulations in a stepwise series of keys is distant; *e.g.,* d–C–B♭ or C–d–e, as in Fig. 7-15c.

Figure 7-15c

Corrente, Partita no. 3

C : I   d : V^9

e : V^9

Progressive Modulation

In modulating to a distant key differing in signature from the first key by an *increased* number of flats or a *decreased* number of sharps, the I of each successive key is "dominantized" to become V^7 of the next key. In modulations to distant keys with signatures of fewer flats or more sharps, each I of successive keys is a pivotal IV of the next key.

Opposite Mode Modulation

Modulations of this type are often transitional, providing easy access to a related key. For instance, a modulation is made from A major to e minor, the I of which serves as a II pivot to the related key, D, or IV to b minor. This is more easily confused with a secondary dominant-pivot triad change in mode, than with the distant modulation (Fig. 7-15d), a shift from c minor to F major.

184

Figure 7-15d

Figure 7-15d

II, no. 14

c: I   F: V⁷

Stepwise Modulation

Intermediate keys in the circle of fifths are bypassed in stepwise modulation, C–D–E or C–B♭–A♭. Having fewer chords in
common, these modulations depend on common tones between
keys and melodic sequences for a convincing effect. Common
tones between I of one key and V⁷ of the next (tied in Fig.
7-16a), and between dominants of both keys (Fig. 7-16b), link
such modulations.

Figure 7-16a–b

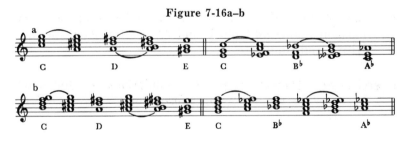

a

C   D   E   C   B♭   A♭

b

C   D   E   C   B♭   A♭

We have seen, in Ch. 5, that the diminished seventh chord,
structurally composed of minor thirds and sounding the same
in root order or inversion, moves equally well to both the major
and minor I. Its equally spaced structure makes it possible to
use *each tone* of the chord as leading tone of both related and
distant keys (Fig. 7-16c). Observe that one or more tones of
the d7 are enharmonically respelled in accord with the new
key. Two nondominant d7 chords *in the key* (Fig. 7-16d) are
altered forms of II⁷ and VI⁷. These may also function as

dominants of related or distant keys (Fig. 7-16e). Note the use of the d7 in the *Two-Part Invention #13,* measures 13–17. The stepwise modulations are e–d–c, with a change of mode to C; d7 serves as substitute for V⁷ofV before the d7 of a.

Figure 7-16c–e

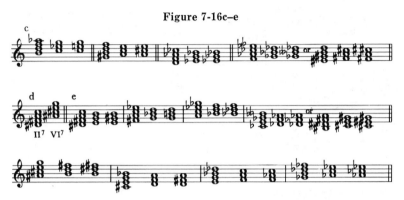

Exercise 5a. Write a brief progression in four-part harmony in F. (1) Modulate to a distant key progressively, with an increased number of flats. (2) Starting similarly in B, modulate to a distant key by progressive steps to a key with fewer sharps. (3) Do this starting in A♭ to a distant key with fewer flats and (4) from D to a key with more sharps. Alter Fig. 3-11d chromatically to move progressively to a distant key.

Exercise 5b. Use the opposite mode modulation in four-part harmony, starting from E and A♭. Do the same starting with d and f minor.

Exercise 5c. Employ stepwise modulations in four-part harmony in the following succession of keys: G–F–e; g–a–B.

Exercise 5d. Use the d7 chord in brief modulatory progressions taken from Fig. 7-16c and e.

Exercise 6. Write passages in two-part counterpoint, using each type of modulation employed in Ex. 5. Return to the original key in some of these.

Analyze several Bach chorales. With your present knowledge you will find it a rewarding experience. Apart from their

186

intrinsic worth, they constitute a compendium of harmonic, modulatory and nonharmonic tone practice.

Continuous Imitation

Each line in previously written passages employing imitation pursued a different course after the initial unit and its imitation. Passages in which a second voice continues in imitation of the first voice, wholly or in part, as in Fig. 7-17a, are *canonic*. Such passages are frequently employed in inventions and in fugal episodes.

Figure 7-17a

The Canon

Music in which a complete melody is imitated throughout is a *canon*, a term derived from the Greek—meaning *a rule*.*

Canons are written for two or more voices, and range from simple round-canons like "Three Blind Mice" to complex compositions in multiple voices, with imitation either in contrary motion, retrograde motion, augmentation or diminution, as

---

* Early canons were written on a single line, as in Fig. 8-3a—sometimes without specific indication of the number of parts, the interval of imitation or the point where the second (or third and fourth) parts pick up the beginning. J. F. Bridge (in his book *Double Counterpoint and Canon*) offers the explanation that the term, in its original meaning, referred to an explicit or enigmatic sentence preceding the music that gave a clue to the rule of performance, the number of parts, their point of entry, etc.

well as double and triple canons; *i.e.,* two or three canons combined. Some canons have added parts; others are written around a chorale hymn. Some have an internal repetition of a section. Our work will be limited to canons that are less complex, to canonic episodes in inventions and to the invention in canon form. From the time of John of Fornsete, to whom the thirteenth century canon "Sumer Is Icumen In" is ascribed, composers have been intrigued with the challenge and intricacies of canonic composition.

Strict canon proceeds according to the rule that the imitating voice must reproduce the leading voice exactly in its note-to-note intervallic movement. Notes are freely chromaticized and changes of intervals are made in the imitating voice of the free canon. Canons in the unison are those in which the notes of the following line are the same and on the same level as those of the leading line. The common round, described later, is generally written in this way. Canons in the unison present few problems if the lines are kept far enough apart to avoid frequent and prolonged voice crossing. Except for some rounds, two-part unaccompanied canons at the unison are uncommon. More often there is either an additional free third voice or the canon is constructed around a set melody. Although the following illustrations in two parts are largely self-sufficient, an occasional note of the missing added part completes the harmony. The beginning of a two-part canon in the unison is shown in Fig. 7-17b. The violin part in this excerpt is imitated by the melody line of the keyboard accompaniment.

Figure 7-17b

Canons can be written without difficulty when the imitating line begins an octave or two lower or higher than the first note of the leading line (Fig. 7-17c). This is described as a "canon in the octave" or "canon at the octave." Observe the change indicated by arrows. Except as a matter of discipline, there is no advantage to undeviating strictness. On the contrary, such minor changes facilitate modulation and are regarded by many writers as acceptable in strict canon.

The first voice or *leader* commences in either the upper or lower part. The imitating line or *follower* enters anywhere from a single beat later to an entry after several measures. The listener finds it difficult to grasp the line of a canon where the follower enters after a single beat because the ear hears little of the leader at the beginning. More of the beginning is heard in the compound meter of Fig. 7-17c. (See the complete canon in the Appendix, p. 321.)

Figure 7-17c

V'on Himmel hoch, Var. 1

Leaders that are two or more measures long provide greater freedom in shaping the line. Such canons are easiest to write and grasp. There is a time gap of two long measures before the follower enters in *Invention I, no. 2*. The follower in Contrapunctus 12 of *The Art of Fugue* enters after four measures, and after eight measures in Contrapunctus 13. It is best, for the present, to introduce the follower after one or two measures. Its entry is clearest when it starts on the same beat of its measure as the leader. Hence a leader beginning on an up-beat is imitated by an up-beat entrance in the follower. The follower, after a time gap of a measure in Fig. 7-17b, starts on the same half beat as the leader.

There are two methods of writing a canon. The first, described below, is more suitable to the diatonic canon and an entrance of the follower after a measure or more. The second approach is better for modulating canons in which the follower enters after a measure, a half measure or less; *i.e.*, before the leading line has assumed any recognizable features. This will be demonstrated in Ch. 8.

Two-part Canon in the Octave

The basic process in writing a two-part canon in the octave is illustrated in Fig. 7-18. (1) Write the leader, L. (2) Copy this an octave or double octave lower as the follower, F'—copy it an octave or two above if the leader is in the lower part. (3) Extend the leader, L', counterpointing it to the follower. (4) Tack this counterpoint onto the follower, F'. Continue this process of transferring each new portion of the leader to the follower, then counterpointing it until the close, described later. Mechanical as it is, this approach, with perhaps some minor adjustments, will produce a satisfactory canon if the entry of the follower is delayed for some time and if the precepts described below are observed.

Figure 7-18

Several problems must be anticipated and resolved to produce a good two-part canon. The first tones or the first measure of the leader should be distinctive enough in line, skips or rhythm to make its imitative entry stand out against the continuing leader. (See Fig. 7-18 and read the section on the invention theme in Ch. 8.) Each addition to the leading line should be a natural and interesting prolongation of it without recourse to immediate repetition or sequence of the entire beginning (Fig. 7-19a). A figure taken from any part of the beginning may be extended or developed as described in the section on motival play. (See Fig. 8-6.) Do not restrict the

190

leading line to an extremely narrow range. Note the wide range in Fig. 7-17c. Long notes on successive first beats, or cadential endings on them (Fig. 7-20a), break the line into disjunct bits of melody. Avoid returning to the same note on successive first beats if possible. Play the first measure of Fig. 7-18 and then the upper part of Fig. 7-19b. Avoid this sudden slowdown in rhythm or a drastic change in rhythm (Fig. 7-19c). In general, do not have too many different rhythms in the course of the line. An occasional tie, syncopation or brief rest is often sufficient to vary the rhythm. Do not use a rest after a tendency tone unless its resolution comes immediately after the rest.

Figure 7-19

The leader should preferably start with a tone or tones of I or dominant harmony. The dominant note is generally used for a leader commencing on an up-beat. The leader, as subsequent follower, should provide a good bass for the counterpoint, as in Fig. 7-18. A leader composed of tonic and dominant tones only may result in monotonous reiteration of this harmony as the canon progresses (Fig. 7-20a). It is therefore advisable to include a tone or tones of subdominant, supertonic or VI harmony in the opening. Harmonic alternatives are, of course, available and should be weighed with each addition to the line. A chord tone of the leader may be treated as a nonharmonic tone in the follower, starred in Fig. 7-20b. Avoid an invariable concord on the first beat. The follower in some canons starts on a discord; *i.e.*, a suspension or other nonharmonic tone. Melodic independence suffers when parallel thirds and sixths are used for too long a stretch (Fig. 7-19a). Avoid octaves on strong beats where possible.

Figure 7-20

In summary, the leader should evolve as a good melody with a sense of flow and direction. It should contrast in rhythm and line as counterpoint to the follower, while providing a continuing choice of harmony as it becomes part of the following line.

The canon has no specified length. Vocal canons vary in length, from a brief four or five measures to some of considerable length. The round-canon with balanced phrases of two or four measures takes on, in three or more voices, some sense of form. Instrumental canons should run to not less than eight or ten measures. We will set a limit of approximately 24 measures to those written in the next exercises. The two-part canons in *The Art of Fugue* run from 78 to 109 measures.

Canons also vary in the way they terminate. *Finite* or *closed* canons end without repetition as a whole, on a perfect cadence. *Infinite* or *perpetual* canons may be repeated without end unless some device is used to terminate them. These are commonly written in three or more parts.

Since the leader starts before the follower, it will naturally end earlier. The leader must end in a manner that will give the follower a cadential ending. If the time gap between them is a measure or less, the leader may end on the tonic tone, the follower finishing alone. More often the leader will go on with a free ending or codetta, seen in the notes in brackets (Fig. 7-21a). A leader in the lower part can close on a held tonic tone, the follower in free imitation providing a plagal cadence (Fig. 7-21b). An interesting way to handle the free ending with the leader in the lower part is to use a deceptive cadence

(Fig. 7-21c). V⁷ofV and the d7 may be used, as well as VI. Examine how Bach handles the long free ending of the canon in the octave (Fig. 7-21d).

Figure 7-21

We indicated earlier that figures taken from the leader and employed in motivic play endow the line with a sense of cohesion. In lengthy canons a return to the leader opening may be made near the close. Bach brings in the leader (Fig. 7-17c)

after 13 measures. Before this return the tag end of the leader (Fig. 7-22a, #1), repeated in the follower (#2), must fit the return of the opening. This device, incidentally, is used before announcing the theme in the second or third section of the invention in canon form. The opening and its imitation in this example is continued for two and a half measures only. The canon concludes with an additional four measures.

The leader opening can also be used in the closing measure (Fig. 7-22b). The fragment of the leading line is abandoned in the follower and a free ending is supplied.

Figure 7-22

Exercise 7a. Write several leaders, preferably one measure long, in $\frac{4}{4}$ and $\frac{6}{8}$, or two measures in $\frac{3}{8}$. Use different major and minor keys. Start some of them in the lower part. Develop these beginnings as canons in the octave. Use endings like those shown in Fig. 7-21. Do not use chromatic tones, except for the raised and lowered tones of the melodic minor upper tetrachord and, if necessary, an occasional unaccented auxiliary. Check your leading line step by step, so that a good melody is developed.

Exercise 7b. Write a canon in the unison that is eight-ten measures long. The leader beginning should move up sufficiently to avoid voice crossing with the follower.

Exercise 7c. After examining the canon in the Appendix, write a canon in the octave which closes with a return to the leader beginning, as in Fig. 7-22b.

8

Canon (cont.); The Invention Theme; Types of Episode; Double Counterpoint at the Octave

Modulation in the Canon

Canons that include modulations and secondary dominant-triad harmony are far more interesting and challenging than those that are largely diatonic. Several factors should be borne in mind in writing them. (1) The leading tone is strongly indicative of a key. It is therefore difficult to abandon the original or a new key when the leading tone is present in the leader and then picked up by the follower. The leading tone in the follower may, however, change in function to root or fifth of dominants in related keys. For instance, the leading tone of C can be the chord-fifth of V^7 in a, the root of V^7 in e, and by chromatic alteration, the chord-seventh in V⁷ofF. (2) Should it be necessary to use the leading tone, it may be chromatically altered or treated as a nonharmonic tone in the follower. The lowered leading tone in minor does not hamper modulation; *e.g.*, the B♭ in c minor may lead to the keys of E♭, A♭ and f. It can also be used as a passing tone.

(3) Closely related keys, however, have many tones in common that can be used in the leader without recourse to the leading tone of a new key. The note E, for instance, is in I of C, a and e, as well as in V⁷ of F, d and a. The root of a C triad may become the seventh of V⁷ in G in the follower. Skips of a third, particularly the minor third, fit tonic and dominant harmony of more than one key. The third (E–G, for instance) is in I of C and e, in VI of G and in V⁷ of d and F.

(4) Modulations should not range so far from the original key as to make a return difficult. Canons called *circular canons* are designed to modulate by step or in progressive modulation, returning to the original key after completing the circle of keys.

Modulation can produce an exciting effect in· canons where the follower enters shortly after the leader, a half measure or a measure later. Under these circumstances the "tack on" method of development has limited value. As each addition is made to the leader, it may be necessary to revise the follower accompanying it. For instance, labelling the first three measures of the leader, A–B–C, and those of the follower, A′–B′–C′,

A–B–C

A′–B′–C′,

it may be necessary to alter B′ if a modulation is desired at C; working backward, it is then necessary to change B. The process of working forward and backward, explained in detail below, is one in which nonharmonic tones in the leader become chord tones in the follower, and vice versa. A simple auxiliary may be used in the leader, anticipating its next use as the leading tone of a new key. Definitive tones that will contradict an intended key in the follower must be shunned in the leader. While these considerations are borne in mind, a good line must, nevertheless, be shaped in the scant elbow room afforded by a follower entering closely after the leader. A section of a simple modulatory canon in the octave is shown in Fig. 8-1, to illustrate this process. (It should be understood that other alternatives are possible.) The reasons for each step taken in arriving at this result are given at each point as the fragment of canon is developed in Fig. 8-2. Play Fig. 8-1, then play each part separately.

Figure 8-1

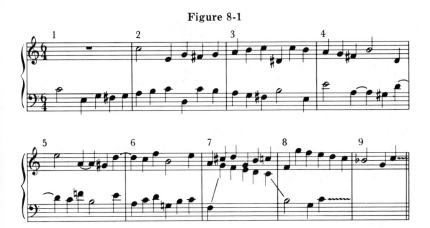

The auxiliary is consciously used in Fig. 8-2a, measure 1, to function next as leading tone of G in the follower. The last half of measure 2 is written first. This takes care of setting up the new key, while leaving room for a bit of maneuvering. The note G in the follower is treated as an appoggiatura. The half measure in brackets, with II of G in mind, is then written (Fig. 8-2b). Two of several possible alternatives are shown. The second with the skip of a seventh makes a better line and clearer harmony.

Figure 8-2a–b

After transferring this as follower in measure 3, it may be counterpointed as in measure 1 of Fig. 8-2c; *i.e.*, remaining in G. This is good if a return to C is desirable. Measure 2, also acceptable, provides a counterpoint leading to a; in this event the G♯ in the follower to come will keep the lines in a. This key can lead as II to G and back to C. It seems preferable, at this early point, to modulate further by making the chromatic change in the follower (Fig. 8-2d).

Figure 8-2c

The last half measure of counterpoint to this is then written (measure 1, Fig. 8-2d). A vacant half measure may be prefixed, as in measure 2 of Fig. 8-2a. A change in rhythm is desirable here, since the lower part, up to this point, runs in quarter notes for two and a half measures. The change can be made as in measures 3 or 4 of Fig. 8-2d. The wider skip in measure 4 is better related to the skip at the beginning, and the omission of G permits a later G♯ leading to a.

Figure 8-2d

This is transferred to the upper line. The harmony suggested is dominant of a. Four counterpoints in this key are shown in Fig. 8-2e. The line is somewhat weak in measure 1; there is insufficient contrast in the parallel motion of measure 2; a striking octave skip to a discord would be preferred in measure 3; we adopted measure 4, with the suspension and the needed rhythmic change.

Figure 8-2e

The counterpoint to the follower in Fig. 8-2f excludes G♯ to make a further key change possible. Sequential skips, bracketed in measure 1, is one alternative. We adopted the second measure, in which the suspension ties in with the previous one, while providing the discord on beat 1.

200

Figure 8-2f

To continue the leader with sequential skips, as in measure 1, Fig. 8-2g, would extend the skips for too long, making both lines similar in skips, direction and rhythm. Some change of rhythm in the follower would be necessary if the skips were retained (measure 2 of Fig. 8-2g). Working backward, this alteration must be made in the leader (Fig. 8-2g, measure 3). Observe that G♯ is omitted in the leader, making a return to C major possible. Abandoning the skips, a new figure, in sequence

Figure 8-2g

(measure 4), is preferred. This counterpoint, transferred to the follower, is altered (C♯) to include a V⁷ofII. The two-measure leader unit of Fig. 8-2h, as well as measures 3 and 4, both of which provide a contrasting line—was discarded in favor of a simple scale line (measures 7 and 8 of Fig. 8-1). Note that the chromatic change in measure 9 of Fig. 8-1 may lead to F or d minor as the canon continues.

Figure 8-2h

Other ways of directing the course of this canon should concern us less than an insight into the method used to achieve the result in Fig. 8-1.

Exercise 1a. Write several brief canons that modulate to closely related keys, starting with simple leaders in major and minor that are one measure long in $\frac{4}{4}$ and $\frac{6}{8}$.

Exercise 1b. Do the same with half-measure leaders in these meters.

The Infinite Canon

Canons that return to the beginning in endless repetition as a whole (Fig. 8-3a) are *perpetual* or *infinite* canons. Written as a single line, the entrance of the follower is indicated as (2) in measure 2. When the leader completes its line (the repeat symbol in Fig. 8-3a) it starts all over again as in Fig. 8-3b (in

Figure 8-3a–c

Telemann, *Thank the Lord*

brackets), accompanied by the last measure of the canon, X′, formerly X in the leader. Clearly the leader at X must counterpoint both its follower Y and as X′, the beginning of the repetition. After any number of repetitions of the whole canon, the leader prolongs the first held note (*fermata*) of Fig. 8-3a while the follower continues to the same fermata, as written out in Fig. 8-3c.

Observe that both parts at X conclude in tonic harmony, and that the beginning of the repetition (measure 3, Fig. 8-3b) is also tonic. Although many infinite canons end and begin again in tonic harmony, others end on step 5 with implied dominant, as in Fig. 8-3d. This produces a better return to the repetition. After several repetitions of the whole, the canon concludes with an added measure, as in Fig. 8-3e.

Figure 8-3d–e

Examining the canon in the octave (Fig. 8-4), note that Bach uses V in measure 5 preceding the return of the leader opening in measure 6. The suspension in measure 6 changes that measure slightly from measure 1. Since the suspension is picked up

Figure 8-4

by the follower in measure 7, the repeat sign is pushed forward
to the end of that measure, instead of at the end of measure 5.

Exercise 2a.   Write an infinite canon in the octave, with a one-
measure leader in the upper voice before the follower
entry. Use diatonic tones and dominant harmony before
the return of the leader opening.

Exercise 2b.   Write an infinite canon in the octave that modulates from major to the relative minor and then to the
dominant key in the measure before the repetition. Start
the leader in the lower voice.

Exercise 2c.   Write a modulatory infinite canon with an entry
of the follower after a half measure in $\frac{4}{4}$.

Canons at the Fifth and Fourth

The follower may be located at any interval above or below
the leader. Canonic writing at the fourth and fifth above and
below is a useful preparation for canonic passages in inventions and fugues. Canons at the fourth and fifth can be strict.
Strict imitation at the fifth above or fourth below can result
in a leader in the tonic key and a follower in the dominant key
if the leader contains skips in dominant harmony and returns
to the leading tone frequently (Fig. 8-5a). Under these circumstances the leading tone should be used sparingly and skips
in dominant harmony should be avoided as the leading line
continues (Fig. 8-5b). As in canons at the octave, notes in the
leader may subsequently be sharped, flatted or made natural in

204

the follower. A leader like the one in Fig. 8-5a may create similar difficulties in strict canon at the fourth above or fifth below when step 4 is imitated by step 4 of the subdominant key (Fig. 8-5c).

Other diatonic skips in the leader generally remain in the key in the follower; *e.g.*, leader steps 1–4, follower steps 5–1, etc.

Figure 8-5

Canons at these intervals should modulate after at least two or three measures. Each extension of the leader should be regarded as tentative, since its imitation at the fifth or fourth should imply the required harmonic or modulatory conditions. Observe the key changes in Fig. 8-6, a portion of a canon at the fifth below.

Figure 8-6

Von Himmel hoch

Exercise 3a.   Write a complete finite canon in major at the fifth above. Suggested modulations are: to the dominant, then by change of mode to the supertonic of that key, to the supertonic of the original key, the original key, and to the subdominant key returning to the original key.

Exercise 3b.   Write a canon in minor at the fourth below that modulates to several keys.

Exercise 3c.   Write a modulatory canon in major at the fifth below.

Canons at the second, third, sixth and seventh which require continual modifications present no further problems. Those at the second, like canon at the unison, are subject to frequent voice crossing. An examination of the Bach *Goldberg Variations* is well worth the time devoted to it; each third variation is a canon at a successively wider interval.

Exercise 3d.   Write four brief canons in different keys at the second, third, sixth and seventh.

Other devices in canon construction are reserved for advanced contrapuntal study in canon and fugue. These include

206

inverted canon—*i.e.*, steps and skips made in any direction by the leader, taken in the opposite direction by the follower— and canon in augmentation and diminution, in which the notes of the follower are twice or half as long as the notes of the leader. Still another device is canon cancrizans, or "crab" canon, in which the follower starts with the last note of the leading line, proceeding backwards to its first note as it counterpoints the leader.

Canonic Sequences

The melody in preceding examples of the canon is an evolving line in which any immediate repetition or sequence of a section of the leading line is avoided; *e.g.*, Fig. 8-6. Sequences in canonic writing are, however, used as a unifying factor in the episodic passages of inventions and fugues. Brief motives, or longer units derived from a theme or subject, are extended in sequences which are canonically imitated, as seen in the slurred units of Fig. 7-17a. Observe the initial two-measure unit in the upper line followed by a sequence and a modified sequence in the next four measures. (Notes in parentheses are added to show unmodified sequences.) This sequential line is canonically imitated in the lower line. Examine the means used to vary the sequences in measures 5 and 6, as well as the last three measures, which demonstrate how to bring a canonic sequential passage to conclusion.

Canonic sequences may either remain in the key, as in this example and in Fig. 8-7a, or modulate, as in Fig. 8-7c. See also Fig. 7-15a and the partially canonic sequences in the *Two-Part Invention #7*, measures 3–5. Note the way the passage is brought to a cadence. The passage in Fig. 8-7a is based on dominant harmony. Sequences of triads down in thirds, with the daggered tones forming sevenths, is the harmonic basis of Fig. 7-17a.

Fifth-fall progressions in triads, sevenths and secondary dominants are best as harmonic bases for such passages. The harmonic scaffolding of Fig. 8-7c is shown in Fig. 8-7b. Note the fifth-fall progressions, the passing tone effect of chord sevenths and the modulation leaving and returning to d minor. (See Fugue no. 12, measures 22–24, W.T.C. I.)

A simple step-by-step approach to constructing canonic sequential episodes in two parts is demonstrated in Fig. 8-8. A five-note scalewise figure in the progression I–IV (Fig. 8-8a) is continued in sequence and canonically imitated in VII–III,

Figure 8-7

d:I   F:VI⁷ II⁷   V⁷   I⁷   IV⁷   VII⁷

d:II⁷   V⁷   I⁷

Fantasia and Fugue in d minor

Figure 8-8a–c

I   IV   VII   III

208   CH. 8

VI–II and V–I. A chord skip, replacing the quarter notes, is imitated from part to part in Fig. 8-8b. This is filled by a passing tone in the first example (Fig. 8-8c) and, successively, with a passing tone and chord skip, and with an auxiliary and chord skip.

The canonic sequences of Fig. 8-8d are converted from diatonic harmony to chain dominants by chromatic alterations. A modulation to the relative minor is effected by such alterations (Fig. 8-8e) and to the dominant key via secondary dominant-triad progression and chain dominants (Fig. 8-8f). Note the slight melodic changes. A distant key may be reached by such chromatic modifications (Fig. 8-8g). Bear in mind that any dominant in a chain series can be made the V^7 of the new key.

Figure 8-8d–g

Exercise 4a. Write several canonic sequences in diatonic passages that cadence in the key, as in Fig. 8-8d, first example.

Exercise 4b. Write several similar passages using chain dominants with a cadence in the key, as in Fig. 8-8d, second example.

Exercise 4c. Use chromatic alterations in canonic sequences to modulate to closely related keys, as in Fig. 8-8e and f.

Exercise 4d. Write several canonic sequences in passages that modulate to distant keys.

Canonic overlapping of an invention theme and fugue subject is called *stretto*. This will be used later in our work.

The Inventions

Bach wrote an instruction book for his young son, Wilhelm Friedemann, which included a set of two-part polyphonic clavier pieces each entitled "Praeambulum" (prelude), and another group in three parts called "Fantasien." (See the frontispiece.) These pieces, with subsequent insertions and refinements, were completed in 1723 and renamed "Inventions" and "Sinfonias," respectively. The sinfonias were entitled "Three-Part Inventions" in later publication. Bach also applied the title "Inventions" to four sets of simple pieces in homophonic style for violin and clavier with figured bass. Each of these inventions is a collection of pieces resembling a miniature suite. They are nonimitative and have little in common with the two-part inventions.

Composers of the seventeenth and early eighteenth centuries used titles for their instrumental compositions that were often loose and indefinite in meaning. "Partita," originally meaning "variation," was used for a suite. "Sinfonia," an instrumental introduction to a vocal work or an instrumental interlude between parts of a vocal work, was Bach's title for three-part inventions. Similarly, there is no substantial difference between some of the Bach three-part fugues and inventions.

Bach's foreword to the *Two-Part Inventions* and *Three-Part Sinfonias* states that the pieces, among other reasons, were presented as examples of good "inventiones" (ideas) and how to develop them well so that the student would get a strong foretaste of composition. His evident purpose was to offer a variety of themes and then demonstrate different methods of developing them.

The Two-part Inventions

These inventions differ from each other in various ways. The themes range from a simple motive to some that are four measures long. Inventions no. 2, 8 and 14 are wholly or partly canonic. Others, like no. 10 and 13, are more homophonic than polyphonic. Inventions no. 12 and 14 are similar to pieces that Bach often chooses to call "Prelude." Four inventions, no. 5, 6, 9 and 11, employ two themes simultaneously. The last invention of the set is similar to a two-part fugue. The term "invention," then, is not used to describe a specific form or manner of treatment.

Pursuing Bach's intent, we will adopt several of them as models, imitating the simple (nonfugal) type first. Simple inventions develop both brief motives and themes, *i.e.*, melodic units composed of at least two different motives. The theme offers more material for development and is more nearly like a fugal theme (subject) than the short motive.

The Simple Invention, General Organization

The components of this type of invention are: (1) the *theme*—this is imitated in the octave at the beginning and then recurs later at different intervals, in different keys and frequently in modified form; (2) the *counterpoints* to the first and subsequent imitations—these generally vary with each theme entry in simple inventions and in some fugal inventions, and (3) the *episodes*—development passages in both simple and fugal inventions in which the theme as a whole does not appear.

Inventions, like fugues, move through a planned series of modulations. These key changes, consummated with a pronounced cadence and followed, in some instances, by different treatment of the material, suggest a sectional division of the invention. Where there is no cessation of rhythmic momentum and the cadences are barely perceptible, a division into sections is more arbitrary than real. Many inventions, however, show a clear division into two or three sections, but there is no invention "form" as such, *i.e.*, a pattern that describes the design of all inventions. We may now proceed to a closer examination of each component.

The Theme and the Subject

The *theme* is a fairly complete musical idea that is the principal and often the only source of material constituting the invention. Theme and subject (S) of the fugal invention are alike in all respects, except that some subjects end with a modulation. We will therefore examine their characteristics at the same time, referring temporarily to both as "theme" except where there are elements of difference. Two-part inventions will be designated by a Roman I; three-part inventions by a Roman II. Excluding brief motivic ideas like those in I, no. 1 and 13, our models are invention themes and the shorter subjects of the *Well-Tempered Clavier*. These reveal Bach's fecundity in creating themes that are strikingly original, diverse in character and composed of elements that lend themselves to development.

Generally one or two measures in length, the theme has distinctive features that make it instantly recognizable as it recurs in the course of the work. The themes of your inventions should have obvious or latent melodic resources that can be manipulated in ways that are described later. The first note will be either step 1 or 5, which is on the strong beat, or, when preceded by a rest, on the half beat after it. On occasion the theme may start on an up-beat, as in I, no. 3, in which case its ending overlaps the beginning of the imitation. (See Fig. 8-9f.) Themes of the two-part inventions generally end on step 3 or 5, which harmonize well with the first note of the imitation (step 1 or 5). Most three-part invention subjects end on step 3. Note that the S in II, no. 4, ends on step 3 after a suspension in measure 2. Subjects that modulate end on step 1 of the dominant key (I, no. 15) or on step 3 of that key (II, nos. 7 and 12). Themes and subjects end on the strong beat or on the secondary accent in $\frac{4}{4}$ and $\frac{6}{8}$.

Some subjects, like that in II, no. 3, are followed by a codetta (beats 1 and 2 of measure 3). This link affords a smooth key change that is especially necessary in moving from a minor S to its imitation in the dominant minor key (II, no. 13). Read the material on codetta, p. 246.

Themes and subjects vary not only in length but in contour, structure, rhythm and range. The theme in I, no. 4, has a gable-type contour. Themes like this, constructed almost entirely of a scale line, yield little material for episodic development; compare it with the more promising S, W.T.C., II, no. 14. The broken chord motivic idea (I, no. 13) is also insignificant. Bach relies more on harmonic than on contrapuntal interest in this invention. Some themes have a clear upward or downward line, as in Fig. 8-9f, or a less obvious line, indicated by arrows in Fig. 8-10c and in the undulating line of Fig. 8-9a.

The first motive of the theme should have some arresting melodic or rhythmic feature. This may be a characteristic skip at or near the beginning, as in Fig. 8-10a and c. Some themes have a repeated note beginning (Fig. 8-9b). (See also W.T.C., II, fugue no. 5.) Others rotate around one note before moving off in a definite direction, as in II, no. 12. Notice the turn opening motive of Fig. 8-10e. The S in Fig. 8-9c, opening with an auxiliary figure and skip, keeps reverting to one note. Simple repetition is generally undesirable in a theme; the melodic interest in this theme lies in the changed direction and intervals of the notes in brackets.

Although these themes and the three below open with mo-

Figure 8-9a–c

tives that are different in character, each is designed to seize our attention with every theme entry. Two crisp notes signal the theme opening of Fig. 8-9d. A solid opening is the distinctive feature in Fig. 8-9e. (See also Fig. 8-10a.) Many themes open with a bustling motive, like those in Figs. 8-9f and 8-10f. Compare them with similar openings in the inventions.

Figure 8-9d–f

A different motive may follow the first, as in Fig. 8-10a, or it may be succeeded by more than one, as in Fig. 8-9b. A sequence of the opening motive is used in Fig. 8-10b, and a sequence of the second motive is seen in Fig. 8-10c. Notice that the fourth, shown in brackets, is the governing interval. Note also the line indicated by arrows. While sequences unify a theme, they do not add different material for later episodic development. They should be used sparingly in short themes. Unvaried sequences, as in Fig. 8-9e, are less interesting than modified sequences. Compare Fig. 8-10d, no. 1, with the opening of the original, no. 2. Compare no. 3 with the original (Fig. 8-9a). Observe how the high F improves an otherwise mechanical sequence. Sometimes a specific skip at or near the opening is used later sequentially to round off the theme (Fig. 8-10e).

The illustrations in Fig. 8-10d imply that the first draft of a theme is only the beginning of the process. Each way of extending the theme from its opening motive should be explored to achieve the most interesting result. The line as a whole should be reviewed. A change of a note or interval or, as we will see later, a rhythmic alteration, may give it a novel twist. The theme constantly recurs throughout the invention. Every motive, each fragment of line, each rhythmic element

214

Figure 8-10a–e

is potential material for development. Bach can evolve a highly ingenious work from a simple and seemingly unpromising subject. Such themes and subjects are not for the tyro with his limited contrapuntal experience. Nor should he attempt working with a highly chromatic theme like that of Fig. 7-6c. It is generally better to avoid themes like that of Fig. 8-9f, which splits into two equal halves.

Remarks previously made regarding the implied harmony of the canon leader apply equally to the invention theme. (See Ch. 7, p. 191.) The theme should be one that can be harmonized naturally with tonic and dominant harmony, and preferably should include a subdominant, a subordinate triad or secondary seventh harmony. Bach at times favors a V^7ofIV–IV early in the theme, as in invention II, no. 3, beats 2 and 3. The simple invention theme does not modulate; it must end on a tone of I. Fugal invention subjects that end with a modulation move to the dominant key only. The codetta in Fig. 8-10f modulates back to the original key.

Two-part invention themes vary in compass from a fifth to a twelfth. Most of them range from a seventh to a tenth. Subjects for use in three-part inventions should not exceed a range of a ninth. It is difficult to manage a wider range in this texture, since either hand playing two voices should not be required to span more than an octave. Then, too, the counterpoint may be forced to follow a wide-ranging theme to keep within a practical hand span. Voices may get too close and frequently cross in a three-part invention with a narrow ranging theme, *i.e.*, a fifth or sixth.

The rhythm of a theme, inextricably bound up with its melodic line, is sometimes more significant than the line itself. Inventions with themes in uniform rhythm—*e.g.*, I, no. 11, and II, no. 1 and 10—must rely on an interesting thematic contour and rhythmic variety in their counterpoints to offset monotony. Some themes are rhythmically active at the start and taper off at the close (Fig. 8-10f). Other themes of the "head and tail" variety have a slower rhythmic beginning and a rhythmically busy ending, as in Fig. 7-5b. A theme with a tail of this length is unsuited to the invention. A better example is seen in Fig. 8-10g. This rhythmic activity in the tail motive is often transmitted to the counterpoint accompanying the imitation.

Figure 8-10f–g

Long notes placed off the metric accent, as in Fig. 8-9a, the syncopation in measure 2, Fig. 8-9f, a short rest like that in Fig. 8-10a, measure 2, ties or rhythmic variants like the second measure of Fig. 8-10d, no. 2, can transform a prosaic theme into one of gripping interest.

Test each theme written in Ex. 5. How do your major themes sound in minor, and vice versa? Minor subjects that avoid the leading tone near the end evade a conflict with step 3 of the dominant minor in the answer. Break the theme down into motives and try the inversion of one recombined with the other. Invert the whole theme. A single note change may produce a better inversion. The S, particularly in a three-part invention or fugue, is overlapped at times (*stretto*). Try this with the one-measure subjects for later use.

216

Exercise 5a.   Write ten or more invention themes, both in major and minor, one and two measures long. Incorporate more than one motive in these themes. Some of these should start after a short rest. Do not modulate. Be mindful of necessary revisions.

Exercise 5b.   Write five major subjects that modulate to the dominant key.

The theme is the heart of the invention. A weak theme, like a weak heart, affects the total organism. After reconsideration, you may find it advisable to discard a number of your themes.

The first imitation enters an octave lower than the first entry of the theme, at the same time or shortly after the last note of the theme. The intervals at this juncture are important. The last note of the theme and the first note of the imitation should form an interval of a third, a tenth, a fifth, a twelfth or an octave, even when the imitation enters after a rest. Examine Fig. 8-11 before working out Ex. 6.

The theme in Fig. 8-11a ends on step 3, forming a tenth with the imitation beginning. The theme ends on step 5 in Fig. 8-11b, forming a fifth (12th) with the first note of the imitation. The theme ends on step 5 in Fig. 8-11c. Two tones carry it to the beginning of the counterpoint, forming a tenth with the imitation, which starts after a rest. In Fig. 8-11d, the theme ends on step 5; the imitation starts on step 5, forming an octave. The succeeding notes of the counterpoint are gen-

Figure 8-11

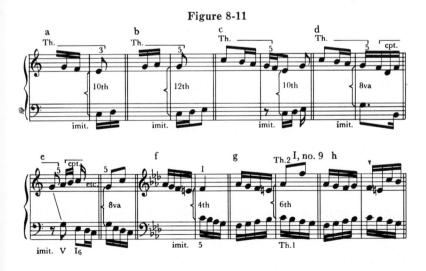

erally in dominant harmony. The same tones are used in Fig. 8-11e, except that the imitation enters after a rest. Here too, the counterpoint should be in dominant harmony. If the theme starts on step 5 and ends on step 3, the interval of a sixth will produce I_4^6 harmony. Avoid this if possible. Do not end on step 1 with a theme that starts on step 5. It will result in the fourth of Fig. 8-11f. Note how Bach evades this interval, ignores the resolution of the leading tone, yet nevertheless is forced into the I_4^6 (Fig. 8-11g). Except for the fixed double theme here, the F of the fourth could be used as an accented passing tone (Fig. 8-11h). As a rule, then, avoid a fourth and sixth at the point where the theme ends and the imitation begins.

The counterpoint to the first imitation is written in the same way as the material counterpointing the canon follower in the octave. It should flow in a natural manner from the end of the theme, rather than as a foreign addition to it. This does not necessarily mean sequential extensions; the counterpoint may be an additional source of episodic material, particularly when the theme is short or in uniform rhythm. The counterpoint should be in contrast to the imitation in line and rhythm, while it is well integrated with the theme. Examine the counterpoint in measures 3 and 4, upper part, of the following inventions: I, nos. 3 and 15; II, nos. 2 and 10; see also I, no. 7, the last half of measure 1 to beat 1 of measure 2. The first counterpoint in the simple invention is not associated with subsequent theme entries with any degree of consistency. It may reappear, however, especially in the last section. Counterpoints that accompany a S fairly regularly are called *countersubjects* (CS). They are used frequently in fugal inventions and in fugues.

Exercise 6.   Write each theme of Ex. 5a on the treble staff. Imitate each one an octave lower in the following measure or measures. Write a counterpoint to each imitation, giving due regard to the intervals formed by the theme endings and imitation beginnings.

The Episode

Developmental passages in which the theme as a whole does not appear are *episodes*. They follow theme entries in the first section of a two-part invention or the exposition of a three-part invention, and are used in later sections as well. These

218

passages are constructed from any expository material, from theme or subject, from the counterpoint, the countersubject or the codetta. When the theme is very brief or motivic, as in I, nos. 1, 4, 7 and 13, the resources for episodic development are severely limited. In these instances Bach uses these motives in modulatory passages characteristic of the episode or resorts to unrelated but analogous material, as in I, no. 13, measures 14–17, and in I, no. 10, especially the end of the episode, measures 10–13. Subsequent references, unless specifically indicated, are to excerpts from the two-part inventions.

Apart from the contrast it offers to theme entries, the principal function of an episode is to lead the lines to a cadence and generally to a theme entry in a new key. A direct modulation is often made early in the episode. The key is then established in the rest of the passage, as in no. 1, measures 4–7. Long episodes usually assume the nature of motivic development, constituting, in some instances, the major portion of a second or third section (no. 13, measures 14–17). Such episodes build to a climax before the cadence, as in no. 15, from the middle of measure 7 to the beginning of measure 10, or taper down to the cadence (II, no. 3, measures 12–14). Brief episodes, a measure or so long, are used between the first theme entries and are designated here as interludes. (See II, no. 4, measures 3 and 5, and no. 8, measure 4 to the middle of measure 5.) It leads to three S entries before the beginning of the second section in the middle of measure 7. There may be no key digression in interludes.

Various devices unify the episodic passage. Among those used are antiphonal responses with alternately long tones in the other voice (Fig. 8-12a). These passages generally culminate in two rhythmically active parts. Compare this with no. 1, measures 15–18, where the motivic theme and inversions of it alternate antiphonally. (See also no. 14, measures 4 and 5, and II, no 13, measures 8-12.) Motivic fragments are used antiphonally in Fig. 8-12b. While material in antiphonal responses

Figure 8-12a

may be dissimilar, the two examples below are instances of antiphonal responses that are canonic.

Episodes composed of free melodic sequences are common. Any thematic material may be the source of the initial unit. A motive derived from the CS, and expanded by using its skip, is the initial unit in Fig. 8-12c. The second half of measure 1 is a sequence, and the whole measure is then repeated in sequence in measure 2. The initial motive starts a series of short sequences in measure 3, which is imitated in the lower voice in the last measure. Observe how Bach brings this episode to a close with a descent to the cadence and a reference to the first motive of the S. Added stems in the upper voice are used here to show the scalewise derivation of the fragments in the lower voice, alternating in direct and contrary motion. The episode modulates from minor to the relative major.

Figure 8-12b

Examine the episodic sequences in no. 6, measure 9, to its cadence in measure 18; no. 10, measure 4, to the cadence on the dominant, measure 14; no. 13, measure 3, to the middle of measure 6. See also II, no. 10, measures 9 and 10, in which the second half of the S is used in sequences.

An episode composed of canonic sequences is shown in Fig. 8-12d.

Figure 8-12c–d

II, no. 8

The material of the first episode is often utilized in later sections. A common device is to repeat the earlier material with the voices interchanged.

Double Counterpoint at the Octave

The second S entry (answer) in Fig. 8-13a is accompanied by a CS. Seven measures later the same material is ·used, but the upper voice, dropped two octaves, becomes the lower voice (Fig. 8-13b). This interchange is called *double counterpoint.*

Figure 8-13a–b

Art of Fugue, Contrapunctus III

The interchange works equally well if: (1) part A drops a single octave, making it the lower voice (Fig. 8-13c) ; (2) part B is raised an octave, transferring it above part A (Fig. 8-13d) or (3) if part A drops an octave and part B is raised an octave (Fig. 8-13e). Shifting the voices by two octaves, here and in Fig. 8-13a, is double counterpoint at the fifteenth. These examples demonstrate that one voice may remain stationary while the other is shifted above or below it, or both voices may be shifted in opposite directions. If both parts originally are more than an octave apart, as in Fig. 8-13f, dropping A an octave, as in the next measure, will not effect an interchange.

Figure 8-13c–f

The technique of devising lines that work equally well when the original lines exchange their material at any interval is also called *invertible counterpoint.** This technique is essential in writing the fugal invention and the fugue. For instance, the S in I, no. 15, is imitated in the lower voice and accompanied by a CS in measure 3. The S re-enters in the upper voice in measure 5, accompanied by the CS, which is now below it. The latitude in range of each voice, permissible in two-part polyphony, must be restricted in three-part writing if invertible counterpoint is used. Assuming a three-voice texture, there is no problem involved when the two voices of Fig. 8-14a are interchanged in Fig. 8-14b. The upper part of a different CS (Fig. 8-14c) has a range of more than an octave. An interchange of parts, resulting in the voice crossing of Fig. 8-14d, creates a confusion of line. Furthermore, if the parts appeared *originally* with crossed voices, as in Fig. 8-14d, lower voice notes which lie above the upper voice will, at that point, again lie above that voice in the interchange (Fig. 8-14c). Parts intended for interchange at the octave should not cross voices.

Double counterpoint at the octave does not seriously affect the altered relationship of the parts in the matter of consonance and dissonance. You will see from Fig. 1-3 that concords

---

* Instead of the term "invertible counterpoint," the author adopts the term "interchangeable counterpoint" from *The Technique and Spirit of Fugue*, Oldroyd, to avoid confusion between inversion (notes moving opposite to the direction of the original notes) and invertible, interchanged voices.

CH. 8

Figure 8-14

inverted remain concords and discords remain discords. Major intervals become minor, and vice versa. The diminished interval becomes augmented. Perfect intervals remain perfect. Note that the perfect fifth, starred in Fig. 8-14a, becomes a perfect fourth. It is generally better to use as few perfect fifths as possible in order to avoid the fourth in the interchange.

Our immediate concern is the use of interchanged parts in episodes. Bach starts the episode of II, no. 10, at measure 9, with the second half of the S in the lower voice; the next measure is a sequence of it. The upper voice in measure 9 is a broken chord and tied note. Compare this with the second episode, starting at measure 17, where, by an interchange, the running sixteenths are now in the upper voice, with the broken chord and tied quarter below it. The eight-measure episode in the second section of I, no. 9 (Fig. 8-15), includes one of the best examples of double counterpoint. Examine the double theme first, measures 1–4, to discover the source of the episodic material.

Figure 8-15

The parts in the first two measures are interchanged in the next two, with a change of key. Observe that a sequence in both parts, measures 25 and 26, is continued for another measure in the lower part. Bach runs both parts in sixteenths on the dominant, measure 28, before the final entry of the double theme in the home key. This is an exceptionally long episode but one well worth close analysis. An interesting example of double counterpoint by *inversion* is seen in Fig. 8-16. Both themes of a two-part double fugue, A and B, are interchanged and inverted in the second measure.

Figure 8-16

W.T.C. II, P. no. 20

Additional polyphonic devices that are used more effectively in the three-part fugal invention and in the fugue are described in detail in Ch. 10. These are: *augmentation*—doubling the note values of a S; *diminution*—halving its note values; *cancrizans*—running the S backward, from last note to the first, and *stretto*—the canonic overlapping of the S by itself. These devices are mentioned in passing because fragments of theme or counterpoint, used in one of these ways, may crop up in a subordinate role in an episode.

The length of the first episode depends on the length of the theme, the planned number of entries and the size of section 1. An episode after several entries of a brief theme is apt to be longer than one following entries of a longer theme. The harmonic route to the cadence will, accordingly, be shorter or longer. Other than a direct plunge into the new key, the briefest route from major to the dominant key is V^7ofVI/II– V^7–I and from minor to the relative major: I–V^7ofIV/II, V^7 of the new key, I. Such routes may be inconveniently short, particularly for later sections. In that case, a direct modulation to the desired key is followed by a digression to other related keys before returning to the new key, or a series of secondary dominant-triad units are used. In any case, the harmonic route to the cadence must be mapped out in advance. Any device planned for section 1 may have a bearing on the number and length of later episodes.

The following exercises make use of the themes written in Ex. 5a and of the counterpoints written to them in Ex. 6. Episodes constructed from major themes and their counterpoints should modulate to the dominant key or to the relative minor. Minor theme material should modulate to the relative major or to the dominant minor key. This does not preclude transitional modulation on the way to these keys. Remember that only a portion of the theme may be used in episodes, as well as material from the counterpoint. Any recombination of motives from both sources may be used.

Exercise 7a.   Write an episode that is largely antiphonal, with material drawn from one of your major themes. Do the same with material from one of your minor themes.

Exercise 7b.   Write a sequential episode, with material taken from another of your major themes. Do the same with material from a different minor theme.

Exercise 7c.   Write an episode in canonic sequences, with material extracted from a third major theme, then write another with material drawn from a minor theme.

The ending of an episode in double counterpoint need not be, and often is not, the same as the ending of the original unit. Some changes may be necessary to draw the episode to a good cadence. In some instances, particularly in a second or third episode, a slight change in the beginning of the episode in double counterpoint may be required to make it mesh with the preceding material.

Exercise 7d.   Start with a two-measure episode; continue for another two measures with interchanged voices and a modulation.

9

Sectional Organization of the Simple Invention; Canon as Invention; The Two-part Fugal and Double Invention

The Simple Invention, Section 1

The best way to approach the composition of an invention is to plan it as a whole. The key of each section is set in advance, harmonic routes to cadences are plotted, theme entries are sketched in and episodic materials and various devices are explored and selected, at least tentatively. This should be your procedure after some experience in composition. At our present stage a section-by-section approach is more practical.

Section 1 begins with a theme announcement in the upper voice, either alone or accompanied by a simple bass line, as in I, nos. 13 and 15. This line, called an *auxiliary bass,* is merely

227

harmonic support; it extends to the first note of the imitation. Starting with the tonic note, it establishes the first beat for themes that commence after a rest. A tone of the auxiliary bass is also placed on the beat, under dotted notes and suspensions in the theme. The auxiliary bass has no further role in the two-part invention. Although optional in these compositions, it is used in all three-part inventions. Examine the auxiliary basses in the inventions.

The imitation, an octave lower, follows the initial announcement. Except for half-measure motivic themes, it starts on the same beat or fraction of it as the initial entry. Review the material in Ch. 8, p. 217, describing intervallic points of juncture between theme endings and imitation beginnings. While additional entries of a short theme may be used, there need be no further entries of a two- or three-measure theme in section 1. The third entry of a short theme is often preceded by a brief interlude (Fig. 9-1). Its irregular entry here, in the same voice as the one preceding it, is excused by its location in the lower octave. Examine the Prelude of the *English Suite no. 4,* in which a two-and-a-half-measure interlude separates the first two theme announcements and two additional entries at the fifth. Bach uses additional entries at the fifth with the brief themes of I, nos. 1 and 7. We will confine entries in the first section to imitation at the octave, reserving entries at the fifth to the fugal invention.

Figure 9-1

Prelude, English Suite no. 2

The counterpoint to the imitation, as previously described, flows without interruption from the end of the initial entry. Subordinate in importance, it should not overshadow the imitation. Counterpoints to any additional entries are not consistently the same. It is essential to avoid a distinct cleavage between theme ending and the beginning of the counterpoint. The theme, then, should not end on a long note.

The imitation or last entry moves directly to the episode, sometimes after a brief link. The first episode, simpler in character than those of later sections, is composed of material related to the theme. Sequences of thematic motives are commonly used. The Fantasia of *Partita III*, similar to a two-part invention but somewhat longer, starts with the theme shown in Fig. 9-2a. The episode begins with half of the theme in sequences, which are then imitated (Fig. 9-2b). Examine the whole first section, ending in measure 31. An initial motive in sequential episodes (Fig. 9-2c) may require alteration to extend the line (Fig. 9-2d) or to conform to the required harmony (Fig. 9-2e).

Figure 9-2

Fantasia, Partita no. 3

Since little can be extracted from the motivic theme of I, no. 7, it may be necessary to employ the whole theme or to resort to extraneous material in its episode. The interesting S of Fig. 9-3a is rich in motivic content. A wide variety of initial episodic units can be derived from it to launch the passage. Examine each unit of Fig. 9-3b to discover its source in the S. Look for various recombinations of motives, rhythmic changes, changes by motive augmentation and diminution, and by inversion or retrograde motion. Note changes in the size and direction of skips, skips in sequence, etc. Each unit may begin a sequential, antiphonal or imitative passage. Devise a number of such units from some of your themes in preparation for Ex. 1.

Figure 9-3

The harmonic route to the cadence closing section 1 is planned before proceeding any further with the type of episodic unit selected. It may then be necessary to alter that unit chromatically. The rest of the material must conform to that route. The goal of section 1 of a *major* invention is a cadence in the dominant or relative minor key. Section 1 of a *minor* invention cadences in the relative major or dominant minor key. The modulation may occur close to the cadence; if made early, it should be confirmed by material in the rest of the passage. A minor climax, with both parts rhythmically active, is commonly developed prior to the cadence. The first section should not be disproportionate in length to the whole invention. Six to 10 measures in $\frac{4}{4}$ and approximately 12 to 18 measures in $\frac{3}{8}$ are sufficient.

Exercise 1a.   Write a first section that modulates to the dominant key, using a two-measure major theme from Ex. 5a, Ch. 8.

Exercise 1b.   Write another that modulates to the relative minor, using a one-measure major theme from the same exercise.

Exercise 1c.   Starting with a two-measure minor theme, write a first section that modulates to the relative major key.

Exercise 1d.   Take the first section to a cadence ·in the dominant minor key, using a one-measure minor theme.

Section 2

Section 2 of nearly all two-part simple inventions commences with a theme entry in the cadence measure of section 1, and in the key of that cadence. This section is not a replica of the first in a different key. Since the theme appeared first in the upper part, it is preferable, though not obligatory, to put this entry in the lower part. This is a simple matter with a theme that began on step 1. The cadence note of the lower part is step 1 of the new key. A theme starting on step 5 is handled in the new key as shown in Fig. 8-11d and e. In moving from one section to the next, it is necessary to realize that the cadence is not only momentary but that the cadential note is often the first note of a theme entry beginning section 2. This dovetailing of the ending of one section into the beginning of another is sometimes described as *elision* or a *telescoping effect*. We reiterate this point because, in some instances, the first note or two of the theme at the beginning of the next section must be altered on account of the cadence note. Compare the upper voice in the first measure of Invention I, no. 11, with the theme in the same voice, measure 11.

The second section may start with the theme inverted. Section 1 of the Prelude 10, W.T.C. II, starts with the theme shown in Fig. 9-4a. The second section starts with the inverted theme (Fig. 9-4b). For most of the way, the episode employs imitations of half of the theme inverted. Examine this section from the double bar to the a minor cadence, 24 measures later, with particular attention to the way this fragment is used in modulations. This prelude is similar to a simple two-part invention, except for the repetition of section 1 and the repetition of the remainder.

Figure 9-4

While a single entry of a long theme is sufficient, a second entry at the octave may be used. This may come in close succession or after a nonmodulating interlude. The theme may be shifted in the measure after the first entry; *e.g.*, from its beginning on beat 1 to beat 3 in $\frac{4}{4}$ and to beat 4 in $\frac{6}{8}$. Subsequent entries, if any, may start on any scale step of the key or of the key to which this section moves, as well as on any beat. Counterpoints to these entries generally differ from each other and from those in section 1.

Various episodic resources and devices are available for use in section 2. More interesting combinations of motivic material can generate a sequential series. Two or three sequential measures may be followed by an interchange of parts in different harmony or in a different key. (See no. 8, measures 21–23, and 24–25; also no. 9, measures 21 and 22, and 23 and 24. Note the key change in the latter and the relationship of the material to the double theme.) Bear in mind that both lines should be germane to the thematic source. The less important line, based on different motivic material, may include inversions of the motive, changes in skips, rhythm, etc. Canonic or partly canonic sequences is another episodic device. (See no. 3, measures 9–11; also see Fig. 7-15a. Note the antiphonal responses in I, no. 3, measures 24–31.) Part of a long theme may be employed in a series of imitations. A choice of material or devices is contingent on reserving the most interesting episode for section 3, unless, as in no. 9, the second section is the most significant.

Section 2 almost invariably modulates to a related key or returns to the original key. Major inventions that modulated to the dominant in section 1 modulate to the relative minor of the original key, or to the supertonic key, in section 2. Major inventions modulating to the relative minor in the first section cadence in the dominant key, or return to the original key, in section 2. Minor inventions with a first section cadence in the relative major key move to the dominant minor or, as in no. 15 (a fugal invention in two sections), return to the original minor key. Minor inventions with a section 2 starting in the dominant minor return to the original key or, as in no. 11, move to the subdominant key. Intermediate modulations between cadences of sections 1 and 2 are common.

On occasion a fairly solid cadence divides this section in two. Examine no. 3, measures 12–23 and measures 24–38; also no. 7, measure 7 to the middle of measure 9 and from there to the middle of measure 13. The length of section 2 varies. It may be as long or longer than section 1 if the third section is short.

Exercise 2a. Analyze the harmonic and modulatory path of the following second sections of major inventions: no. 1, measures 7–15; no. 6, measures 21–42; no. 8, measures 12–26; no. 10, measures 14–27; no. 14, measures 6–12; also no. 3, measures 12–38, and no. 5, measures 12–27.

Exercise 2b. Do the same with the following second sections of minor inventions: no. 4, measures 18–38; no. 7, measure 7 to the middle of measure 13; no. 13, from the middle of measure 6 to the middle of measure 13; no. 15, measure 12 to the close; also no. 2, measures 11–23; no. 9, measures 17–28, and no. 11, measure 11 to the middle of measure 16.

Exercise 3a. Write second sections to the first sections composed in Exs. 1a and b.

Exercise 3b. Write second sections to inventions begun in minor in Exs. 1c and d.

Section 3

Most two-part simple inventions are in three sections. The last section includes one or more theme entries in the original key, either at the beginning or near the close of the section. The location of these entries generally depends on the cadence key of section 2. The third section will start with an entry in the original key when section 2 ends either in that key or in the dominant major key. (See the canonic invention no. 2, five measures before the end, and the double inventions nos. 5 and 9, six measures before the end.)

Major inventions cadencing in the original key move to the subdominant key in the last section before closing in the first key. A measure of transition between sections 2 and 3 may be used when section 2 does not cadence in the original key or its dominant, and a last section beginning in the original key is desired. One such measure bridges the keys of g♯ and E in no. 6, measure 42; section 2 of no. 9 moves into the third section with a measure of dominant transition, seven measures before the close.

Regardless of the key in which section 3 begins, it generally moves to the subdominant area before closing in the home key. In short third sections V^7ofIV–IV takes the place of a modulation to the subdominant. Examine no. 1, measures 5–4 before the close; no. 4, measures 38–40; no. 5, measures 3–2 before the end; no. 7, from the middle of measure 13 to the beginning of the next measure; and no. 13, measure 14 to the beginning of the next measure. A modulation to the subdominant key should not be placed too close to the final cadence, or the cadential I may sound like V of the subdominant key.

Modulation from the dominant minor in section 2 to the original minor key is generally handled in one of two ways. The third section may open with a modulatory episode leading to a belated entry in the original minor key. This can be a refreshing change from opening a section with a theme announcement. Examine episodic openings of the following: no. 13, a half measure on the dominant minor, measure 13, precedes four measures of episode leading to entries in the home key; no. 7, section 2 closes in the middle of measure 13 in the dominant minor. Its short theme necessitates using the whole theme in an episode-like beginning of section 3. An entry with the notes of the first announcement is delayed until the next to last measure in the lower voice.

Another way of moving from the dominant minor to the original minor key is to substitute a major tonic cadence chord (*Picardy third*) for the expected minor I of the dominant minor. Note that no. 4, measure 38, veers off immediately to the subdominant after a cadence in the dominant minor.

Section 2 of the minor invention no. 11 cadences in the less common subdominant key, seven and a half measures before the end. At this point two measures of episode, formed from half of the long theme, usher in section 3, leading to the double theme in the home key. The major invention, no. 3, cadences in the dominant key in section 2, measure 38. The next five measures, sequences of the brief theme, form an episode-like beginning of section 3. The unusual unaccompanied entry with altered beginning follows in the original key.

Some third sections move to a deceptive cadence near the close. See no. 1, six measures before the end; no. 4, four measures before the end, and no. 10, three measures before the final cadence. The measures after the deceptive cadence, providing a less abrupt ending, function like a codetta in homophonic music. (See codetta on p. 246.)

Thematic material or devices previously unused may now be applied in the last episode or episodes. Material previously used may appear in double counterpoint. Canonic episodes are also generally interesting. See the remarkable canonic episode in no. 14, measures 12–16 before the final theme entry. Remember that the episode has both a developmental and modulatory function.

The invention, like most compositions, rises to a high point of interest or climax. A compelling drive to a climax or climactic area is often the distinguishing characteristic of section 3. This applies to all two-part inventions, except for some double and canonic inventions in which the high point is developed in section 2. The third section in these inventions consists merely of one or two announcements of the long theme. The climax is usually located near the end of the section. Its placement may be dictated by the nature of the preceding material, as in no. 1, where this section begins with quiet antiphonal responses, measures 15–18. The motivic theme in the next two measures moves sequentially to a climax (starred in Fig. 9-5a). Observe the sequentially rising lower part, formed of the first four notes of the motive, inverted and augmented.

Figure 9-5a

The long third episode of no. 7, starting in the middle of measure 13, is one of the most interesting episodes of the two-part inventions. The passage reaches one climactic area with the trill in the middle of measure 15, gradually simmering down to its low point in measure 20. Note the rhythmic relaxation in the preceding measure. From that point the passage is built to another climax (measure 2 of Fig. 9-5b). The trill, as Bach uses it, is dramatically effective. We will refer to it again in connection with the use of the pedal point in Ch. 10. Used otherwise, it is no substitute for a vital contrapuntal line.

Figure 9-5b

The passage of rising motivic sequences in the first measure of Fig. 9-5c continues after a dipping curve in the line, with widening skips to the climactic note in the next measure. Do not overlook the contribution made by the rising skips in the lower part and the descending lower line in the next measure, projecting the upper line into high relief.

Figure 9-5c

Cumulative rising sequences of a short motive is one way of developing the unremitting tension leading to the climax. Broad expansion of the theme is another. The last theme entry

236

of no. 5 is expanded by inserting a sequence of one segment of the theme (measure 2 of Fig. 9-5d), lifting the rest of the theme to its climax in measure 3.

Figure 9-5d

Exercise 4. Add the third section to each incomplete invention of Ex. 3. Use an episode beginning and a deceptive cadence in at least one of them. Experiment with different methods of achieving a climactic development before settling on any one of them.

A number of Bach's compositions serving as preludes to fugues and single movements of partitas and suites are similar in character and general structure to various types of two- and three-part inventions. Some differ in no way from a simple two-part invention. An analysis of them will deepen our understanding of the various types. Others, to which we will refer later, are fugal and double inventions. In some instances an invention is imbedded in a longer piece.

Exercise 5. Analyze at least three of the following in regard to section structure, theme entries, episodic source material, devices used, modulations, cadences, etc. (Study the analysis of the invention in the Appendix for guidance). (a) W.T.C. II, P. nos. 8 and 10. (b) Part. III, *Fantasia*, a long invention, of which Fig. 9-2a is the theme. (c) *French Suite no. 5, Gigue.* (d) *English Suite no. 1, Bourrée* no. 1 (this is in phrase structure; the first section and the remainder are repeated). The following are also two-part simple inventions in which a relatively unessential third voice appears at a few points. (e) *English Suite no. 2*, the Prelude up to the *tranquillo* section. Section 1 is longer than in most inventions. (f) Part. V, *Allemande*. (g) *French Suite no. 5*, the *Courante*, which has two additional entries at the fifth in section 1 and a repetition of the whole section.

The Canon as Invention

The difficulty of producing some sense of intelligible design in the canon can be surmounted in the less rigid sectional form of the invention. Our model, Invention no. 2 of the *Two-Part Inventions*, is a superlative example of how to employ the canon in a coherent pattern that adheres to the general structure and modulatory scheme of the invention. Follow the analysis below *with the score in front of you* and with the measures numbered. The abbreviations "l.v." and "u.v." stand for lower and upper voice; measure is abbreviated as "m."

The first two measures, unlike the leader of a canon, is the theme. Recurring in the first and subsequent sections, its length, as we remarked in connection with the canon, is advantageous. This factor, along with the theme's beginning after a rest, allows some room for later adjustment. An interesting undulating line compensates for the uniform rhythm of the theme. Its harmonic implications are clear: I–IV–VII⁷–I.

Each section of the canon as invention has the same modulatory objective as the simple invention. Here section 1 cadences in the relative major, E♭ (m. 11). The theme, as in the canon leader, is written so as to permit modulation in the imitation. Observe that the trilled note (step 2 to 3 of c) is also 7–8 of E♭. The imitation is an exact copy an octave lower (m. 3–4). Notice several factors in the counterpoint above it: (1) it flows smoothly and naturally from the end of the theme; (2) it is well contrasted in rhythm; (3) the sequence adds to its coherence; (4) it avoids the leading tone of c, and (5) it makes use of pivotal harmony (VI/IV, m. 4, beat 3).

Measures 3–4, u.v., are now copied in the l.v., m. 5–6. Except for the ambivalence of the first beat in m. 5, the harmony of these two measures is clear and solid (II⁷–V, I⁷–II–V⁷–I₆), remaining in E♭ until the cadence of this section. The episode starting in m. 5 carries section 1 to a close in m. 11. As in most

238

inventions, the episodic material bears some relationship to the theme. The first motive of m. 5, u.v., is extracted from the middle of m. 1 (Fig. 9-6a). Part of the second motive is taken from m. 2 (Fig. 9-6b). Note the sequences (m. 5–6, u.v.), the last of which is abbreviated. Carried out as in Fig. 9-6c, it would lead to I with doubled third. Measures 7–8, l.v., is an exact copy of m. 5–6, u.v. Observe the rhythmic drive to the climax in m. 8, u.v.

Figure 9-6a–c

Measures 9–10, l.v., are an exact copy of m. 7–8, u.v. The motivic material used in the u.v., m. 9–10 (shown in Fig. 9-6d) is derived from the theme. This upper line (m. 9–10) is not transferred to the lower line because section 2 starts with the theme in the lower voice. It is, however, not wholly discarded. (See m. 19, l.v., and m. 20–21.)

Figure 9-6d

Before proceeding with the analysis of section 2, examine the cadence in m. 11. A student might have written a cadence and the two beats before it, as in Fig. 9-6e. Awkward as the extended line is, it prepares a theme entry in E♭ on step 1, as in the initial announcement in c. Bach's remarkable skill is evident in his manipulation of this cadence. The leading tone is suspended, and by the time its delayed resolution appears he manages to slip quickly into g minor. The tones used to delay the resolution are "planted" in g, an excellent example of harmonic fusion. The cadence then is a fusion of relative major and dominant minor in which the theme is set (m. 11–12). Note the beginning of the theme, which could have remained unaltered: G–F♯–G. It may be noted that the rhythmic continuity is unchecked. The a natural in the l.v., m. 11, is necessary in g.

Figure 9-6e

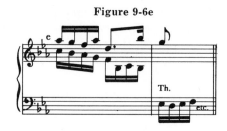

Bear in mind that the l.v. is now the leading voice. The new though related counterpoint in m. 11 and 12 is not used again. Such "free" measures mark one difference between the canon and the canonic invention. The theme is imitated in the u.v., m. 13–14. Bach reverts to the counterpoint accompanying the first imitation (m. 3–4, u.v.), naturally in g. The omission of the g minor leading tone makes a modulation to B♭ possible. This counterpoint appears for a third and fourth time as accompaniment to the theme, though in altered form (m. 23–24 and m. 25–26).

The upper voice, m. 15–16, then picks up the countertheme of m. 13–14. Now compare both parts in m. 15–18 with the parts in m. 5–8. The parts, now in B♭, are interchanged to begin the second episode. The counterpoint below the u.v., m. 19–20 (copied from m. 17–18, l.v.), is taken from m. 9–10. This counterpoint is not transferred in m. 21–22 because Bach intends a climactic area in measures 20–22. Now single-measure imitation is substituted for canonic imitation in these three measures (Fig. 9-6f). The material comes from m. 8.

Figure 9-6f

Free but related counterpoint accompanies the imitations, culminating in the long scale line of m. 22.

Section 3, the last five measures, consists of theme entries in the original key, first above and then below, accompanied by the altered countertheme. Note the altered beginning (l.v., m. 23) to form a solid cadence and the change in m. 24 to remain in c. Compare this measure with m. 4, u.v. Observe also the alterations in m. 26 to insure a good cadence.

Exercise 6a.　Analyze Invention I, no. 8.

Exercise 6b.　Write a canon in invention form modelled on Invention I, no. 2.

The Two-part Fugal Invention

The simple invention starts with a theme which is imitated an octave lower. The fugal invention subject is imitated a fourth or, more often, a fourth plus an octave, below its initial entry. This marks the principal difference between the two types. Later sections of the fugal invention generally maintain the same relationship between entry and imitation, except when the entry is in the lower voice. The imitation is then a fifth or a fifth plus an octave above that entry. The first imitation in no. 10, m. 2, is a fourth below the first announcement. The imitation in m. 15 is a fifth above the second section entry in the preceding measure. Imitations that are a fifth above or a fourth below a preceding entry are described, as we learned earlier, as *imitations at the fifth* because both start with the same lettered note. Notice the imitations in no. 15, m. 3, and in the last half of m. 5. Compare m. 12 and 14.

The theme of a fugal invention, as we know from previous experience with theme construction, is called the *Subject* (S). Its imitation is the *Answer* (A), sometimes called the *Response*. We refer to the imitations in the examples above as answers at the fifth. This is the customary location of the answer though, on occasion, it is at the fifth below or fourth above.

Fugues and fugal inventions, particularly those in three parts, are often similar in regard to length, brevity of subject and relatively simple treatment. Some fugues, however, are longer than inventions, have longer subjects and are more complex. They differ in another respect. The fugue S is un-accompanied, except for one type of double fugue, on its initial appearance. The S of a fugal invention is accompanied by an auxiliary bass when first announced. We will draw on details from fugue examples that apply to the fugal invention, because of their common characteristics.

The Fugal Invention Subject

Except for some attention to the end of the S, little need be added to our previous description of the characteristics of a good subject. The nonmodulating subjects of the *Three-Part Inventions* and short subjects of the *Well-Tempered Clavier* are excellent models. The new factor, an A at the fifth (fourth below) in this two-part texture, may have a bearing on the way the S is terminated. Let us turn momentarily, then, to the A before considering the S ending.

The Real Answer

Strict imitation of the S at any interval other than the octave is a *real* answer. Real answers of nonmodulating subjects are written most frequently at the fifth; *i.e.*, a fifth above or a fourth below, as in Fig. 9-7a. We changed the original order in which the voices entered to demonstrate this and a later point. An answer that is a free imitation of the S is a *tonal* answer. It differs from the S at the beginning, at the end or in both places. Compare the real A in II, no. 10, m. 3 and 4, with the following tonal A in m. 5 and 6. Note the tonal A in m. 2, II, no. 8.

Figure 9-7a

Although a tonal answer may be used in the two-part fugal invention, we will use *nonmodulating subjects* and *real answers only* at this time because: (1) real answers to modulating subjects carry the first entries too far from the original

242

key—for instance, a S starting in C and modulating to G will have an A in G that modulates to D; and (2) tonal answers involve a variety of problems—their solution, and the reasons governing a choice of real or tonal A, will be discussed in Ch. 10.

A real A at the fifth to a nonmodulating major S is a response in the dominant key, except as noted below. See m. 3 and 4 of II, no. 10. See also the first 11 measures of Fugue no. 15, W.T.C. I. Observe the simple chromatic change in m. 10 which provides a return to the original key.

The A at the fifth may remain in the original key if there is no leading tone in the S, as in Fig. 9-7a. This is less true in Fig. 9-7b, even though the S does not contain the leading tone. The skips in the A imply a modulation, and the accompanying counterpoint confirms it. Note the implied harmony at the beginning of the S: I–IV. The A responds with V–I. See the first four measures of Fugue no. 5, W.T.C. II, in which the A in tonic harmony responds to the beginning of the S in sub-dominant harmony. The change of voice entry from the original in Fig. 9-7b results in a I⁶₄ at the juncture point. Occurring occasionally in Bach, this is a practice best avoided by the student. (See Invention I, no. 9, m. 5; also Fugue no. 18, W.T.C. II, m. 5.)

Figure 9-7b

Real answers at the fifth below and at the fourth above are used at times. A modulation is not necessarily involved if step 4 is absent in the S. (See Invention II, no. 1, m. 1–2, the upper and inner voices.) Motives of a S paired with real A beginnings at the fifth below demonstrate this in Fig. 9-7c. Similar units can be used in an A at a fourth above the S.

Figure 9-7c

A real A at the fifth to a nonmodulating minor S is in the dominant minor key (Figs. 9-7d, e and f). It is inadvisable to use the awkward succession of tones D♯ and D natural in close proximity (Fig. 9-7e). These are, respectively, the leading tone of the original key and the third of the dominant minor. Note how far apart such tones are in Fig. 9-7f.

Figure 9-7d–f

Major Subject Endings

Unlike octave imitation in the simple invention, the S ending must mesh with the first note of an A in the fifth. Most two-part fugal inventions and two-part fugues start with the S in the u.v.; this is the order we will follow. Most initial answers start with the last note of the S or a fraction of a beat later if the S starts after a rest. Delayed entry of the A is treated below, as well as subjects starting in the l.v., as in section 2.

The last note of the S is a tone of I of the dominant key (Fig. 9-8a), unless it is a suspension or other accented non-harmonic tone, as in the last unit. A subject starting on step 1, after a rest, may end in the original key (Fig. 9-8b). The best ending for a S that starts on the beat and on step 5 is shown in Fig. 9-8c: the implied V or V⁷ of the dominant key. A subject starting on step 5 and ending on step 1 also implies this harmony with the first note of the real A (Fig. 9-8d). When the S begins on step 5 after a rest it may end on a tone of the original key (Fig. 9-8e) and then, with an additional note or two, meet the A in harmony that implies V or V⁷ of the dominant key. Do not use an ending that implies I⁶₄, as in the next two units.

Figure 9-8

Minor Subject Endings

Joining the end of a minor S immediately to the beginning of an A in the dominant minor is often difficult, because of the conflict between step 7 of the first key and step 3 of the second key. (See Fig. 9-7e.) When the S starts on the beat on step 1 end it on step 5, which is the tonic tone of the dominant minor. A subject entering on step 1 after a rest makes the transition to dominant minor less difficult. It may then end on any I chord tone of the original key and, as in Fig. 9-7f, slip into the new key. Observe that the starred note in this example meets the A at an interval of a fifth. This opening interval is frequently used, particularly with the A in the u.v., in section 2 of the fugal invention. (See Fugue no. 4, W.T.C. I.)

It may be remarked, in passing, that minor subjects which modulate to the dominant minor key somewhere along the line, or even with the last note, make the junction with an A in that key a simple matter. Then, too, the entry of the A may be delayed, permitting the insertion of a modulatory codetta, which is described below. The tonal A, as we shall see, evades an immediate modulation. This is practically the best way to handle a S that starts on step 5, or where the first tones are steps 1 and 5 or 5 and 1. The only ending possible with a S starting on step 5, and a real A, is step 5 of the dominant key, forming an octave with the first note of the A.

Exercise 7a. Write several nonmodulating subjects in major that do not exceed two measures in $\frac{4}{4}$ and $\frac{6}{8}$; or use some of those written in Ex. 5a, Ch. 8, amending them, if necessary, in accordance with the above information. Start some on the beat and others after a rest. Include one or two that lack the leading tone or step 4. Write real answers to each of them at the fifth (the fourth below); write several answers at the fifth below.

Exercise 7b. Write several nonmodulating subjects in minor; or use those written in Ex. 5a, Ch. 8, amending the endings, if necessary, as previously indicated. Write real answers in the dominant minor to each of these minor subjects.

The A beginning does not always fall on the same beat as the S ending. It may be desirable or necessary to delay the entrance of the A. This is done, in some instances, where the S does not modulate—particularly in minor, with the difficult transition to the dominant minor. A brief bit of material that is a measure or less in length follows the last note of the S, linking it with the counterpoint to the A.

The Codetta

The term *codetta* is borrowed from homophonic music, where the phrase or more appended to the last phrase of a section or to the terminal phrase is called "codetta." In this meaning of the term a codetta is infrequently used in inventions and fugues. The last three measures of Invention I, no. 6, constitute an example; so do the measures following a deceptive cadence near the end. Some writers prefer the term "link" for the material between starred points in Figs. 9-9a and c, because it spans the end of the S and the beginning of the counterpoint. In Fig. 9-10 it fills in the measure before an A that starts on the up-beat and continues to the CS. The retention here of the traditional term "codetta" should be understood in the light of these examples and a comprehension of their function. The codetta in Fig. 9-9a: (1) brings the line to a melodic apex and cadence; (2) prepares the way for an A in the dominant, and (3) does so at a point where the A can make a satisfactory entrance. This would be less so with the last note of the S (Fig. 9-9b).

246

Figure 9-9a–b

In minor inventions a S beginning and ending on step 1 (Fig. 9-9c) would have the A at the fifth making the wrong juncture point shown in Fig. 9-9d. This is the reason for the delayed entry of the A and a resort to a codetta. In another instance the leading tone is near the end of the S. Note the awkward proximity of G♯ and in G in the amended version (Fig. 9-9e).

Figure 9-9c–e

Ideally the subject-codetta-counterpoint makes a long continuous line, as in Fig. 9-10, so that the codetta, at least, *seems* to be part of the S. This is particularly true when the last note of the S is short or when the codetta is a sequence of the tail end of the S. If this material does not recur with each or most entries of the S or A it is not part of the S, even though it completes the line started by the S. Remember that the S usually ends on a strong beat. The codetta in this example overlaps the A.

Figure 9-10

codetta

Exercise 8a.   Add brief codettas to a few of the major subjects of Ex. 7a. These codettas should carry the line to the dominant key and mesh with the delayed real A at the fifth.

Exercise 8b.   Add codettas to a few of the minor subjects of Ex. 7b. These codettas should modulate to I of the dominant minor and end on a tone that makes a good interval with the real A beginning.

The Countersubject

The entry of an A and subsequent entries of S and A is accompanied by various counterpoints in some fugal inventions and fugues, and by the *same* counterpoint in others. Counterpoint associated with S and A entries in a fairly consistent manner is called a *countersubject* (CS), as previously mentioned. The CS in the fugal invention (Fig. 9-11a) and in the two-part fugue (Fig. 9-11b) is coupled with the first A and with subsequent entries of S and A. The CS of Fugue no. 24, W.T.C. II (given in part in Fig. 9-10) is less consistently used. Since S and A re-enter in different major and minor keys, the CS, naturally, will be adapted to those keys. Furthermore, episodic material preceding such entries may run into the S and CS in a way that compels a modification of the beginning of the S, A and/or countersubject. Compare the CS of Invention I, no. 15 (shown in Fig. 9-11a), with its re-entry in m. 5 (last beat), 12, 14, 18 and the last beat of m. 19.

Figure 9-11a

I, no. 15

248

The countersubject should have some features that offer a distinct contrast to the subject. Repetition of a motive from the S may be a unifying element, but it reduces by that much the contribution of new material for episodic use. Observe the differences between A and CS in Fig. 9-11a in regard to the rhythm, and the skips in the S against generally stepwise motion in the CS. Uniform rhythm in one against varied rhythm in the other is often encountered, as well as differences in the high and low point of each. The CS may be sequential whether the S is sequential or not. Contrary motion, perhaps in part, and the entrance of the CS after the A beginning, as in Fig. 9-11b, serve to establish the individuality of the CS. Examine the changes at the end of this CS in Fugue no. 10, W.T.C. I, and m. 11, 13, 20, 22, 30, 32 and 39, which are exclusive of those in which the CS is used in episodes.

Figure 9-11b

The CS in these measures appears in both upper and lower voices. It is, therefore, necessary to write it in double counterpoint at the octave. This is fairly simple. Avoid a fifth between voices, if possible, because it becomes a fourth when S and CS are interchanged. The range of the CS is also no problem in two-part writing. When S and CS are more than an octave apart at any point, or when the range of the CS exceeds an octave, follow the instruction on double counterpoint (p. 222).

The point where the CS begins and ends may be unclear in some inventions and fugues, when the S sweeps onward into the CS or through a codetta without a perceptible dividing point. The CS may also be shorter than the A. Compare the first with later entries of the CS to determine its actual span. The CS should end on a chord tone.

Exercise 9a.   Write countersubjects to the answers of Exs. 7a and b.

Exercise 9b.   Write countersubjects after the codettas of Exs. 8a and b. These are delayed entries of the CS.

Second Entry of A or S

The two-part fugal invention may move either from its S and A directly to an episode, to re-entry of its A and countersubject with interchanged parts in the dominant or, less often, to re-entry of the S in the lower voice but at a different octave than the initial entry. Let us consider these alternatives.

The choice depends on the length or brevity of the subject and of section 1, on the number of sections planned and on the over-all key scheme. A long S——A with CS and short episode is sufficient for a relatively short first section. Since the A is in the dominant key, choose a different key for the cadence—preferably the relative key. A cadence in the dominant key is possible with a short S (and short A in the dominant) and a long episode, as in I, no. 10, making a long first section. Long episodes allow enough room for digressions to other keys before reaching a cadence in the dominant. It is generally better to lead major fugal inventions to the relative minor, and minor fugal inventions—as in I, no. 15—to the relative major. A two-section invention will have a different key scheme than one with three sections.

Entries that are not in the original key or cadence key may alternate in a long first section; these are single entries. Any succession of S and A in a related key, or S alone after a distinct cadence, is an indication that this entry or entries begins a new section. (See Fugue no. 10, W.T.C. I, m. 11–14. The first section, m. 1–10, is patterned on the first alternative.)

The second alternative: S——A with CS——CS with A (interchanged parts)——episode to cadence, is the plan of I, no. 15, m. 1–11. Observe the codetta, m. 4, last beat through the next half measure, separating the first and second answers. The strong cadence, m. 5, before the second A is unusual. The pattern of the second alternative works best with a short S.

With regard to the third alternative: S——A with CS——S with CS——episode, an A in the dominant key of a major invention makes it easy to return to the re-entry of the S in the tonic key. Returning to the S in the tonic minor from an A in the dominant minor is less simple. A modulatory measure or less of codetta, as in m. 3, Fig. 9-12, may be necessary. The whole first section is shown. Despite some characteristics limiting its complete usefulness as a model, this fugal invention has a serviceable plan.

The unpromising S is accompanied by an auxiliary bass. The S ending is slightly overlapped by the A. The tonal A in

250

Figure 9-12

dominant minor is accompanied by the first of two alternating countersubjects. The S re-enters in the lower part and in the original key. Brief episodes separate further entries. Observe the free treatment of the S and the first CS shifted in the measure, in the last measure and a half.

Exercise 10a. Write the first section of a fugal invention according to the first alternative described above. In most respects Fugue no. 10, W.T.C. I, may serve as your model. Excepting its lack of an auxiliary bass, it is similar to a fugal invention. The S modulates and the last note of the A makes it a tonal A.

Exercise 10b. Write a first section according to the second alternative. Use Invention I, no. 15 as your model.

Exercise 10c. Write another first section, according to the third alternative. Use the general scheme of Fig. 10-12, with or without additional imitations. (See p. 282.) Employ a better S and CS.

Bear in mind that any material from the S, CS or codetta is available as episodic material.

Composing the rest of the fugal invention is a matter of an initial decision concerning the whole plan, the number and length of sections and the bearing of S length on the number of entries. A short first section should have at least two additional sections. A second section is sufficient if section 1 is long. Invention I, no. 15 has two sections. The over-all scheme of section 2 in this invention is: a S entry in the lower part and in the key of the cadence. It is answered at the fifth above; this real A is followed by an episode leading to the S entry in the original key, in the lower voice and imitated an octave higher. Note the motive of broken thirds, imitated in the lower voice, to close the invention.

Fugue no. 10, W.T.C. I, has four sections: m. 1–10; 11–19; 20–29, and 29 to the end. Observe the important role of the CS in episodes and the frequent use of canonic sequences. The measure in octaves before the beginning of section 3 is an unusual and masterly stroke.

Exercise 11a. Analyze Fugue no. 10, W.T.C. I, in detail; *i.e.*, S and CS entries, modulations, episodic material, devices, etc.

Exercise 11b. Complete at least one of the fugal inventions started in Ex. 10.

The Double Invention

The distinguishing characteristic of the double invention, and of one type of double fugue, is an initial announcement of *two concurrent* and *equally important themes* which appear jointly at each subsequent entry. These are double subjects in the double fugue. The second entry in the double invention is *at the octave*, with the themes interchanged. Octave imitation is the main factor differentiating the double invention and double fugue. The double subject, similarly with parts interchanged, is answered at the fifth in the double fugue. Three of the two-part inventions are double inventions: nos. 6, 9 and 11. (See also Prelude no. 20, W.T.C. II.) Inventions no. 5 and 12 are double fugues.

Since the double invention and double fugue have much in common, we will draw on all the above-mentioned compositions for examples. It may be of interest to know that a longer and more involved type of double fugue starts with a single S that is fugally developed. This reaches a second S with a different CS, which is also fugally treated. Both subjects are then combined in the rest of the work.

The Double Theme

The first essential is to create two themes in good counterpoint that work well in double counterpoint at the octave. Each theme should have the features of a good theme. The lower theme, however, may be quite simple in a texture of three or more voices. Examine the chromatically descending second theme in the first two measures of the three-part invention no. 9. This invention is a double fugue. The dual themes are double subjects; the imitations in m. 3–4, upper and middle voices, are answers at the fifth.

The theme appearing first in the upper voice will be identified as theme A, here and when it appears later in the lower voice. Theme B is in the lower voice at the initial entry. It is important to recognize the difference between theme B and an auxiliary bass. The latter is nonthematic and has no function other than harmonic support for the first entry.

An examination of double themes and double subjects should illumine the process of setting off one against the other. In no. 5: notice the sequences in subject A, its generally upward direction, its climax and varied rhythm, in contrast to the uniform rhythm of subject B, its undulating line gravitating downward and its delayed beginning in the middle of measure 1. In no. 6: the scalewise themes move in contrary direction; in addition, theme A is syncopated. In no. 9: observe the difference in profile and rhythm, the alternation of sixteenths against eighths from voice to voice and the different terminal points; theme A ends in m. 5; theme B ends in m. 4. In no. 11: the themes are two measures long. Theme A, in uniform rhythm, contrasts with the diversified rhythm of theme B. Bach seizes on the five-note scale line in theme A, m. 1, beat 3, extending it and running it in sequence. The last two beats of m. 2 consists of the motive of beat 2, m. 1, inverted. Note the chromatically downward course of theme B and the syncopated ending. In no. 12: the subjects are a measure and a half long. Subject B, first in a uniform rhythm of sixteenths and then in eighths, has a sequential line. Theme A is atypical, consisting of the repeated notes, the long trill and a half-measure tail.

Exercise 12a. Play each of the themes and subjects described above, separately and together.

Exercise 12b. Write five double themes in different major and minor keys. End one pair on I of the tonic key. Use a long dominant with another pair, as in no. 9, m. 3; avoid the I$_4^6$ telescoped ending and beginning of the interchanged voices in the next measure. Test each pair of themes by interchanging the voices.

The Double Invention, Section 1

Following the initial entry of the dual theme, section 1 of each double invention is outlined below. Examine each one, with particular attention to the way the second entry is approached, the episodic content, the harmony and the modulations. In no. 6: one measure of codetta (m. 4) is used to maintain the phrase structure of this invention. The codetta also skirts a beginning on a unison when the themes are interchanged. The episode, starting in m. 9, carries the section to a cadence on I of the dominant key (m. 18). A three-measure codetta closes the section.

254

In no. 9: the themes are interchanged (m. 5), with the previously noted alteration at the beginning of theme B. The scale in the preceding half measure leads to theme A. Note the different added part (m. 8) before the episode starts in the next measure. Most of theme A and all of theme B (altered to fit modulations to c and g) are used in this episode, which cadences in the dominant minor (m. 17).

In no. 11: since theme B initially did not enter until almost a half measure after theme A, the second entry of theme A is accompanied by a codetta added to its initial entry. The parts could have been simply interchanged here. Bach ingeniously shifts theme B forward another half measure, so that now it is almost a whole measure behind theme A, then inverts and abbreviates it. Two measures of modulatory episode (m. 5–6) precede a third entry of the themes in d (m. 7–8). The episode that follows brings the section to a cadence in that key. Especially noteworthy is the extension of the syncopated motive to the climax of the section (m. 9), with the lower part in m. 9–10 extracted from beat 2 of theme A.

Since the themes are already contrasted, the episodes consist, as a rule, of coupled segments of both themes. Observe this in no. 12, m. 5–6, and in the other inventions. Note the antiphonal passage in no. 12, m. 7–8. Prelude no. 20, W.T.C. II, is an unusually interesting double invention in two sections. It demonstrates, among other things, Bach's ability to imply rich harmony merely with two voices. The single-measure double theme, repeated with interchanged voices in m. 2, reappears after a measure of interlude, twice at the fifth. Two- and three-measure episodes intervene between further entries. Section 1 closes at the double bar in dominant harmony of the original key.

Exercise 13. Write the first section of a double invention patterned after section 1 of either no. 9 or no. 11.

The Double Invention, Section 2

The second section leads off with theme A in the lower voice and in the new key. Theme B accompanies it in the upper voice. This beginning is used in all of the double inventions, with the exception of no. 11. It is also used in the double fugues of Inventions nos. 5 and 12. The themes are interchanged in Prelude no. 20, W.T.C. II, but both themes are inverted. Some adjustment is usually necessary at the cadence, where the end of section 1 and the beginning of section 2 are telescoped. Two beats in a free part take up the slack before theme B starts in m. 12, no. 5; the first note of theme A must be changed in no. 9, m. 17; the first two notes of theme B (f♯ minor) must be changed in no. 12, m. 9. (Observe the change in the beginning of theme A in this measure.)

The length of the second section depends largely on the length of the double theme, the number of interchanged entries and the nature of the episodes. Section 2 of no. 5 runs from m. 12 to m. 27. The episode following second entries in f minor is made up of one-measure sequences (m. 20–22); segments of both themes are interchanged in m. 25–26, cadencing in the original key. Section 2 of no. 6 extends from the double bar to m. 42. After two entries in the dominant key, the episode moves through several keys before concluding in the relative minor of the dominant key. Its material is drawn mainly from the codetta. A single entry of the double theme of no. 9, m. 17, is followed by an episode in which m. 23–24 is an interchange of the preceding two measures. Sequences carry the episode to a cadence in the original key.

Section 2 of no. 11 opens with two measures of episode. Part of theme A (its beginning changed because of the cadence in m. 11) is imitated in m. 12. Both themes then enter in the subdominant key, with parts interchanged from m. 3–4. Theme A alone is now imitated at the octave (m. 15). The upper part is free to bring the section to its cadence. Prelude no. 20, W.T.C. II, is in two sections. Both themes are inverted and interchanged after the double bar. Two- and three-measure units of episode alternate with the double theme in contrary and direct motion, leading to the final entry in the original key, one measure before the close.

Exercise 14. Write the second section of the double invertion begun in Ex. 13.

The Double Invention, Section 3

This section is generally brief. In no. 9: one entry of the long double theme and an added measure brings the section to a close. The last entry must be in the original key. Observe the different beginning of theme B in m. 29. Bach could have simply written it as in m. 1–2. Looking back to the eighth note skips that start in the lower part of m. 25 will reveal the reason for the change.

In no. 11: starting in the middle of m. 16, the section opens

256

with two measures of episode, based on a long section of theme A and a sequence of it. The upper part is free. Compare it with the upper part in m. 12. The episode is followed by the double theme, shifted in the measure (m. 18). The extension of the syncopated motive is taken from m. 9 and set in the original key. Employing material previously used in a different key serves to unify the work. Observe the extension of theme A with brief sequences (m. 20–21) and the scale line rising to a climax. The last two beats of m. 21, an inversion of the beginning of theme A, l.v., is imitated in the upper voice. Examine the consummate craftsmanship with which these last four measures are brought to an effective close.

Exercise 15a.   Analyze the third sections of nos. 5 and 6.

Exercise 15b.   Complete the double invention started in Ex. 13.

Exercise 16.   Write a double fugue modelled on Invention I, no. 5.

10

Three-part Counterpoint; Three-part Canons, Inventions and Fugues; Tonal Answers; The Countersubject; The Interlude; The Exposition

Three-part Counterpoint

The literature of eighteenth century polyphonic music in three parts is far more extensive than that in two parts because imitations and episodic material can be distributed in a more interesting manner in the fuller texture. The implied harmony becomes more explicit, lines and rhythm can be more diversified, climaxes and trenchant devices like stretto and pedal point are more effectively developed. The texture also fluctuates in density as one or another voice drops out momentarily and returns.

Imitative and partly imitative compositions in two voices with continuo were written by such early Baroque composers as Merulo, Grandi, Frescobaldi and other predecessors of Bach. The bass, functioning as mere support in the early trio sonata, gradually gained a measure of parity with the upper voices. Bach's trio sonatas for organ, his three-part fugues and inventions, masterpieces of three-part imitative writing, are noteworthy for thematic diversity, melodic freedom, balanced distribution of rhythmic and melodic interest between voices and ingenious use of various devices.

Although Bach's contrapuntal lines move along a well directed harmonic course, linear movement transcends conventional rules of doubling, voice spacing, resolution of tendency tones and, on occasion, normal harmonic progression.

Doubling and Voice Spacing

Our first step in three-part writing is based on a triadic framework. While complete triads are now available, few contrapuntal passages, reduced to a harmonic framework, display a progression of complete triads in the normal voice leading and spacing of Fig. 10-1a. Free melodic movement more often

Figure 10-1

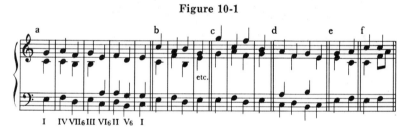

I   IV VII6 III VI6 II V6   I

results in incomplete triads at various points, with consequent tone omission and doubling, as well as wider spacing between chord tones. The triad fifth is omitted in Fig. 10-1b; it is doubled and the roots of two triads are omitted in Fig. 10-1c; the third, including the third of V, is doubled when necessary (Fig. 10-1d; note the unison). At times a doubled third and a fifth represent a triad (Fig. 10-1e). It is unwise to omit the third; when this occurs the third usually appears on the next fraction of the beat (Fig. 10-1f).

Voice spacing like that in Fig. 10-2a is not uncommon. It will seem less capricious when the tones are viewed as sketch points for the free three-voice movement in Fig. 10-2b. References to each voice are hereafter abbreviated as u.v., m.v. (middle voice) and l.v. Note that the m.v. in Fig. 10-2a may be placed on either staff.

Figure 10-2

In the interest of good resonance it is preferable to keep the m.v. closer to the u.v. than to the l.v., unless that voice runs relatively high, *i.e.*, in a range from E below, to G above, middle C. Avoid a low m.v. coupled with a low l.v. Three-part counterpoint written for three instruments or for the organ permits wider spacing between voices than that written for the piano, where the normal octave span of the hands must be taken into account. The m.v., which may be more than an octave from either of the outer parts, should not be more than an octave—or a ninth at most—from *both* of these parts *at the same point*. Bach at times leaps an octave or a seventh in one of the parts to avoid impractical spacing. While any line may cover a range of approximately two and a half octaves in the course of its entire length, extreme high and low points should seldom be used, and then only when melodically justified by sequences, climaxes, etc. Examine the *Three-Part Inventions* for the highest and lowest note reached by each voice. The best practice is to confine the voices to an area central between these extreme points but to avoid hovering around them.

Voice crossing over an adjacent line, which is sometimes necessary, should not be prolonged—to avoid confusion of voices. The m.v. rarely falls below the l.v. A departure from this general practice may be seen in Inventions II, no. 10, m. 16–17.

Several factors in Fig. 10-3a, an excerpt from a simple three-part invention, are relevant to the exercises that follow. Observe the imitations of the scalewise motive, slurred in this example. Note the parallel motion in thirds in m. 2 and 3 and the contrary motion at #3. Here an exchange of the same tones (A–C in contrary motion, C–A) is filled with a passing tone. Note also the skips of a third in contrary motion in chord tones of V⁷, #1, and V⁷ofIV, #2, similarly filled with a passing tone. Two adjacent parts may join momentarily on a unison, as in m. 2. The rest in m. 1 sets off the entry of the m.v., eliminating a unison. Observe the harmonic rhythm and the dominant harmony across the bar-line. Notice rhythmic differences between parts and the long-held notes in the u.v. which as tied notes become suspensions. Study the harmonic framework of the passage (Fig. 10-3b).

Figure 10-3a–b

A brief scalewise motive in direct and contrary imitation (Fig. 10-3c, #1) provides the motivic material for the passage. The u.v. and m.v. are antiphonal. Note the parallel sixths followed by parallel thirds (tenths) at #2; the chromatic change at #3 (D♯–D natural) anticipates the modulation to f♯; the suspension at #4 forms a seventh chord. Examine the harmonic framework of the passage (Fig. 10-3d).

Parallel motion in thirds and sixths between any pair of voices may be freely used if not carried too far. The passage in Fig. 10-4 is based on a prolonged V triad. The nonharmonic tones in the m.v. and l.v. are auxiliaries and passing tones. The

Figure 10-3c–d

E: V⁷ f♯:IV⁷V⁷ I IV⁷—— V⁷ I

m.v. runs in parallel thirds with the moving line of the l.v. Although Bach runs two lines in parallel motion for several
measures on occasion, there is a resulting loss of melodic independence. Examine Inventions II, no. 7, m. 3–6. The u.v. and
m.v. run in parallel thirds and, after a brief interruption, in
parallel sixths. This is in accord with the slow expressive
character of this invention. The line and rhythm of the l.v.
offsets a slavish duplication of one voice by another in parallel
motion. We will discover subtle ways of handling these parallels later. Note that each voice in Fig. 10-4 has a different
uniform rhythm.

Figure 10-4

G: V⁷

Triadic Framework in Three-part Counterpoint

The following exercises are designed to develop facility in
three-part writing by progressive steps and with specific
means. The initial harmonic framework consists of triads in
root position and in first inversion. A passing seventh may be

added to V, as indicated in Fig. 10-5a. Any good nonsequential progression, such as those in Ex. 1, Ch. 2, may serve as the framework. Similar in purpose to the guidelines in a sketch for a painting, the upper tones of this framework are tentative. Tones of the u.v. and m.v. may be exchanged if required by linear development, or one of them may double the tone of the l.v. The l.v. is least subject to change at present. It may be desirable to substitute a chord of similar function; *e.g.*, II_6 for IV, VII_6 for V, to produce a better result.

The three-part harmony of Fig. 10-5a is elaborated in two of the parts with single-beat figures in a basic rhythm of sixteenths (Fig. 10-5b). Any two voices may be so developed; a start could have been made with the outer voices or with the middle and lower voice. (Review the various examples shown in Figs. 2-6b, 2-8a, 2-16a, 2-19, 2-21b, 2-22a and b.) The figure may start after a brief rest, as in Fig. 10-5c. Chord tones, for the present, remain on the beat. Tones that follow may be any type of unaccented nonharmonic tone (passing, auxiliary or changing tones; an échappée, a turn, an unaccented appoggiatura) or another chord tone. Accented nonharmonic tones may be used on the half beat. The same figure may be used throughout, or it may alternate with or be succeeded by a different figure. The second voice may imitate the figure, imitate it in inversion or employ a different figure. Common tone ties may be used, but not suspensions as yet. It may be necessary to tie a shorter note to a longer one, as in Fig. 10-3a, m. 6–7.

Figure 10-5a–c

The third voice is then elaborated. This voice may be relatively simple, with passing tones between chord tones, as in Fig. 10-6. It may include free imitation of the figure (Fig. 10-5d) or run in uniform rhythm (Fig. 10-5e). Bear in mind that it should be possible, at every point, for one hand or the other to play two of the lines. It is generally unwise to run all three parts in sixteenths for more than a beat or a beat and a half.

Figure 10-5d–e

Improving each line is the next step. An added note where the rhythm bogs down or a note changed or eliminated here and there may be sufficient. The note C at #1 (Fig. 10-5e) eliminates parallel fifths; the F♯ at #2 forms an incidental V⁷ofV. Passages written in these early exercises are non-modulatory. Figures and figure-groups, rather than motives related to themes, constitute the melodic material. The passages take on the character of invention and fugal episodes when related to themes or subjects and when secondary dominants and modulation is used later. The simple model, Fig. 10-5, is based on Fig. 10-6, which demonstrates Bach's manner of employing similar motives in an episode. Note the pattern in the lower voice. It should be understood that all exercises in passage writing refer to three-part counterpoint.

Exercise 1a. Write several passages in different major and minor keys, observing the instructions and procedure presented above. Use a triadic framework.

Figure 10-6

Fugue in a minor

Exercise 1b. Write several passages in major and minor in $\frac{6}{8}$, in a basic rhythm of eighths.

Exercise 1c. Use two-beat figure-groups like those in Fig. 2-19b, c and d in similar passages. Repeat the process with single-measure units in $\frac{3}{8}$.

While a change of chord on each beat is often applicable to brief imitative figures, there are numerous instances in which it is preferable to prolong a chord for a measure or more, particularly where any voice carries a broader melodic line (as in Fig. 10-7c). Variety in harmonic rhythm is also necessary to offset regular one-beat chord changes. A single note altered or added, as in IV–II–II⁷, produces a harmonic area of similar function. The tonic triad is extended for a measure in Fig. 10-7c; the preliminary sketches for this measure are shown in Fig. 10-7a and b. Incidental chords may be formed by nonharmonic tones (starred in Fig. 10-7c; an échappée and passing tone form V⁷ with the note of the l.v.).

Figure 10-7

Exercise 2a. The motive shown in the u.v. of Fig. 10-7d is used consistently in section 2 of II, no. 7, starting in m. 14. Note that V⁷ governs the whole measure. Analyze this episode, m. 18–24, noting the harmonic changes produced by nonharmonic tones in the other voices and changes in the motive as the passage moves from b to D.

Exercise 2b. Write a passage in major and another in minor in varied harmonic rhythm that includes extended triads. At least one of these triads should be carried across the bar-line. Maintain some consistency in the design of each part.

We learned in Ch. 2 that a series of triads in first inversion may move scalewise up or down, as in Fig. 10-8a. Parallel motion here in thirds, in sixths and in uniform rhythm deprives the lines of independence while producing a harmonic rather than a contrapuntal effect, despite the stretto indicated by brackets. Parallel fifths result from another arrangement (Fig. 10-8b). It is generally better to move one voice in contrary motion or by skip, as in Fig. 10-8c, the framework for Fig. 10-8d.

Figure 10-8a–c

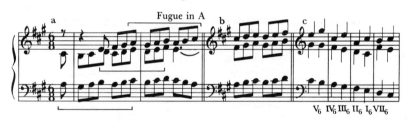

The simplest way of evolving a coherent passage like Fig. 10-8d is to develop every voice in a framework that has a regular pattern. The upper and lower voices here lend themselves to sequences, imitations of a brief figure or rapidly mov-

Figure 10-8d

ing lines in uniform rhythm. A simple motive, borrowed from W.T.C. II, Fugue no. 1, is used in free imitation in Fig. 10-8d. Observe how Bach employs it in modulating (m. 13–22 of this fugue).

Exercise 3a. Write a u.v. in running sixteenths, employing the framework of Fig. 10-8c. Develop the other voices.

Exercise 3b. Write a passage in a different key, using the same progressions in $\frac{6}{8}$, in a basic rhythm of eighths.

Exercise 3c. Write a m.v. to Figs. 3-12b and c. Drop the l.v. an octave if necessary.

The patterned movement of chord tones in harmonic sequences makes it relatively easy to spin melodic sequences in all three voices. While three-part sequences are common in episodes, the texture is often reduced to two voices prior to a S entry which restores three-voice texture. Episodic sequences, usually moving toward a new key, may be built on triads, seventh chords or both in alternation, or on secondary dominants, any of which may serve as pivot chords (Fig. 10-9).

Figure 10-9

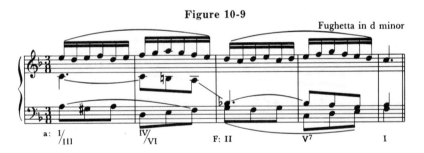

Fughetta in d minor

Examine the development of Fig. 10-10b from the triad sequences of Fig. 10-10a. Minor changes in these sequences convert triads to seventh or to secondary dominant chords. There may be some interplay between two voices in direct or inverted imitation, as in Fig. 10-10c. The rest in the u.v. replaces the implied chord tone. A busy background like the l.v. is not necessarily the most essential line in fugal episodes.

Exercise 4a. Write a sequential passage based on the progressions of Fig. 10-10a, in a key other than C. Do not try to make all three lines equal in interest. The best procedure

268

Figure 10-10

is to develop one salient line which may or may not be most active in rhythm. Add the other lines in contrasting rhythm and line. Write that voice last which is least active rhythmically.

Exercise 4b. Write several sequential passages based on any of the progressions in Ch. 2, Exs. 6, 7, 8, 14 and 15.

Exercise 4c. Add a m.v. to Fig. 3-11d, lowering its lower voice an octave.

Seventh Chords in Three-part Counterpoint

The closest approach to a complete seventh chord in three-part counterpoint is one that omits the fifth in V^7, in secondary sevenths and in secondary dominants (Fig. 10-11a). The essential chord-third is perforce omitted in second inversions, making a secondary dominant indistinguishable from a secondary seventh (Fig. 10-11b). It is therefore necessary to fill in the third immediately. The third is the least essential tone in

Figure 10-11

VII⁷; and the fifth is unessential in the VII⁷ form of secondary dominants (Fig. 10-11c). Doubling in any seventh chord reduces it to the barest essentials, a doubled root and a seventh (Fig. 10-11d). It is inadvisable to double any tone of VII⁷ or of that form of secondary dominant.

Exercise 5a. Using different major and minor keys for each unit of Fig. 4-11b, c and d, extend each unit with similar figures or figure-groups in two parts for at least two measures. Base these extensions largely on progressions of V⁷: V⁷–I (with inversions), V⁷–VI, V⁷–IV₆–V⁶₅, V⁷–II (or II⁷)–V⁷. Use chord tones on the beat. Then take the l.v. of each extended unit down an octave and add a m.v.

The material of the preceding exercise may be adapted, with slight alterations, to include secondary dominants or a modulation (starred in Fig. 10-12).

Figure 10-12

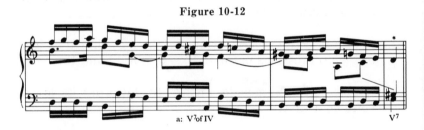

a: V⁷of IV   V⁷

Exercise 5b. Start with several units of the preceding exercise with the added voice. Continue with similar material, employing different secondary dominant-triad harmony in each unit. Write these units in different keys.

Exercise 5c. Add a m.v. to Figs. 5-8c and 5-9b.

Exercise 5d. Write several passages based on the progressions in Exs. 3 and 7, Ch. 5.

Any fifth-fall progression of triads or seventh chords may easily be converted to a series of chain dominants which remain in the key or modulate, as in Fig. 10-13a. Compare Fig. 10-10b with Fig. 10-13a.

Exercise 5e. Write sequential passages based on Figs. 5-4a, 5-5a and 5-6c.

270

Figure 10-13a

Secondary seventh chords in fifth-fall progressions, or triads alternating with secondary sevenths, are frequently the bases for passages in melodic sequences. See Fig. 6-11d, noting the suspension effect of the tied seventh. Observe also how the third of a triad or seventh chord, repeated or tied, becomes the seventh of the next chord in fifth-fall progressions. These are adapted to imitation as well (Fig. 10-13b). Notice the exchange of upper parts and the sequence in the l.v.

Figure 10-13b

The following three-part exercises are based on four-part progressions illustrated in Ch. 6. Eliminate the *tenor* part of each progression.

Exercise 6a.   Use the progressions of Fig. 6-8a in sequential elaboration of at least two parts, in a basic rhythm of sixteenths.

Exercise 6b.   Transpose Fig. 6-8b to G, developing the upper parts in canonic sequences. Use a basic rhythm of sixteenths; add a coherent l.v.

Exercise 6c.   Transpose Fig. 6-8c to F, then elaborate the l.v. and at least one of the upper voices in a basic rhythm of eighths, in $\frac{6}{8}$. Do this also with Fig. 6-8d, in the key of D.

Exercise 6d.   Develop passages from the imitations based on seventh chords sketched in Fig. 6-16c, d, e and f.

Suspensions in Three-part Counterpoint

Suspensions are exceptionally important in blunting the edges of block harmony, in contributing to rhythmic independence, in evolving the long melodic line, and in providing a tang of discord to the texture. Review the material on suspensions in Chs. 5 and 6.

The following exercises, which require melodic elaboration of three-part harmony, are based on four-part examples in Ch. 5. The bass part will be retained as l.v. Elimination of one of the other voices may alter the chord in a few instances. The interval of suspension is between the l.v. and the suspended note. Resolve the suspension directly, as shown in Fig. 10-14a (an elaboration of Fig. 5-22a), or with a repetition of the suspension, as shown in Fig. 10-14b. The exercises may be written first without suspensions, as in Fig. 10-14c, and then altered, as in the preceding example. Modulation is not employed in Fig. 10-14c.

Figure 10-14

Exercise 7a. Using a basic rhythm of sixteenths, employ simple resolution of suspensions with Fig. 5-22a. Omit the tenor part; write in B♭; establish a clear melodic pattern in at least one voice and some variety in rhythm

272

between voices. Do this in D with Fig. 5-22b, omitting the alto voice from the framework, and in E♭ with Fig. 5-22c, omitting the soprano voice. Use a basic rhythm of eighths. The tenor and alto in the first two measures invite imitative figures.

Exercise 7b. Add a third voice to each unit of Fig. 5-29 and extend it for several measures with a similar figure. Use different major and minor keys.

Suspensions are used with secondary sevenths in Fig. 10-15a and with secondary dominants in Fig. 10-15b and c. The intervals of suspension-resolution in the last alternate between 7–6 and 2–3. The suspension shifts from voice to voice.

Figure 10-15

V⁷ of IV   V⁷ of III   V⁷ of II   V⁷ of V

Exercise 7c. Transpose Fig. 10-15a to A major. Develop the l.v. sequentially in a uniform rhythm of sixteenths. Transpose Fig. 10-15b to E, treating the l.v. in similar fashion. Write brief contrapuntal passages that include suspensions, based on the harmony of Figs. 6-14a, b, c and d (secondary sevenths in minor). Use a different minor key for each one.

Exercise 7d. Add a sequential upper part to Fig. 10-15c in a basic rhythm of eighths. Eliminate the tenor part of Fig.

5-24 and elaborate the progressions of secondary domi-
nant-triads in a basic rhythm of sixteenths.

Auxiliary embellishments of suspensions are starred in Fig.
10-16a. Delayed resolutions are shown in Figs. 10-16b and
c. These correspond to Fig. 6-17, #2 and #10. Review the
material on delayed resolutions of suspensions in that chapter.

Figure 10-16a–c

Exercise 8a. Write several passages in major and minor
similar to those in Fig. 10-16. Include the other types of
delayed resolutions shown in Fig. 6-17.

We mentioned earlier that parts moving in parallel thirds or
sixths were not truly independent and that there were other

274

ways of handling these parallels. Observe how delayed resolutions in Figs. 10-16d and e artfully conceal the parallel motion and diversify the lines. See II, no. 12, m. 27–28. Examine the m.v. and l.v. in m. 42–44 of the W.T.C. II, Fugue no. 15, in which parallel thirds are treated like the sixths in Fig. 10-16d.

Figure 10-16d–e

Note the parallel sixths between the l.v. and m.v. (Fig. 10-17b).

Double suspensions such as those starred in Fig. 10-16f are less frequently encountered. (Also see Fig. 7-9c.)

Figure 10-16f

Exercise 8b. Write a u.v. and m.v. similar to that in Fig. 10-16d; add a l.v. in running sixteenths which differs from the broken chord figure of that example. Interchange the upper voices and write a different l.v.

Two parts are often treated as in Fig. 10-17. A long-held chord tone becomes a suspension when tied. The second part imitates the first in canonic sequences in Fig. 10-17a; each part is individually sequential in Fig. 10-17b; both voices engage in antiphonal dialogue in Fig. 10-17c. Note the rhythmic imitation. At some points the long-held note, when tied, is merely a common tone.

Passages like these are first sketched in three-part harmony with suspensions and resolutions. The chord tones starred in Fig. 10-17a become the anchor points for the added third part.

Figure 10-17

Exercise 8c. Write three passages similar in treatment to each example of Fig. 10-17. Such passages are frequently characteristic of episodes in inventions and fugues.

Exercise 9. Review accented passing, auxiliary and changing tones in Ch. 5, as well as appoggiaturas. Re-examine the illustrations (Figs. 5-10 through 5-21). Then add a third part to several two-part passages from Exs. 12a and b, 13b and 14c, Ch. 5.

Three-part Canonic Writing

Canonic imitation in three-voice texture is employed in various ways: (1) a free third part is added to a two-part canon; (2) two-part canonic sequences are accompanied by a free third voice (this is frequently used in invention and fugal episodes); (3) a fixed melody, such as a chorale tune, is accompanied by a two-part canon; (4) all three parts are used in canonic imitation.

Figure 10-18a

Goldberg Varations, no. 24

Two-part Canon with Added Voice

It is relatively easy to write a two-part canon at the octave with an added voice (Fig. 10-18a). This may be approached in one of two ways: construct the added part as the canon progresses, or write the canon first, then add the third part. The latter process is recommended. The added part, which may be in any voice, can fill in missing chord tones (starred in Fig. 10-18a), double chord tones or supply an unexpected harmony (m. 3). The canonic parts, in such instances, should be analyzed for alternative harmonizations. When the added voice or follower is made the l.v. it determines the harmony to which the other voices must be accommodated. Bear in mind when writing the two canonic parts that fifths, fourths and octaves can be used, since the added part supplies missing chord tones. Avoid the fourth between upper and lowest voice.

The follower may enter after any reasonable time span and at any interval. A longer time span and imitation at the octave occasions the least difficulty.

Some canons are placid in rhythm. An active rhythm should, then, be used in the added part. Use contrasting rhythms in places with long-held notes and at those points where the canonic parts have similar rhythms. The added part may incorporate figures and rhythms from the canon to articulate it with the other parts. The follower imitates the leader by inversion in Fig. 10-18b. Imitation by inversion need not be strict. Review inversion on pp. 105 and 106.

Figure 10-18b–c

Goldberg Varations, no. 12

Von Himmel hoch, Var. 5

Bach takes the chorale tune "From heaven above to earth I come" in two-part canon by inversion and adds a free third part (Fig. 10-18c). These canonic variations are worth close study.

Exercise 10a. Add a free third part to several two-part canons written in Ex. 1, Ch. 8.

Exercise 10b. Add a free third part to the canons at the fifth written in Exs. 3a, b and c, Ch. 8.

Exercise 10c. Write a two-part canon with imitation by inversion, then add a third part. Write the leader; copy it inverted in the follower; counterpoint the follower, then invert that, etc.

Canonic sequences are written between two voices with an added part, as in Fig. 10-19a; or after several measures, with the sequence in the third voice (Fig. 10-19b). Episodes in which this device is used may be extended by transferring the canonic sequences from one pair of voices to another, such as from the u.v. and m.v. to the m.v. and l.v., with a change of key. Review two-part canonic sequences in Ch. 8; re-examine Figs. 8-7 and 8-8.

Figure 10-19

Exercise 11a. Add a free third part to several of the canonic sequences written in Ex. 4, Ch. 8.

Three-part Canon

Principles governing good two-part canon writing apply to the three-part canon; *i.e.*, evolve an interesting leader, maintain rhythmic contrast between voices and harmonic variety. The voices of the three-part canon are called the *leader,* the *first* and *second follower.* The simplest canons are at the unison and octave (Fig. 10-20a), with entries after one or two measures. Octave spacing between entries is easily controlled by bringing one part close to the entry of the next. The leader may start in any voice; the followers may be in successive octaves or in any arrangement in which one follower is an octave above and the other follower an octave below the leader. The imitation need not be strict.

Figure 10-20a

This type of canon is similar to the four-part round-canon, in which the first follower usually enters after a half phrase or a phrase and two additional followers enter after a similar time span. Imitation in many simple rounds is at the unison. The harmony is often an alternation of tonic and dominant, but closely related modulations are not uncommon. Rounds, as seen in the diagram, are perpetual canons.

Leader: Phrase A——— B⌇⌇⌇ C⌇⌇⌇ A———, etc.
1st Follower: A——— B⌇⌇⌇ C⌇⌇⌇ A———, etc.
2nd Follower: A——— B⌇⌇⌇ C⌇⌇⌇ A———, etc.

To write a round, write the leader; add the first follower directly over it; write a third contrapuntal part above both. Try the parts interchangeably.

Followers may enter after any number of beats, after a phrase and at any interval. The problems vary with differences in entry time span and intervals. Followers in Fig. 10-20b enter after a half measure at the fifth successively. Three parts of a four-part canon are shown in this example. The first small note-head indicates the entrance of the fourth part; notes of

that part (in brackets) fill in essential chord tones. Infinite
canons such as this serve our purpose less than entries adapted
to fugal use, *i.e.*, at the fifth by the first follower and at the
octave or fifth by the second follower.

Figure 10-20b

Pleni Sunt Coeli

Exercise 11b.   Write a brief three-part canon in which the
followers imitate the leader at the octave, as in Fig.
10-20a. Review canon endings, p. 192.

Exercise 11c.   Write a short three-part canon in which the
first follower imitates the leader at the fifth and the second follower at the octave.

Three-part Inventions and Fugues

Most three-part inventions, except for their auxiliary basses,
are three-part fugues. It is therefore feasible to examine the
features of both simultaneously, bypassing simple inventions
with octave imitation—like Invention no. 2, Prelude 18, W.T.C.
I, and Prelude 5, W.T.C. II. Unless specified otherwise, all
numbered references are to the Three-part Inventions.

Some fugues of the *Well-Tempered Clavier* are longer than
the inventions and some have longer subjects, but it must not
be assumed that the inventions as a whole are more simply
organized. Invention no. 8, for instance, is more complex than
fugues no. 9, W.T.C. I, and nos. 1 and 15, W.T.C. II. Every
device used in the fugues, with the exception of augmentation,
is employed in one or another invention. Few inventions, unlike
more than half of the three-part fugues, have a countersubject.
Although some fugues are similarly constructed, most inventions are sectionally divided by clear cadences. The character
and resources inherent in its thematic material give each fugue

and invention its unique design. It is therefore meaningless to speak of fugue or invention "form."

The following are recommended for analysis as supplementary to the three-part inventions and fugues: Parts. nos. 3, 4, 5 and 6, the gigues; Part. 4, the *allegro* section of the overture; Part. 6, the fugue in the toccata; P. 19, W.T.C. I; Ps. 15 and 19, W.T.C. II; English Suites nos. 3, 5 and 6, the gigues; the P. of 5; the *allegro* from the P. of 6.

The Exposition

Some degree of uniformity is evident in the way most inventions and fugues begin. The opening segment, in which each voice enters in turn with the subject, is the *exposition*. The second entry, usually at the fifth, is the answer, as we learned earlier. The subject re-enters immediately in the third voice or after an interlude, except in irregular expositions. This re-entry at the octave is also called a subject; an imitation of the answer at the octave is similarly called an answer. While any order of entry is possible, the most common patterns with or without interludes are:

Upper voice:	S				A
Middle voice:		A	or	S	
Lower voice:		S			S

Eight of the *Three-Part Inventions* and all but three of the three-part fugues in the *Well-Tempered Clavier* start with one of these two schemes. We may, then, regard them as the norm and others as less common.

An additional S or A follows the first entries in some instances. Such *redundant* entries are part of the exposition when the S is in the original key and the A is in the dominant. An entry at any other level is simply called an imitation. See the redundant subjects in Inventions no. 1, m. 5; no. 6, m. 6; no. 7, m. 7 and no. 13, m. 21; also see W.T.C. I, Fugue no. 3, m. 10 and no. 7, m. 11.

A group of two or three entries, instead of a single redundant entry, may follow the exposition, immediately or after an episode. These entries, in the original key or leading off with the A in the dominant, form a *counter exposition*. A clear example with three such entries is seen in W.T.C. I, Fugue 9, m. 6–10. This is preceded by an episode. The function of a counter exposition is to keep the first section within the orbit

282

of tonic and dominant keys, as in W.T.C. I, Fugue 15, m. 20–31; here the three entries are by S inversion.

Some expositions are irregular—for example, two simultaneous entries in Invention no. 7, m. 3 and 5; the initial entry of the S, overlapped in stretto by the A, in W.T.C. I, Fugue 19 and W.T.C. II, Fugue 3. While Bach resorted to these unusual patterns for good reason, they are not models for beginners.

The exposition moves on to an episode or to additional imitations at different levels or in different keys. Before we proceed any further let us re-examine some factors previously discussed in connection with the two-part fugal invention.

Some subjects admit a harmonization that includes a secondary dominant-triad progression (Fig. 10-21a).

Figure 10-21a

The subjects of all three-part inventions and of all but four fugues of the three-part fugues do not modulate. Examine these four: W.T.C. I, nos. 7 and 19; W.T.C. II, nos. 15 and 20. The S ends in the dominant in the first example, returning via a codetta to the original key as the A enters. The codetta here is not part of the S, although it appears with the first entries and has an important episodic role. The codetta appears in the exposition in two additional entries but is dropped later. A codetta-like unit appearing consistently with each entry is the tail of the S; it is not a codetta. One, two or three notes linking the end of the S with the CS is not a codetta. The codetta is generally used to modulate to the dominant in preparation for an A entry in that key. If it follows the A, it must be altered to permit the S re-entry in the original key. (See Invention no. 12, m. 4.) Examine the codettas in W.T.C. II, Fugues 12, 15 and 24. Review the material and codetta examples on p. 246. Note the entrance of the A in Fig. 10-21b before the end of the codetta.

Figure 10-21b

The Auxiliary Bass

The auxiliary bass, as explained in Ch. 9, accompanies the first entry of the S, implying one possible harmonization. Observe the difference in harmony in Invention no. 3, m. 1–2, and the harmonization in m. 6 and 7. The auxiliary bass provides the root of I under the last note of each S ending on step 3. Exceptions are: no. 7, the S ends on the third of V, with the root in the auxiliary bass; no. 14, the S ends on step 1, with the chord-third in the auxiliary bass. The chromatic line under the S of no. 9 is not an auxiliary bass; it is the second S of a double fugue.

The auxiliary bass should be simple. It generally continues to the third entry, as in nos. 1, 6, 7, 8 and 10, and usually becomes more active rhythmically as accompaniment to the second entry. It ends with the beginning of the interlude when one is used. (See nos. 4 and 14.) The auxiliary bass runs on into the CS in no. 3, which normally would follow the S in the same voice. In most instances the auxiliary bass does not re-appear later. Exceptions occur in no. 4, from the last half of m. 8 to the first half of m. 10 and in m. 13–14; note the repetition of the auxiliary bass with the A in nos. 12 and 13.

The Tonal Answer

An answer that differs from a *strict* imitation of the S is a tonal A. Changes, however slight or extensive, which convert a real A to a tonal one serve two purposes: (1) They turn a modulating A back to the original key. Such changes usually occur in the last part of the tonal A. (2) They keep the A beginning in the original key for at least a note or two, before the A veers over to the dominant key. While only three of ten inventions selected for study have tonal answers, the proportion is much higher in the three-part fugues of *The Well-Tempered Clavier*—18 tonal to 10 real answers.

A tonal A is generally the response to certain types of S—

as, for instance, subjects that modulate. The beginning and ending of a lengthy S modulating to the dominant is shown in Fig. 10-22a. A real A (#2), modulating to a dominant further removed, makes it difficult for the S to re-enter in the original key at this point. A modulatory episode would be required for that purpose. The simple change starred in #3 brings the A back to the original key. Observe that the scalewise S ending is preserved in the A. Successive skips of a third and a seventh conclude the S in Fig. 10-22b. The real A winds up in the dominant of the dominant. It is therefore altered as in #3. Note that the A at the star is changed to an imitation at the fifth below. The skips are preserved and the last four notes of the S, steps 4–3–2–1 of the dominant key, thereby become the same steps in the tonic key. Tonal answers should conform in contour, skips and rhythm to the S insofar as possible. There are fewer answers of this type because relatively few subjects modulate. The S of Fig. 10-22b is followed by a codetta—codettas generally modulate to the dominant. It is interesting to note that this codetta moves from the modulating S back to the original key for the entry of the tonal A. The tonal A, as seen below, brings it back to the original key.

Figure 10-22

Tonal answers of the second type are far more common; *i.e.*, those beginning in the original key. While real and tonal answers are used with nonmodulating subjects, certain specific characteristics of the S beginning, with exceptions noted below, usually determine whether one or the other is used. At this point, and in some later examples, it is sufficient for our purpose to show only the beginnings of S and A. A tonal A is used when the S begins with a skip between steps 1 and 5, as in Figs. 10-23a and b. These same tones, in reverse order, are retained in the tonal A. Step 5 of the S becomes step 1 of the A, and vice versa. Retention of these important tones in the A prolongs the original key for about a beat. Subsequent tones of the A must be in the dominant key; particularly, steps 3 and 6 of the S must be steps 3 and 6 of the dominant key in the A. The exception to this exchange of steps 5 and 1 occurs when the S starts on the beat and ends on the leading tone. Step 1 in the A responding to a beginning on step 5 cannot be used against the leading tone. A real A is used. An auxiliary embellishing either step is tonally reproduced in the A (Fig. 10-23b).

Figure 10-23a–b

Since the second purpose of a tonal A is to retain the original key at the beginning of the A, and since tones of the dominant key, except its leading tone, are also tonic key tones, the point of modulation is often unclear. This is particularly true when there is no leading tone in the S or, as in Fig. 10-23c, where the original leading tone receives a tonal response. The notes bracketed in this A, as well as the counterpoint, retain the tonic key much longer than with most tonal answers. Where there is no leading tone in the S, it may be necessary to introduce it in the CS or counterpoint to establish the dominant key.

The modulation comes earlier when the S is short, as in Fig. 10-23d. Note that the second response to step 5 (starred) is not step 1 but step 5 of the dominant key.

286

Figure 10-23c–d

A tonal A at the fifth below will keep the exposition in the original key. See Invention no. 1, m. 2, where the modulation to the dominant devolves on the counterpoint to the A. A tonal A is used with a S beginning with skips in the I triad (Fig. 10-24a). Observe that only the first note is changed in the response. The starred notes in Figs. 10-24b and c are tonally altered. (See Fig. 9-10.)

Figure 10-24a–c

While this type of response is generally used with skips in I, there are some exceptions. See the real A in Fugue 15, W.T.C. II and Fugue 10, W.T.C. I, which is a real A except for the last note; also see the "little" Fugue in g minor. Skips in the IV chord, however, receive a real A (Fig. 10-24d), since the response is in the I chord.

Figure 10-24d–e

When step 1 of the S moves scalewise down to step 5 (four steps), the A moving down scalewise from step 5 to 1 cannot

THREE-PART INVENTIONS AND FUGUES 287

reach step 1 in four scale steps. The A may be tonally altered to retain its scalewise beginning in the original key, as in Fig. 10-24e, or a real A is written. Observe that steps 6 and 3 are answered by the same steps in the dominant key. This is the invariable response to insure a modulation to the dominant.

Real answers are used when the S begins in a manner other than that described above. The real A, as we saw in the preceding chapter, is an exact imitation in the dominant key. Review that material. It is clearly impossible to preserve the opening five scale tones of Fig. 10-25a (steps 1–5) with a four-tone tonal A (steps 5 up to 1), as shown in three versions of such an answer (Fig. 10-25b). Tonal responses to steps 1 and 5 do not apply here.

Figure 10-25a–b

A subject starting on step 1 and moving up scalewise in an indirect manner also receives a real A in most cases (Fig. 10-25c). This also applies to subjects with scalewise motives between steps 1 and 5 near the beginning (Fig. 10-25d). An exception is shown in Fig. 10-25e. Bach retains the original key in m. 3, modulates to the dominant (#1), then uses VofII–II (#2) before a S re-entry in the original key.

Figure 10-25c–e

A major S that starts with scale steps 1 up to 6 may receive a real A in steps 5 up to 3 without giving the impression of a modulation (Fig. 10-25a). (See Invention no. 6.) In this circumstance the A must rely on the counterpoint to consummate the modulation.

The subjects in the following exercises are to be written in major and minor. Slight rhythmic modification of the first note of the A is permissible. This also occurs in later entries.

Exercise 12a.   Write tonal answers to the modulating subjects written in Ex. 5b, Ch. 8. The A may begin before the S ends, as in Fugue 20, W.T.C. II.

Exercise 12b.   Write tonal answers to one or two minor subjects that are followed by a modulatory codetta. Bear in mind that the A often starts before the codetta concludes, particularly if the S begins on an up-beat.

Exercise 12c.   Write several one- and two-measure nonmodulating subjects that start with a skip in steps 5–1. Write the tonal answers. Add auxiliary basses to the subjects.

Exercise 12d.   Write several two-measure subjects that start with skips in the I triad. Write the tonal answers.

The Countersubject

Different counterpoints accompany the A and subsequent entries in most three-part inventions. Several inventions and many three-part fugues have a countersubject. Review the material on countersubject in the preceding chapter. There is no problem with the CS to a real A when that CS must also be used with the S re-entry in the original key. The CS is simply transposed to that key. (See Invention no. 3, m. 6–7.) There may be a problem with a CS accompanying a tonal A because the S differs from its tonal A. A slight modification at the beginning of the CS to a nonmodulating S is all that is necessary. Considerable alteration of the CS is required when it is used with the re-entry of a S that originally modulated to the dominant key. The CS must first fit a tonal A that returns to the tonic key, and then fit the S re-entry which starts in that key but modulates to the dominant. The relatively infrequent use of modulating subjects does not warrant more than pointing up the problem. Compare the CS in W.T.C. I, Fugue 18, m. 5–6 (m.v.) with m. 3–4.

The CS undergoes frequent changes to adjust its beginning and ending to a preceding or following episode and to provide a fresh harmonization. Compare the CS in W.T.C. I, Fugue 2, m. 3–4 (m.v.) with m. 7–8, 11–12, 15–16, 20–21 and 26–27. Trace the changes in W.T.C. I, Fugue 7. Bach takes the liberty in W.T.C. II, Fugue 10, of beginning the CS in one voice and completing it in another. (See also Invention no. 3, m. 19.) Subject and CS are occasionally planned in double counterpoint at interchanges greater than an octave. This technique is discussed later. The CS accompanies most, if not all, S entries. There are dubious instances in which the appearance of the CS is sporadic or abbreviated. The delayed arrival of a CS should not be confused with the late entry of a second S in one type of double fugue. In Fugue 18, W.T.C. II, this S appears in m. 61 as a chromatic line which joins the first S in m. 97. At this point it joins the S consistently. Invention no. 13 first has a gable scale-line CS and later a broken chord CS.

Exercise 13a. Write two different countersubjects to each tonal A of Ex. 12. Do not use intervals greater than an octave between S and CS, to avoid difficulties when they are later interchanged in adjacent voices.

The Subject Re-entry

The third voice leads off with a S re-entry which appears at or near the conclusion of the A or after an interlude. It is preferable to locate the S re-entry on the same beat as its initial announcement. In some cases an immediate re-entry is feasible; *i.e.*, with the last note of the A, a note or two later or slightly overlapping the end of the A. In other instances the re-entry must be delayed. This is mainly due to the difference in key between the A and the re-entering S. The ending of a major A in the dominant key may not fit the beginning of the re-entering S in the tonic key.

290

A major S may re-enter immediately if it starts on step 5 and the A ends on step 3 of the dominant key. See W.T.C. I, Fugue 21, m. 9. The adjustment is usually simpler after a rest (Fig. 10-26a). See Invention no. 8, m. 3. An A ending on step 1 of the dominant key forms a fifth with a S starting on step 1. An interlude is frequently used in this situation. See Invention no. 14, m. 3. A major S starting on step 1 cannot re-enter immediately against an A ending on step 3 of the dominant key (Fig. 10-26b). An interlude is generally necessary in minor because it is difficult to return to the tonic minor after an A in the dominant minor.

Figure 10-26

The A in this invention is followed by another A. This merely postpones the interlude; the second A modulates back to the original key. A similar example is Invention no. 10, m. 6.

The Interlude

The function and character of the interlude should be clear from the above. Episodic in appearance, the interlude is transitional. Its main function is to provide a smooth S re-entry in the exposition, particularly when an immediate re-entry is awkward or impossible. It differs from the codetta and episode in location and function. The codetta prepares the way for an A in the dominant; the episode is developmental as it moves between one group of entries and another. An interlude is used in some instances even where a direct entry is feasible. (See

W.T.C. I, Fugue 16, m. 4.) The interlude then serves to prolong two-part texture and to break up consecutive entries. A redundant S or A may be preceded by an interlude. Interludes are generally one or two measures long. They are used in more than half of the W.T.C. three-part fugues. Examine the interludes in Invention no. 4, m. 3; no. 13, m. 9–12; also those in the following fugues: W.T.C. I, nos. 6, 8, 16 and 20; W.T.C. II, nos. 2, 12, 14 and 24.

Free Parts

One or two free parts, depending on whether or not a CS is used, accompany the re-entry of the S in the exposition. With a rhythmically active S the free parts may consist of little more than supplementary chord tones. (See Invention no. 6, m. 6; no. 1, m. 3 and F. 4, W.T.C. II.) The free part should be rhythmically inactive when both S and CS are active, as in Invention no. 3, m. 6. Inconsequential though it may be, the free part is sometimes planned to accompany the S and CS at one or more later points with the parts interchanged, as will be explained later in triple counterpoint. A busy free part may be used with a slow-moving CS (Fig. 10-27a). (See also Invention no. 13, m. 13 and F. 3, m. 5, W.T.C. I.)

Figure 10-27a

It is sometimes preferable to restrain the rhythmic activity of the parts in the exposition, as in Inventions nos. 7 and 13. In the absence of a CS the rhythmic activity is often divided between the free contrapuntal parts in rhythmic imitation. (See Fs. 11 and 12, W.T.C. II.) In any case, all three parts should not be rhythmically active at the same time. Examine the parts accompanying the S re-entry in F. no. 9, W.T.C. I.

The free parts may bear no direct relevance to thematic material. At times a free part will pick up a thematic motive. Compare the bracketed unit in Fig. 10-27b with that part of the S enclosed in a broken bracket.

Figure 10-27b

Exercise 13b. Analyze the regular expositions of the following inventions from the beginning to the measures indicated. In some, redundant subjects and/or answers follow the first entries: Invention no. 3, to m. 8; no. 4, to m. 5; no. 8, to m. 4; no. 12, to m. 9; no. 13, to m. 16; no. 14, to m. 5.

Exercise 13c. Using at least one major and one minor S and the tonal answers of Ex. 12, complete the invention expositions, employing the auxiliary bass. Include codettas and interludes if necessary. Harmonize the first note of the S re-entry with dominant harmony if the S begins on step 5 in the l.v.; this will avoid a six-four chord. Bear in mind that the CS accompanying the reentry should not be in the same voice in which it previously appeared.

Exercise 13d. Analyze the expositions of the following three-part fugues: W.T.C. I, no. 2, to m. 9; no. 3, to m. 7; no. 6, to m. 8; no. 7, to m. 8; no. 13, to m. 7; W.T.C. II, no. 1, to m. 13; no. 12, to m. 16; no. 19, to the middle of m. 8; no. 24, to m. 21.

Exercise 13e. Complete at least two three-part fugue expositions, using the subjects and countersubjects written in Ex. 12.

The rest of the invention or fugue is developed from the thematic material stated in the exposition. Some of these compositions pursue a simple, if somewhat irregular, alternation of S entries with episodes. Others, more intricately organized, present the S in a progressively more interesting light, in free imitation, inversion, augmentation or stretto. Subject and CS appear in double counterpoint and, with an added part, in triple counterpoint. The dominant pedal point sets the stage for an impressive S entry. Various resources are tapped for the episodes. These devices are described in the next chapter. An understanding of their nature and use is essential in completing the inventions and fugues started in Ex. 13.

11

Triple Counterpoint; Three-part Episodes; The Pedal Point; Stretto, Augmentation, Diminution; Double Counterpoint at the Twelfth; Three-part Fugues

Triple Counterpoint

We previously interchanged two parts in a process called double counterpoint. Three parts are in *triple counterpoint* when two or three parts are shifted to voices different from those in which the parts first appeared. The original material may be parts in an episode or in an exposition. For instance, the S re-entry in the exposition (Fig. 11-1a) is in the l.v.; the

CS is in the m.v. and the free part is in the u.v. (#5 in the table below). These parts are interchanged in Fig. 11-1b, as in #3 of the table, which lists each way in which three parts may be interchanged.

#1	#2	#3	#4	#5	#6
S	S	CS	CS	Fr. Pt.	Fr. Pt.
CS	Fr. Pt.	S	Fr. Pt.	CS	S
Fr. Pt.	CS	Fr. Pt.	S	S	CS

All six arrangements rarely appear in the same fugue. The number of interchanges depends on the length of the composition and on the inclusion or exclusion of other devices.

Bach uses arrangement #6 in m. 19–20 of this fugue; #2 is used in m. 24–26; as well as #3 (Fig. 11-1b) in m. 27–28 and #5 in m. 46–47. Note the slight changes at the starred notes in Fig. 11-1b. Bach makes considerable changes in the free part in m. 10–11, using the interchange of #1. See also the changes in m. 44–45, using the arrangement of #3, and m. 52–53, interchanged as in #1 above.

Such slight changes, particularly at the beginning and ending, are permissible in triple counterpoint to obtain a satisfactory result. The interchange usually differs in key from the key in which the parts appeared originally and from the keys of subsequent interchanges.

Figure 11-1a–b

Writing parts that are to be used later in triple counterpoint is not as difficult as it may seem. Two parts, the S and CS, are already in double counterpoint at the octave, since they

must be used—one above and below the other—in further
entries. The free part, usually formed from a simple motive,
as in W.T.C. I, Fugue 21, or from a few chord tones, is added
in a way that fits above, below or between the S and CS. It
is merely necessary to test the free part an octave above and
below these two parts. Not all arrangements work out well. A
part in the l.v. forming parallel first inversions with the other
parts at any point must remain in that voice, lest parallel six-
fours or parallel fifths result in the interchange. The other
parts can be interchanged. Shifting the l.v. is possible if there
are not more than two or three consecutive first inversions and
if the parts can be modified without too much distortion.

Examine the triple counterpoint in the following: F. 21,
W.T.C. I, m. 9–13, m. 13–17, m. 22–26, m. 37–41; in P. 19,
W.T.C. I, compare the first two and a half measures with m. 4
through half of m. 6, m. 9 (with up-beat)–10, and m. 6–5
before the close; in F. 2, W.T.C. I, compare m. 17–18 with
m. 19 in the same episode; in F. 12, W.T.C. I, compare m. 7–10
with m. 13–16, 19–22 and 28–30.

Parts in an episode that are sufficiently dissimilar may be
interchanged later in triple counterpoint. Compare the episodes in Invention no. 10, m. 9–10 with m. 17–19; Invention
no. 12, m. 5 to the middle of m. 6, interchanged in m. 24 to the
middle of m. 25. Compare the episode parts marked A, B and
C in Fig. 11-1c with the interchange in Fig. 11-1d, noting the
modifications.

Figure 11-1c–d

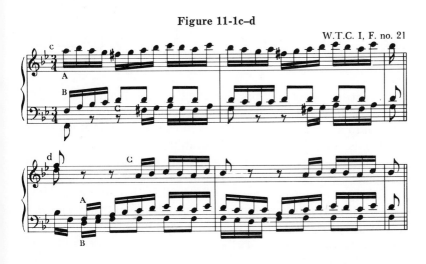

Exercise 1.   Interchange the parts of one of your expositions
    from Ex. 13c and e, Ch. 10, revising the free part if

necessary or substituting a different free part. Try this with several of the five other arrangements, then transpose two of them to related keys.

Three-part Episodes

The third voice adds a new dimension to the various types of episode used in two-part inventions and fugues. For instance, a motive such as the one in Fig. 11-2a may be imitated in an additional voice or, while two parts are occupied with antiphonal responses, the third part may proceed with an independent line of sequences, as in Fig. 11-2b.

Figure 11-2a–b

W.T.C. I, F. no. 13, trans.

W.T.C. I. F. no. 7

Constructing effective episodes requires as much craftsmanship and diligence as creating a good exposition. The time devoted to analyzing the examples in the three-part inventions and fugues cited below should be amply rewarding. Mark off the S entries in your scores, then analyze what Bach does in the episodes. What is the source of the material? Which distinctive type of episode, as described below, is employed? How does Bach lead into and out of an episode? What material immediately preceding the episode is woven into it and what material in the episode foreshadows an entry of the S or CS? It should be evident that an episode is not set between entries like a block of concrete between two other blocks. Any strand of material which may have accompanied the preceding entry—*i.e.*, a portion of CS following a S re-entry, the S tail or a codetta—frequently runs on into the episode and generates a series of sequences or some other developmental process. While an episode may terminate in a cadence as the S enters, here, too, all threads are not snipped off. Continuity is maintained with an unbroken strand that runs into the CS or free part. Note also that episodes have a key destination, usually the key of the next entry. Episodes which reach the new key too soon often detour to related keys before returning to the new key.

Review the material on episodes in Ch. 8. Examine each illustration in the text which is referred to below.

Broadly considered, episodes are either sequential or imitative. A finer distinction must be made regarding the latter as imitative, antiphonal or canonic. The distinctions fuse in canonic sequences which are both sequential and imitative. Two different episodic types, as cited above, may be used at the same time, or one may follow another in the same episode. Salient material treated one way may be handled differently in a later episode. For instance, a motive from the S beginning is used antiphonally in m. 9–12 of Invention no. 12 and sequentially in the four measures before the close. Any type of episode may be repeated in a different key or with interchanged parts.

There is no prescribed number of episodes that a fugue or invention must have. The over-all plan, which is largely determined by the nature of the S, may make it possible to use devices like stretto, augmentation, etc. which will reduce the number of episodes. Nor is there any fixed rule regarding the length of an episode. This is governed by the sectional length of material drawn from the exposition and by the type of episode that is employed. Note the long two-part episode in W.T.C. I, F. 3, m. 34–42.

Sequential Episodes

A single sequential line, often in active rhythm, is accompanied by two nonsequential parts in some episodes. These free lines may consist of nothing more than consecutive chord tones, as in Invention no. 6, m. 13–15. This episode starts two measures earlier, with imitations of the last four notes of the S. The chord tones of nonsequential parts may be slightly elaborated with scale fragments or other nonsequential motives, as in Invention no. 1, m. 7 to the middle of m. 8. The sequential line (l.v.) is an inversion of the first half of the S. (See F. 6, m. 10–12, W.T.C. I, and F. 21, m. 19–21, W.T.C. I; the material is used in double counterpoint in m. 30–32.) An accompanying nonsequential line may be more elaborate, as in Fig. 10-12 (l.v.). Sequences may be modified or extended. Review modified sequences on pp. 51–52.

Two different sequential lines are used in Fig. 10-16c. The m.v. consists of supplementary chord tones. (See also Fig. 10-10b and F. 10, m. 35–36, W.T.C. II; the sequences in triplets stem from the last part of the S.) The most common sequential episode engages all three parts in sequence. This is easily devised in fifth-fall progressions. As a rule, all three parts are not rhythmically active at once. A single line of sequences is active in F. 24, m. 50–53, W.T.C. II; the chord tones in the other voices form sequential lines. Note the same usage in Fig. 10-16b with suspended chord tones. For a clear idea of the way to achieve this effect, reduce the upper parts to quarter-note chord tones. The m.v. in Invention no. 10, m. 28–30, runs in continuous sixteenths in sequences derived from the last half of the S. Observe how rhythmic activity is alternated in the other sequential voices, to avoid simultaneous sixteenths in all three. Examine the episodic sequences in F. 7, m. 22–23, W.T.C. I. The l.v. is in continuous sixteenths; the u.v., in sixteenths for two beats, subsides with eighths and a rest; the m.v., first in quarter notes, picks up the running sixteenths. This episode continues as in Fig. 11-2b. (Also see Fig. 10-9.) A free nonsequential voice may join two-part sequences in sequence at a later point, as in Fig. 6-11d. In all of the next exercises modulate to related keys.

Exercise 2a. Write an episode with sequences in a single part and chord tones in the free parts. Use material drawn from any exposition in Ex. 13, Ch. 10. Plan the harmony so as to reach a related key other than the dominant or subdominant. The chord tones may be slightly embellished. Write a second episode using sequences in two parts and a free third part. Take material from a different exposition of the same exercise. Extend this episode by continuing one sequential line as a free nonsequential part, transferring the sequences to the line originally carrying the free part.

Exercise 2b. Compose at least two episodes with sequences in all three parts, with material taken from a third expo-

300

sition. Rewrite these episodes in triple interchange of voices and in different related keys, including the subdominant. It should be possible to splice these and other episodes of Ex. 2 into the fabric of our original inventions and fugues.

Imitative Episodes

We indicated the close relationship between imitative, antiphonal and canonic episodes earlier. The distinction between them can be recognized by comparing the voice-to-voice imitations of Fig. 11-2a with the antiphonal episode (Fig. 10-14b) and with the canonic episode in Fig. 11-2c. Imitations are shifted from voice to voice in the first example; the antiphonal episode is a dialogue between two voices, in which one voice alternately holds a long note (or breaks off) while the other voice speaks. The dialogue may be imitative or not, as in Fig. 11-2b. (See also Fig. 6-24.) The specific feature of the canonic episode is that the material overlaps, as in Fig. 11-2c.

Figure 11-2c

W.T.C. II, F. no. 14

Examine the following imitative episodes: Fig. 7-10d; in W.T.C. I, F. 24, m. 41–44, the motive of eighth notes, taken from the first measure of the S, is shifted to successive voices. These imitations are written first, with the modulations in mind; the running sixteenths are added next. In F. 19, W.T.C. II, the tail of the S is used in an interesting imitative episode, starting in the middle of m. 21 and continuing through the first half of m. 23; it resumes in the last half of m. 24. Note how this prepares the final entry. In Invention no. 7, m. 18–24, an episode based on half of the CS is expanded in the last measure. A common device is to use the head of a S in brief imitations prior to a complete entry. (See Invention no. 3, from the middle of m. 14 through m. 17.) The same device is used antiphonally in Invention no. 4, m. 5.

* This unit bears some relationship to the end of the S. Although this beginning is not an exposition, some writers regard the unit as a new S in a multiple S fugue.

Exercise 2c. Write at least two imitative episodes that modulate to keys other than those used in Ex. 2a.

Antiphonal Episodes

It is not obligatory to maintain three parts continuously from the S re-entry in the exposition to the end of an invention or fugue. The relief afforded by an occasional reduction of the texture to two parts is discussed later. An antiphonal episode lightens the texture, producing the aural illusion of two-voice texture. Note how the two antiphonal voices of Fig. 7-7d may sound as a single line in the preceding example. Observe the same effect in Invention no. 10, m. 17–19. This pseudo-two-part texture is effective prior to a S entry. (See Invention no. 8, m. 4–5.)

Examine the following antiphonal episodes: W.T.C. II, F. 19, m. 14–15. Observe how the S ending in m. 13 is imitated in contrary motion in that same measure, leading to the antiphonal response before the S re-entry. In F. 14, W.T.C. II, a free part in running sixteenths accompanies nonimitative antiphonal parts starting in the middle of the measure, 14 measures before the close, and continuing for the next two and a half measures. A motive from the S beginning of F. 2, W.T.C. I, is used antiphonally in m. 9–10; sequences in the l.v. are derived from the CS. The episode leads to an entry in the relative major key. Examine Fig. 6-15a. Antiphonal parts using the last four notes of the S alternate in contrary and direct motion in Fig. 10-3c. (See also Figs. 10-16a and 10-17a and b.)

Exercise 2d. Using a short motive from the S of one of your expositions, write an antiphonal episode with a free third part. Write another antiphonal episode using a longer unit from the CS, with sequences in the third voice. Rewrite this in triple counterpoint.

Canonic Episodes

Episodes of this type are different in character from brief canons which have a progressively changing leading line. One sequence is overlapped by similar material in another voice in canonic sequences. Clear examples are seen in Invention no. 3, m. 8–9 (the upper and lower voices) and in Fig. 11-2c. Overlapping is less clear in F. 6, W.T.C. II, from the middle of m. 19 through m. 20. The eighth notes following the triplets are overlapped by a similar unit. Canonic sequences, as a rule, should not be extended for more than a few measures; some are written in two voices only.

Exercise 2e.   Write at least one episode in canonic sequences with a free third part, and another with an independent third sequential part. Write a brief episode with canonic sequences in all three parts. Use material from one of your expositions.

Variety of Texture

The number of voices may be reduced in the course of an invention or fugue and increased at or near the end. A reduction to one voice, as in Invention no. 6, m. 18 and m. 36, is rare. We referred earlier to an effective way of lightening the texture by using antiphonal three-part episodes. Writing the free part in long notes, with occasional brief rests, is another way. A change to two-part texture may be in order in one or two places in the course of a fugue or invention, as relief after an intense passage. This, however, depends on the character of the composition. A vigorous S may call for a drive without letup in three-part texture, from the end of the exposition to the close. Each part in Inventions nos. 3, 10, 12 and 14 barely pauses, and then only for a measure or less.

The change to two parts should not be made too soon after a conventional exposition. It may be made prior to a redundant entry, as in Invention no. 13, m. 9–12. Otherwise a reduction to two parts should not be made until after the episode that follows the exposition, after a counter exposition, or after additional imitations. The cadence telescoping the end of an exciting episode and a S entry, particularly a tranquil S, is a logical point to revert to two-part texture. The part that drops out should end on a chord tone. It may be desirable to change to two parts for a special purpose—such as beginning a new section with the inverted S or, as in Invention no. 8, with a two-part stretto (middle of m. 7–9). Single-beat rests do not affect the prevailing texture.

The number of parts may be increased to bring a fugue to a resounding close. A cursory examination of the last measure or the last few measures of the three-part fugues reveals the frequency of texture ampler than three voices or closing chords in four or five parts. (See the close of F. 3, W.T.C. I, and the final entry of the S often played in octaves in F. 2, W.T.C. I, which closes with a repetition of the S and a chordal accompaniment over a pedal point.) See Fig. 11-3c, the last two measures.

Pedal Points, Dominant and Tonic

A note that is prolonged or repeated, generally in the l.v. while the other voices move over it, is a *pedal point*. The dominant note of any key drawn out in this manner is a *dominant pedal point;* a tonic note, usually the tonic of the original key, similarly used, is a *tonic pedal point.* A protracted dominant tone by itself, held unresolved for several measures, produces mounting strain that is released only by its eventual resolution. As a pedal point, its tension is sharpened by discords produced with the upper lines, as in Fig. 11-3a, m. 6.

Upper lines moving in dominant and tonic harmony over a dominant pedal point do not have the same biting effect. (See W.T.C. I, F. no. 15, m. 62–64, and Inventions no. 3, m. 18; and no. 11, m. 24–28, noting the discord in the last measure. The dominant pedal usually starts in dominant harmony or on a I$_4^6$. The pedal tone is held, repeated or embellished, as in Fig. 11-3b. Bach at times uses a trill on the dominant note, as

Figure 11-3b

in Invention no. 2, m. 15–16. Material for the upper lines is drawn from thematic sources.

The dominant pedal is a striking device in building up a climax. Strategically located, it leads into the beginning of a new section, as in Invention no. 12, m. 13. It is also effective toward the close, as in the last four measures of this Invention. Bach's skill in heightening dramatic tension is evident in his piling stretto over the pedal in W.T.C. I, F. 11, m. 36–40 and a pseudo-stretto in W.T.C. I, F. 15, m. 62–63.

The tonic pedal point is almost invariably used in a codetta-like ending. The voices continue over the held tonic note in what amounts to a prolonged plagal cadence (Fig. 11-3c). The harmony before the last tonic is subdominant, V^7ofIV–IV, or the major or minor II^7. Examine the last measures of Ps. 1, 9 and 16, W.T.C. II.

Figure 11-3c

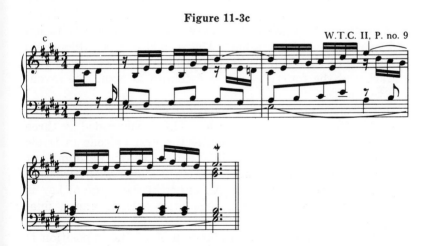

Our experience in writing two-part inventions and various types of episodes is sufficient preparation for completing the uncomplicated type of three-part invention. The broad outlines of several inventions, starting *after* the exposition, are sketched below as concrete models to follow without necessarily sticking to details. The modulatory scheme, however, is important. Types of episodes better suited to your thematic material may be substituted for those in the selected model. The S may be altered to suit the circumstances. (See Fig. 4-21c.)

In Invention no. 3: an episode in canonic sequences (m. 8–9) follows the exposition. The S enters in the relative minor; another episode, after the codetta, is formed from the last four notes of the S. This is used antiphonally in direct and contrary motion, bringing the section to a close in the relative minor of the dominant key (middle of m. 14).

Section 2 starts with an imitative episode, using the opening motive of the S. The section closes with a pedal point leading to its cadence in the subdominant key. The final section consists of three entries, the first in the subdominant key; the next two, as answers, complete the invention.

In Invention no. 4: the exposition is followed by one measure of antiphonal episode (m. 5) that leads to a free imitation. This, extended, closes the section in the relative major (middle of m. 8). Section 2 starts with an entry in that key and another at the octave. Note the use of the auxiliary bass in the l.v. The upper parts in the episode following are antiphonal against a sequential l.v. A free imitation, extended, closes the section in the dominant minor (middle of m. 13). Section 3 opens with the S in that key, followed by an A in free imitation and two additional imitations. The second one is extended to m. 20, where the S enters in the original key. The A, a free imitation at the fourth above, is extended to bring the invention to a close.

In Invention no. 10: an episode derived from the last half of the S (m. 9) follows the exposition. This is succeeded by three modulatory imitations, followed by the first episode in triple counterpoint. Another entry in the relative of the dominant key closes section 1 (m. 22). Section 2 starts with two free imitations in the same voice. An entry in the original key is followed by a three-measure sequential episode and a final entry in the original key.

In Invention no. 12: the redundant A of the exposition is followed by a long antiphonal episode starting in m. 9, which culminates in the same motive moving over a dominant pedal of f♯, the relative minor key. Section 2 starts with an entry in that key (m. 15). The seven-measure episode that follows includes the codetta inverted, a pedal point and a repetition of the first antiphonal episode. Compare these two episodes. Section 3 starts in m. 24, with an entry in the original key followed by an imitation at the octave. Observe the next short episode with sequences of the codetta. Now compare the voice parts with the material from the middle of m. 7 into the next half measure, noting the interchanged parts. The close of this invention is preceded by a dominant pedal.

The details of these inventions are omitted for a reason other than the likelihood of obscuring the broad structural layout. At this point you should pursue the analysis further with answers to the following questions: (1) How does each bit of material, however unimportant, relate to something in the exposition? (2) How is each episode linked with what precedes and follows it? (3) Why is one type of episode used and not another? (4) What modifications are made in the S, CS (if there is one) or codetta, and particularly, why? (5) What occurs immediately before the change to require it? (6) Is the S shifted in the measure and, if so, why? (7) Does Bach at any point do something other than the expected, and why? (8) How is an entry prepared? (9) How are extensions of the S made? (10) What is the harmonic route to each cadence? (11) How does Bach move away from cadences? Where Bach conducts a line in an unexpected manner, re-write the line as it would normally proceed to discover his reason for doing so.

Exercise 3a. Analyze each invention listed above with answers to such specific questions, after examining the Invention analysis on p. 323 of the Appendix.

Exercise 3b. Complete two inventions, using your expositions of Ex. 13c, Ch. 10. Follow the general plan outlined for any of the above inventions. Use triple counterpoint if possible. It may be feasible to include a pedal point or entries with an inverted S. Reserve the most interesting episode for the third section. Note how episodic material runs into and is carried over the S entry in Fig. 10-6.

Episodes are one of the principal sources of variety in the simple invention and fugue, each one projecting thematic material in progressively fascinating guises. In more sophisticated inventions and fugues the subject becomes the center of interest when it is presented in inversion, in stretto, in augmentation and diminution and in a relationship to the CS at intervals greater than the octave.

Stretto

Canonic imitation of the subject in one or more voices, as mentioned earlier, is called *stretto*. The S in Fig. 11-4a is overlapped by itself at the octave in a second voice. The third voice is a free part. Two entries at the octave overlap the S before it comes to a close (Fig. 11-4b). Note the slight change in the m.v. Strict imitation in stretto is neither essential nor always practical. Alterations that do not warp the S unduly are permissible. Shortening or lengthening the first note may provide a better adjustment in some instances.

Figure 11-4a–b

A response in stretto may begin at any point along the line of the S, providing, of course, that it is in harmonic agreement with the initial entry for most of the way. The principles of canon writing are applicable to stretto. Note the short time interval between entries in Fig. 11-4b. Such entries are in "close stretti." They are more difficult to bring off because the second and third entries must be in agreement with the first for the greater part of the way. More often one voice overlaps the first entry before it comes to an end. The third voice then overlaps the second entry, as in Fig. 11-4c. Note the answers at the fifth.

Entries in the exposition are *separated* from each other. Stretti that bring S and A together at increasingly shorter time intervals create an exciting, and at times tempestuous, effect. Stretto is rarely used in the exposition. (See F. 19,

Figure 11-4c

II, no. 14

W.T.C. I and F. 3, W.T.C. II.) Incidentally, an answer in the exposition that begins a note or two before the close of the S is not considered to be in stretto. Stretto is used after a redundant S and A in F. 11, W.T.C. I, m. 25; a series of stretti appear after two redundant answers in Invention no. 8, m. 7; note the two-part texture and the changes.

More often stretti like those in Figs. 11-4a and c are used in the second section or later. When there are several stretto passages used, the close stretti of Fig. 11-4c are reserved for last. These passages should not be in the same key. A free part is used in two-voice stretto since, obviously, it is impossible to fit a CS to entries of the S in different places. Close stretti generally work out better with a short S.

The S in inverted form may be used in stretto against itself or against the A in direct motion (Fig. 11-5a). The inverted A is used in stretto against the inverted S in F. 6, W.T.C. II, m. 17–18. The entries in stretto may alternate in motion, as in Fig. 11-5b.

Figure 11-5a–b

W.T.C. I, F. no. 6

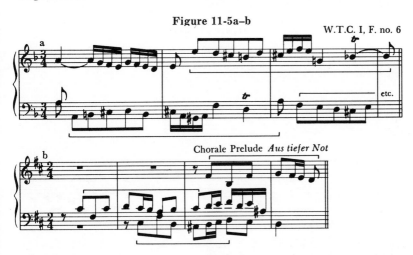

Chorale Prelude *Aus tiefer Not*

Some subjects are not suitable for treatment in stretto. Others may not work in close three-part stretti. Some subjects are too long, so only a portion is written in stretto, either in direct or contrary motion. (See F. 8, W.T.C. I, m. 54–55 and F. 15, W.T.C. I, m. 51–53.) An entry like the one in brackets (Fig. 11-5c) is a *pseudo-stretto*. Subjects may be constructed with stretto in mind. In that case the S is not constructed as a whole. The S and its overlapping imitation at the octave, fifth or both, is developed step by step as in canon.

Figure 11-5c

Working out a stretto passage is generally a matter of *systematic* experimentation. Overlapping the S at the octave is the easiest. Write the imitation separately an octave above or below, then move it along the line of the S to where the most concords on the beat occur and the fewest changes are required. Do this also with imitations at the fifth and fourth above and below. If this does not work out, try it in the same way with a different interval. Sometimes the quickest approach is to reduce the S (Fig. 11-5d) to its essential tones (Fig. 11-5e). Then try *that* at different levels and at different points along the line (Fig. 11-5f).

Figure 11-5d–f

If the S starts on an up-beat or after the beat, the best beginning of the stretto is at a similar rhythmic point. Be on the lookout for parallel fifths and octaves. Avoid more than two consecutive seconds, sevenths and ninths. Changes in the size of skips and chromatically altered notes make modulation feasible.

Exercise 4a. Work out stretti in two voices with some of the subjects written in Ex. 5, Ch. 8. Add a free part, borrowing a motive or more from the S. Bear in mind that it is not necessary to have a concord on each beat; that the free voice may fill in the harmony; that it is preferable to avoid the same rhythm in both voices in the area where the stretto begins.

Exercise 4b. Work out passages in which the second voice is in stretto with the first and, after the S ends, the third voice is in stretto with the second.

Exercise 4c. Work out one or two stretti in which the third voice overlaps the first two.

Augmentation

Doubling the note values of a S, a CS or of any salient thematic motive is called *augmentation*. Used with relative infrequency in fugues, this device is fairly common in chorale elaborations. An augmentation of the S may be simply accompanied by two free parts. A passage takes on greater vitality when the S in its original rhythm values is counterpointed against its augmentation (Fig. 11-6). The S, half as long as the augmentation, may move on to a free part while the third voice enters with the S against the second half of the augmentation. Bach, at this point, uses the inverted S (Fig. 11-6). An augmentation

Figure 11-6

W.T.C. II, F. no. 2

does not work well with a long S. It is usually repeated at a later point in a different voice and key. (See m. 19–21 of this fugue; note also the close stretto six measures before the close.)

Examine the augmentations in F. 8, W.T.C. I, m. 62–67; in m. 77–82 the augmentation is accompanied by the S in the l.v. and by an augmentation in free rhythm in the m.v. Fragments of a S are frequently used in augmentation in an unobtrusive free part.

Diminution

The converse of augmentation, *i.e.*, halving the original note values of a S, is called *diminution* (Fig. 11-7a). Treatment of the S in diminution is not common because diminution tends to upset the basic rhythm motion except with subjects in long notes or slow tempo. Careful scrutiny of an invention or fugue will, however, uncover bits of thematic material in diminution (Fig. 11-7b). Bach occasionally uses a few notes from the head of a S in free diminution at the tail (Fig. 11-7c).

Figure 11-7

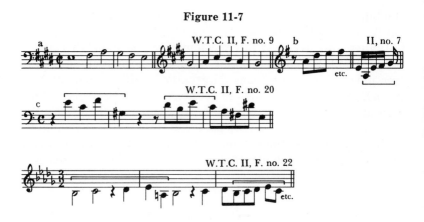

Exercise 5.   Experiment with one of your shorter subjects against its augmentation, as in Fig. 11-6; then, after a short episode, use the augmentation in a different voice and key.

Retrograde Motion

A device that is rarely used is a statement of the S backwards from last to first note. *Retrograde motion,* also called *cancrizans,* is difficult to grasp aurally unless the S is extremely short. This device, applied to a brief motive from the S, is occasionally used in a free part.

Double Counterpoint at the Twelfth

Our prior experience with double counterpoint was limited to an interchange of two parts at the octave. Although this is the most common type of double counterpoint, the S and CS or two episodic parts are sometimes interchanged at intervals wider than an octave. The material of a lower part, for instance, may be shifted a tenth or twelfth above the upper part, and vice versa. With the exception of double counterpoint at the octave, the shift at the twelfth is the most practical.

The principal reason for resorting to double counterpoint at the twelfth is to obtain a fresh harmonic effect with a repetition of the same material. Compare the difference in harmony between the two measures of Fig. 11-8c. The interchange that takes place when the bottom note of each interval is shifted up a twelfth to become a note of the upper part is shown in Fig. 11-8a. Any interval wider than a twelfth, as in Fig. 11-8b, does not result in an interchange by shifting the lower note up a twelfth. The parts therefore should not be wider than a twelfth apart initially at any point.

Figure 11-8a–b

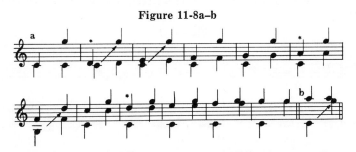

Observe that the consonant intervals of a prime, a third, a fifth, an octave and a tenth remain consonant when interchanged. In two-part texture the starred intervals prove troublesome when interchanged if they must imply the harmony. Every interval, however, may be used in three-part texture because the third voice, which does not partake of the interchange, can supply a chord tone to make the poor interval part of the harmony. For instance, a B added below the fourth (Fig. 11-8d, m. 2) creates a V_6 at that point; a C below the seventh (Fig. 11-8e) forms a VI^7. A single interval of a sixth, as in this example, is easily managed. An initial passage with parallel sixths is another matter: these become parallel sevenths in the interchange, a situation which rules out double counterpoint at the twelfth. Parallel thirds which become parallel tenths, and vice versa, are practical. A poor interval resulting from the interchange—like Fig. 11-8d, m. 2—may be altered chromatically, as in the first measure of Fig. 11-8f. Liberties of this sort may also be taken in order to modulate, as in the next measure.

Figure 11-8c–f

An initial diatonic passage may therefore be altered so as to include a secondary dominant or a modulation with the interchange and, conversely, accidentals in the original passage may be cancelled in the later passage. Part of an A and CS are shown in Fig. 11-9a. The CS is shifted a twelfth above the A

Figure 11-9

W.T.C. II, F. no. 16

314

in Fig. 11-9b. It should be understood that the exchange may be made in the other direction, *i.e.*, retaining the CS in the same location and shifting the A a twelfth below it. This, if practical, will produce a different harmony. Observe the altered beginning of the A. Considerable modification is sometimes necessary to make harmonic sense in the interchange. Note the difference in harmony.

In two-part counterpoint, the narrow intervals do not create any difficulties in spacing between voices when they become fairly wide in the interchange (Fig. 11-8a). There is, however, a special spacing problem in three-part counterpoint; *i.e.*, it is not always feasible to keep one voice at its original level in three-part counterpoint while shifting the other voice a twelfth up or down. A method commonly employed is to shift both voices, one up and the other down, *to the equivalent* of a twelfth. The lower voice in Fig. 11-10a is shifted up an octave while the upper voice is dropped a fifth. The sharp (in parenthesis), unessential to the shift, is an indication that it may be used if a modulation is desirable.

Figure 11-10a

Compare the parts in the interlude before the S re-entry (Fig. 11-10b) with these parts interchanged at the twelfth (Fig. 11-10c). Here a reverse of the shift in Fig. 11-10a takes

Figure 11-10b–c

W.T.C. I, F. no. 2

place—the upper part is dropped an octave, while the lower part is raised a fifth. This passage is transposed from the key in which it appears in m. 17–18 of this fugue, to show the interchange at the twelfth more clearly. Note that the single sixths starred in Fig. 11-10b become sevenths in Fig. 11-10c. Observe that the third note of the upper part in Fig. 11-10c is altered to fit the harmony. Some countersubjects are composed in a way that makes an interchange with the S at the octave and at the twelfth possible. Study the interchanges in F. 17, W.T.C. I, comparing m. 11 and 12 with m. 14 and 15.

We remarked earlier that any interchange adding up to a twelfth is double counterpoint at the twelfth. Compare Figs. 11-10d and e. The A and the delayed CS in Fig. 11-10d is interchanged with the S raised a fourth and the CS dropped a ninth (actually an octave plus a ninth) in Fig. 11-10e. The sum of the interchange is a twelfth. The other voices filling out the harmony are omitted for the sake of clarity. Incidentally, the tail of the S and A differs from the initial entries. The alteration in Fig. 11-10e, from the starred note to the end of the example, shows the freedom taken in such interchanges.

Figure 11-10d–e

Exercise 6a. Experiment with your previously written subjects and countersubjects by retaining some at the same level and shifting the others a twelfth. Make whatever alterations are necessary in the interchange to get a reasonably good harmonic result, remembering that a free third voice will fill out the harmony. Add the third voice.

Exercise 6b. Use an interchange in which one voice is dropped or raised an octave and the other dropped or raised a fifth in the opposite direction.

Exercise 6c. Employ the interchange demonstrated in Fig. 11-10e.

Interchanged parts, with one a tenth above or below the other, is more difficult. Here a prime-tenth; 2nd-9th; 3rd-8va; 4th-7th; 5th-6th; 6th-5th; 7th-4th. Parallel thirds and sixths become parallel fifths and octaves.

No single invention or fugue incorporates all of the devices described in this chapter, nor do these compositions exhibit any uniformity in the inclusion, exclusion and location of any device. We are prepared, at this point, to include stretto in the invention, reserving other devices for the fugue. Inventions nos. 8 and 14 may serve as models; their general layout after the exposition is outlined below.

In Invention no. 8: an episode of antiphonal sequences (m. 4) follows the first three entries, leading to two redundant real answers which bring the section to a cadence in the dominant key (middle of m. 7). Section 2 starts with the A and S in two-voice stretti which continues through m. 11. Starting in the middle of m. 11 is a cluster of four imitations, two of which are successively in the same voice. They wind up in a cadence in the relative minor key (middle of m. 15). Section 3 opens with an episode leading to two simultaneous entries. A single stretto follows immediately. The free voice, using the motive of m. 4, introduces an episode similar to the first antiphonal episode. The invention closes with two entries in the original key.

In Invention no. 14: an episode (m. 5), with material taken from the end of the S, moves to canonic sequences. Two free imitations (m. 7–8) are extended. The modulation to the opposite mode (m. 10) prepares the single entry before the cadence that closes section 1 (m. 12). Section 2 starts with a close stretto. An episode follows. The next entry (end of m. 14) has a pseudo-stretto in the l.v. Three entries follow before another stretto that starts in the last half of m. 18. There is an additional stretto in m. 20–21 in all three parts. A free rhapsodic episode in the last three measures closes the invention.

Exercise 7. Write a three-part invention featuring stretto. It need not follow in detail the inventions described above.

Three-part Fugues

Bach's fugues are remarkably different from each other in character and treatment. Their boundless variety supports Cecil Gray's oft-quoted remark that "after the exposition almost anything may, and generally does happen with Bach." Various writers have advanced conflicting views on fugue "form." These correspond in no great measure to "what happens in Bach." Oldroyd* suggests two schemes following the exposition for use in student examinations. (1) A sequential episode; a single middle entry; a canonic or free imitational episode; two additional entries in stretto; a third episode which is an interchanged version of the first; a final section with optional choice of a number of devices. While this is not a rigid layout, it may not work with certain kinds of subjects which are unsuitable for stretto. (2) A shorter layout eliminates an episode and one set of middle entries. The best procedure for beginners is to follow the general plan of one of the simpler fugues in the *Well-Tempered Clavier*, such as W.T.C. I, nos. 7, 9, 13, 21 and W.T.C. II, nos. 1, 11, 12, 19 and 24.

The fugue may be organized in a simple manner, *i.e.*, an alternation of entries with episodes and a final entry or two in the original key. It may be sectional in design, as in F. 12, W.T.C. II. The entries may be single or grouped in free imitations. The inverted S may be used in one of these group entries. The episodes are varied at least in key. The modulatory plan is similar to that of any two-part invention. Although the second section may start in the dominant key, it is not advisable to use this key if the exposition has more than one A or redundant answers in the dominant key. Pedal point may be included in this type of fugue.

Exercise 8a. Write a simple type of fugue, following the general plan of one of the fugues listed above.

The more involved fugue embraces one or more of the following: stretto, augmentation, entries in double counterpoint at the twelfth; triple counterpoint and pedal points. It is not necessarily longer than one in simple structure. Some preliminary exploration is necessary before a decision is made to use a specific device. Questions to be answered are: Does the S

* George Oldroyd, *The Technique and Spirit of Fugue*. New York: Oxford University Press, 1948.

lend itself to stretto, to coupling itself with its augmentation, to interchange with the CS at the twelfth? Can the parts, either of an episode or of S, CS and free part, be interchanged in triple counterpoint?

Exercise 8b.   Write a fugue of the type described above. Make some experimental sketches, first using one or another of the various devices. These sketches can be altered at the beginning and ending after transposition to fit into your key scheme. Choose the most effective location for these devices.

The knowledge and techniques that you have acquired on satisfactory completion of the work in this text should be a source of gratification. Students aiming to become performing artists should realize that the analyses undertaken and the compositions written, even if unoriginal, have given them a deeper insight into the music of Bach and a greater awareness of the organization and subtleties of polyphonic compositions. Writing music of a high order requires inborn musical gifts as well as knowledge and technique. Coleridge says, "The sense of musical delight, with the power of producing it, is a gift of the imagination; and this together with the power of reducing multitudes into unity of effect and modifying a series of thoughts by some one predominant thought or feeling, may be cultivated or improved but can never be learned." This text was written with the objective of cultivating the musical gifts with which students are endowed.

Appendix

The Complete Canon

Von Himmel hoch, Var. 1

Analysis of a Three-part Invention

¹ The second half of m. 1 implies V⁷ofIV–IV.

² The cadential ending of the auxiliary bass is used in m. 5 and 14.

³ This codetta borders on being an integral ending of the S. It appears with all but the last two entries, and is used here to round out the phrase and to modulate to the dominant. A hasty re-adjustment in the free part would be necessary at this point if the A started at the beginning of m. 3 and if the codetta were omitted. An overly extended codetta like that

in #3 below would be necessary if the entry of the A were delayed until m. 4. It is Bach's evident intention to use the codetta as supplementary episodic material to the limited means supplied by the opening motive. Note the extension of the auxiliary bass to meet the CS.

[4] The free part is used with the S and CS in triple counterpoint in measures 6, 10, 19 and 21–22.

[5] The first appearance of the CS is normally in the same voice as the one in which the S first appears. (See Invention no. 14, m. 2.) Since the S here is relatively long, an overly long auxiliary bass would be required if the CS followed the S in the u.v.

[6] Note the change in the codetta, adjusting it to the return of the S in the tonic key.

[7] The codetta may also be considered as the beginning of the canonic sequences.

[8] With the indicated accidentals the measure would clearly be in b minor. Bach prefers a stronger entrance of the S over a dominant, which has the effect of a dominant pedal.

[9] Compare this half measure with #9 below, where the b-sharp provides V^7ofII, as at #6. This, however, compels an unwanted change in the S: D-sharp.

[10] The CS is abbreviated. Bach could easily have continued it as in #10 below. He prefers the slurred imitative fragments which intimate their use in the next episode.

[11] The first section could have closed in the relative minor with a cadence, as in #11 below. Bach evidently prefers tapering the section off with an episode and a more convincing cadence in the relative minor of the dominant key. Note the augmentation of the tail end of the S in the next m., m.v.

[12] Observe the lightened texture and the single voice effect of the antiphonal upper and middle voices. The motive is an inversion of the end of the S.

[13] Note the thickened texture as the l.v. takes up the motive.

[14] A distant modulation—f♯ minor–G—pivots on the common tone F♯.

[15] See the m.v., m. 17.

[16] The first note of the CS is altered. The CS starts in the u.v. and, with the C natural, shifts to the m.v.

[17] The S in the subdominant key is answered by two entries in the original key. Except for this relationship, the two entries would be regarded as subject.

[18] The four bracketed notes are the last notes of the A. The invention would end with an imperfect authentic cadence if they remained in the u.v. an octave higher; this accounts for the shift to the m.v.

Index

B

Bach, characteristics of his music, influence of, 4
teaching methods of, vi
Baroque style:
approach to cadences in, 146, 181
continuo in, 3–4
harmonic and rhythmic motion in, 74, 89

C

Cadences, 17
approached by tonic six-four, 76
by augmented sixth chords, 181
by secondary sevenths, 146
authentic, 17
deceptive, *see* Deceptive resolutions
in canon ending, 192–93
in inventions, 235
elision of, in inventions, 231
half, 17
harmonic fusion in, 239–40
in modulation, 160
plagal, 17
in the canon, 192
Cambiata, 81
Cancrizans, defined, in canon, 207
in fugue 313
Canon, 187–207
canonic sequences, 279, 302
characteristics of the diatonic, 190–92
circular, 198
endings, 192, 194;
in infinite, 203–4
example in Appendix, 321
at the fifth and fourth, 204–5
finite, 192
free, 188
harmony in, 191
infinite, 192, 202–4
as invention, 238–41
leader length in the *Art of Fugue*, 189
modulation in, 197–98
at the octave, 188
at other intervals, 206

Canon (*cont.*)
process of writing the diatonic, 190–91; the modulatory, 199–201
strict, 188
three-part, 279–81
two-part with added voice, process of writing, 277–78
at the unison, 188
Cantus firmus, defined, 2
Canzona, 3
Chain dominants, 115
in canonic sequences, 209
in modulation, 178
Changing tones, 57–59
accented, 125; *see* Cambiata
Chansons, as canti firmi, 2, 3
Chorales, 3
preludes, variations, 3
study of, 186–87
Chord intervals, implying:
dominant seventh, 86
secondary sevenths, 144
the six-four, 79
triads in first inversion, 34–36;
see Harmony
Codetta:
after deceptive cadences, 235
defined, 246
in double invention, 254
to modulating subjects, 285
in three-part inventions and fugues, 283
in two-part canon, 192–93
in two-part fugal inventions, 246, 247
Consonance, 12
Continuo, *see* Figured bass
Contrary motion, 17, 19
imitation by, 106
scales in, 93
Counter exposition, function of, 282–83
Counterpoint, historical development of, 1–4
Three-part, 259–79, *see* Three-part canon, Fugue, Triple counterpoint
canonic writing in, 277
chain dominants in, 270
doubling in, 260
parallel motion in, 275

Counterpoint (*cont.*)
  Three-part (*cont.*)
    process of writing in, 263–65,
      267–68
    secondary dominants in, 270
    secondary seventh framework
      in, 269, 270–71
    sequences in, 268–71
    spacing in, 260–61
    suspensions in, 272–75
    triadic framework in, 260–61,
      263–68
    voice range in, 261
  Two-part, 23–186; *see* Two-part
    Canon; double, fugal and
    simple inventions
    accented nonharmonic tones in,
      120–35
    appoggiaturas in, 125–28
    canonic sequences in, 207–209
    chain dominants in, 178
    delayed resolution of suspen-
      sions in, 151–53
    distant modulation in, 186
    imitations in, 102–103; with
      suspensions, 135; by inver-
      sion, 105–106; based on sec-
      ondary dominants, 117, 119;
      on secondary sevenths, 150
    melodic contrast in, 66
    modulation to closely related
      keys in, 157; via pivot har-
      mony, 161–63
    one rhythmically active line
      in, 23–25, 29, 36–38, 48–51,
      59–60
    rhythmic independence in, 66–
      67
    sequences in, 69–71; in minor,
      101
    suspensions in, 133–35
    unaccented nonharmonic tones
      in, 23–25, 29, 36–39, 48–51,
      59–60, 81
Countersubject, 248–49, 289–90
  adjustments of, 248
  in alternative entry schemes,
    250
  characteristics of, 249
  modifications of, 289–90
Cross relations, 111

D

Deceptive resolutions:
  of dominant seventh, 75
  to I of a new key, 179
  of secondary dominants, 112,
    116
  to a Neapolitan sixth, 180
Diminution, defined, 224
  in the fugue, 312
Discord:
  harmonic, in V^7, 72
  intervals, 12
  melodic, 119
  in pedal point passages, 304
  in secondary seventh chords, 138
  successive, 91
Dominant class of chords:
  primary: V, 13; VII, 13, 32–33;
    V^7, 72–75; VII^7, 73, 89; V^9,
    73
  secondary, 109–115, 117
    as diminished seventh, 110
Double counterpoint, 221–25, 313–
  16
  adjustments in, 225, 314–15
Double Counterpoint and Canon
  (Bridge, J. F.), 187fn.
  described, 221, 313–14
  in episodes, 223–24
  in interludes, 315–16
  with inverted themes, 255
  at the octave, 221
  with subject and countersubject,
    249
  at the tenth, 317
  at the twelfth, 313–16;
    purpose of, 313
Double fugue, *see* Inventions, double
  inversion of both subjects in,
    224
  types of, 253, 290

E

Échappée, 94–95
Elision:
  of cadences, 231
  of figures, 39
Enharmonic, intervals, 10
  spelling, 185

Motive (*cont.*)
    as material for development, 230
    in themes and subjects, 213–14

N

Neapolitan sixth, 118, 179–80
Nonharmonic tones:
    accented, 119–35, 151–53
    unaccented, 21–23, 46–48, 57–60, 80–81, 94–95, 115–16

O

Organum, 1

P

Parallel motion:
    in fifths, 18–19, 63
    in octaves, 14, 18
    in root movement, 19
    in stepwise first inversions, 33
    in suspensions, 134, 275
    in thirds and sixths, 191, 262–63, 267, 275
    in three-part counterpoint, 262–63
    in two-part counterpoint, 66
Passacaglia, 3
Passing tones:
    accented, 120–22
    chromatic, diatonic, 25fn.
    unaccented, 23
Pedal point:
    defined, 304
    dominant, 304–5
    stretto over, 305
    tonic, 305
Phrase, 17
Plain chant, 1
Polyphony, *see* Counterpoint
Progression, defined, 16

R

Relative motion: contrary, oblique, parallel, similar, 16–17; *see*

Parallel, and Contrary motion
Response, *see* Answer
Retrograde motion, *see* Cancrizans
Rhythm:
    in augmentation, 311
    in auxiliary bass, 228, 284
    of auxiliary figures, 47
    basic, 66
    in canon, 191, 201, 278
    in changing tone figures, 59, 125
    in countersubject, 249
    in diminution, 312
    factor in contrapuntal contrast, in the counterpoint to imitation, 218
    in themes of double invention, 254
    in three-part counterpoint, 262, 300
    flow in Baroque style, 166
    in free parts, 292
    in modified sequences, 174
    patterns of, 67–69
    rhythmic imitation, 102, 276
    rhythmic independence, 66–67
    of themes and subjects, 213, 214, 216
    in the turn, 80
    uniform, varied, 29
Ricercar, 3, 4
Rota, 2; *see* Round
Round, 187, 188
    form in, 192
    three-part, 280–81

S

Secondary dominant chords, 109–117
Secondary seventh chords, 137–48
Sequences, *see* Harmonic, Melodic, Canonic
Stretto:
    close, 308, 309
    defined, 224
    with inverted subject, 309
    process of writing, 310–11
    pseudo, 310
    in three-part inventions and fugues, 308–10, 317

Subject, *see* Theme
    dual, in double invention and fugue, 253–54
    endings, 244–45
    entries in exposition, 282
    in fugal invention, 242
    at intervallic points of juncture with answer, 244–45
    modulation in, 215, 283, 285
    redundant entry of, 282
    re-entry,
      in three-part inventions and fugues, 290–91
      in two-part fugal inventions, 250–52
Suspensions, 128–35, 151–53
    continuous (chain), 131, 134
    delayed resolution of, 151–53, 275
    as dotted notes and in syncopation, 129–30
    resolution of, 129, 132
    in three-part counterpoint, 272–76
    untied, 129

T

Tendency tones, 16
    in dominant seventh, 73, 83
    indirect resolution of, 87
    irregular movement of, 74, 84
Texture density, 268
    variety in, 303

Theme:
    characteristics of, 212–15
    double, 253–54
    inversion of, 231–32
    revision of, 214
    rhythm of, 216
    shifted in the measure, 232
Thorough-bass, 3–4; *see* Figured bass
Ties, common tone, 28
Tierce de Picardie, 155
    in modulation, 234
Transition, in inventions, 234
Triads, 13–20, 31–33, 43–45, 55–57, 76–78
Triple counterpoint, 295–97
    in episodes, 297
    modifications in, 296
    process of writing, 296–97
    with subject, countersubject and free part, 296
Tritone, 10
    in V⁷, 72

V

Voice crossing, 18
    in canon, 188
    in double counterpoint, 222
    in narrow-ranging themes, 216
    in three-part counterpoint, 261
Voice range, in four-part harmony, 15
Vox organalis, vox principalis, 1